# money moves & MINDSET SHIFTS

TIFFANY GRANT

# money moves & MINDSET SHIFTS

## HOW TO REACH THE PATH TO PROSPERITY

WILEY

Published by John Wiley & Sons, Inc., Hoboken, New Jersey.



***Library of Congress Cataloging-in-Publication Data:***

Names: Grant, Tiffany author
Title: Money moves & mindset shifts : how to reach the path to prosperity / Tiffany Grant.
Other titles: Money moves and mindset shifts
Description: Hoboken, New Jersey : Wiley, [2027] | Includes bibliographical references and index.
Identifiers: LCCN 2026019647 | ISBN 9781394364480 hardback | ISBN 9781394364503 adobe pdf | ISBN 9781394364497 epub
Subjects: LCSH: Finance, Personal
Classification: LCC HG179 .G7194 2027
LC record available at https://lccn.loc.gov/2026019647

Cover Design: Wiley
Cover Image: Yeti Studio/stock.adobe.com
Author Photo: Courtesy of the Author

Typesetting: Set in MinionPro-Regular 11/16pt by Lumina Datamatics

SKY10164029_072926

*To my grandfather, who planted the seed of "pay yourself first" in a young girl's mind long before she understood what a harvest looked like. You taught me that wealth isn't about what you have, but about the dignity you keep.*

*To my Nana and Papa, who raised me until I was twelve and provided the first and most important example of what a loving, stable household looks like. Nana, you were the mother I needed, and the values you both instilled in me are the compass I use to navigate the world. I strive every day to be the kind of person you were, and to build a home that reflects the warmth and safety you gave me. I miss you so much!*

*To my mother, for being my greatest support system. From helping me navigate the complexities of my college education to making my move to Jamaica seamless by stepping in to care for my children, your sacrifices have been the foundation of my success. I am eternally grateful for your strength and your heart.*

*To my four children—my heartbeats. Whether you are already here with me or preparing to join us this February, you are the "why" behind every late-night word, every side hustle, and every mile traveled. This book is the map I wish I had when I was seventeen; may it be the floor upon which you build your own magnificent ceilings.*

*To the community of Greensboro, North Carolina. Thank you for being the soil where I grew as an individual and a business owner. Serving on your boards, volunteering with the unsheltered, and supporting our local small businesses allowed me to find my voice and my purpose.*

*And to the community of Negril, Jamaica. You welcomed a stranger and showed her the true meaning of resilience, stewardship, and "one love." You are the proof that when we pour into each other, we all rise.*

# CONTENTS

ABOUT THE AUTHOR xi
PREFACE xiii
ACKNOWLEDGMENTS xvii
HOW TO USE THIS BOOK xix

PART 1
THE INTERNAL REVOLUTION 1

CHAPTER ONE
THE CROSSROADS 5

CHAPTER TWO
CHOOSING EDUCATION 17

CHAPTER THREE
THE BINDER OF CREDIT CARDS AND THE GHOST OF 2008 29

CHAPTER FOUR
MY GRANDFATHER'S LEGACY AND THE BILL YOU PAY FIRST 37

PART 1 Action Guide 42

PART 2
THE ARCHITECTURE OF FLOW 49

CHAPTER FIVE
BUDGETING IS PERMISSION 51

CHAPTER SIX
FINDING YOUR "WHY" 57

CHAPTER SEVEN
YOUR FIRST 30 DAYS 63

CHAPTER EIGHT
THE AUTOPILOT RESET 71

CHAPTER NINE
CREATING YOUR MONEY FLOW SYSTEM 79

CHAPTER TEN
BUILDING YOUR FINANCIAL SAFETY NET 95

CHAPTER ELEVEN
IN CASE OF EMERGENCY, PROTECT THESE FOUR WALLS 105

PART 2 Action Guide 111

PART 3
THE ENGINE OF GROWTH 115

CHAPTER TWELVE
THE INNER GAME OF WEALTH 117

CHAPTER THIRTEEN
OVERCOMING THE SCARCITY TRAP 125

CHAPTER FOURTEEN
SETTING GOALS YOU ACTUALLY ACHIEVE 131

CHAPTER FIFTEEN
THE UMBRELLA METHOD 139

CHAPTER SIXTEEN
THE REVENUE TRAP 153

CHAPTER SEVENTEEN
THE STRATEGIC ADVISORY TEAM 165

CHAPTER EIGHTEEN
THE ART OF THE ASK 177

CHAPTER NINETEEN
BUILDING YOUR BRAND AND ATTRACTING OPPORTUNITIES 187

PART 3 Action Guide 198

PART 4
THE AUTOPILOT LIFE 205

CHAPTER TWENTY
AUTOMATION IN LIFE AND BUSINESS 209

CHAPTER TWENTY-ONE
THE EXPAT GOAL 217

PART 4 Action Guide 241

PART 5
THE LEGACY SHIFT 245

CHAPTER TWENTY-TWO
THE GENERATIONAL SHIFT 247

CHAPTER TWENTY-THREE
THE STEWARDSHIP MANIFESTO 265

PART 5 Action Guide 277

CONCLUSION: YOUR LEGACY IS MORE THAN JUST MONEY 285
THE FINANCIAL WELLNESS CHECK-UP: YOUR PATH FORWARD 291
THE FINANCIAL WELLNESS CURATOR'S MANIFESTO 299

APPENDIX A: THE CYCLE-BREAKER'S GLOSSARY 303
APPENDIX B: THE STEWARDSHIP STACK (TOOLS AND APPS) 309
APPENDIX C: THE CYCLE-BREAKER'S FAQS 313
APPENDIX D: THE SYLLABUS FOR SUCCESS 321
APPENDIX E: THE LEGACY BINDER 329
APPENDIX F: THE LEGACY LETTER 335
APPENDIX G: HOW TO WRITE YOUR OWN LEGACY LETTER 341
BIBLIOGRAPHY 345
INDEX 349

# ABOUT THE AUTHOR

**Tiffany Grant, AFC®, MBA**, is an accredited financial counselor, business consultant, and the founder of *Money Talk with Tiff.* Renowned for her ability to bridge the gap between complex financial mechanics and the psychological shifts required for lasting change, Tiffany has dedicated her career to helping "Cycle-breakers" move from survival mode to a legacy of stewardship.

Her expert advice on wealth creation, strategic business growth, and the "ROI of Peace" has been featured on global platforms including *CNBC*, *MSN*, *Yahoo Finance*, *Business Insider*, and *ESSENCE*. As a former contributor to *Forbes*, Tiffany has documented the intersection of personal finance and entrepreneurship, reaching a global audience with her actionable, down-to-earth insights.

Tiffany's academic and professional foundation is as robust as her practical experience. She holds a bachelor of business administration from the University of North Carolina at Pembroke and a master of business administration (MBA) from the University of North Carolina at Greensboro. In addition to her AFC designation, she is a certified Lean Six Sigma Yellow Belt—a discipline she uses to help her clients build efficient, "autopilot" systems for their lives and businesses.

In 2024, Tiffany performed her own "Strategic Asset Reallocation" by relocating her family and business from the United States to the cliffs of **Negril, Jamaica**. Today, she leads the *Money Talk with Tiff Financial Academy*, a learning portal designed to empower ambitious individuals to reclaim their cognitive bandwidth and build wealth that serves their soul. *Money Moves and Mindset Shifts* is her debut manuscript, written from her veranda in Negril as a blueprint for the next generation of stewards.

# PREFACE

If you are holding this book, it is because you have realized that the math of your life is no longer adding up. Perhaps you have followed all the traditional advice—worked the jobs, cut the coupons, and tracked the spreadsheets—yet you still find yourself in a state of High-functioning Survival Mode. You are earning, but you aren't thriving. You are building, but you aren't at peace.

This book is the bridge between the financial struggle you've inherited and the legacy you were meant to lead.

## THE NEED: WHY THIS BOOK, WHY NOW?

Most financial literature operates on a dangerous assumption: that human beings are rational calculators. We are told that if we just fix the math, we will fix the life. But after a decade as an accredited financial counselor (AFC®), I have seen that the best financial systems in the world will fail if the money ghosts of your past are still driving the car.

There is a profound need for a framework that addresses the biological tax of financial stress—the wear and tear on our bodies and minds caused by chronic scarcity. We don't just need more money; we need a restoration of our psychological capital (PsyCap). This book answers the cry of the Cycle-breaker—the individual determined to ensure that the negative financial patterns of their family tree stop with them.

## THE PURPOSE: FROM SURVIVAL TO STEWARDSHIP

The aim of *Money Moves and Mindset Shifts* is to move you through a total internal and external revolution. My goal is to transform you from a passenger in your financial life into the chief steward of your legacy.

This book is written for

- the entrepreneur caught in the "revenue trap," where high earnings are masking a lack of personal peace;
- the professional who feels like an imposter despite their credentials;
- the parent who wants to provide a "floor" for their children to build "ceilings" upon; and
- the dreamer who feels trapped by their current environment and is looking for a path to a "Life by Design."

## SCOPE AND TREATMENT: THE DUAL-TRACK APPROACH

To satisfy both the psychological need for healing and the tactical need for growth, this book utilizes a dual-track methodology. Every chapter is built around a mindset shift (the internal work) and a money move (the external action). We do not just discuss theory; we implement the architecture of flow—a system designed to automate the "boring" so you can focus on the "beautiful."

We will travel from the linoleum floor of a crisis to the veranda of a life designed with intention, using frameworks like the Umbrella Method for income and the Council of Stewards for professional support.

# SUMMARY OF CONTENTS

The journey is structured into five transformative parts:

## Part 1: The Internal Revolution (Mindset)

Chapters 1–5 focus on excavating your foundation. We address the Hyper-independence Trap, silence the "money ghosts," and shift from an external to an internal locus of control. You will learn to build your PsyCap—the Hope, Efficacy, Resilience, and Optimism required to begin.

## Part 2: Architecture of Flow (Systems)

Chapters 6–11 move into the mechanics of your daily life. We define your "Deep Why," implement the awareness tracker, and build your Four Walls of protection. This section is about creating a system that moves at the "Speed of Peace."

## Part 3: Engine of Growth (Execution)

Chapters 12–19 shift from defense to offense. We explore the universe of income streams and the Umbrella Method. You will master the Art of the Ask, learn to negotiate your value, and build a personal brand that attracts opportunities rather than chasing them.

## Part 4: The Autopilot Life (Lifestyle Design)

Chapters 20–21 are about removing yourself as the bottleneck. We discuss the power of automation and the concept of geo-arbitrage—designing a life that allows you to thrive in the environment that best suits your soul, whether that's a quiet hometown or a veranda in Jamaica.

## Part 5: The Legacy Shift (Stewardship)

Chapters 22–23 address the final turn from personal success to generational significance. We discuss financial socialization, the authorized user launch plan, and the transition from "owner" to "steward." The book concludes with the Stewardship Manifesto and your own Legacy Letter.

Welcome to the revolution. It's time to stop surviving and start stewarding.

# ACKNOWLEDGMENTS

Writing this book has been a journey of a thousand "money moves," and I did not walk this path alone. To reach this final page required a village of supporters, mentors, and truth-tellers who believed in the mission of *Money Talk with Tiff* even when I was still silencing my own money ghosts.

To My Family:

To my maternal grandparents, Nana and Papa: thank you for the childhood foundation that made everything else possible. The values of hard work, love, and community you modeled for me are woven into every chapter of this book. To my mother: thank you for the countless ways you have helped me, especially in ensuring my education and my transition to a new life in Jamaica were successful. Your presence in my children's lives is a gift I can never repay. To my four children: you are my greatest teachers in patience, resilience, and the true meaning of "Human Capital." Whether in the United States or here in Jamaica, you are my greatest investment.

To My Professional Tribe:

To my clients and peers: thank you for allowing me to serve as your financial wellness curator. To my "professional tribe"—the financial professionals across multiple disciplines and credentials who challenge me and grow with me—thank you for the collaboration. To my editor and the team at Wiley: thank you for seeing the value in a story that starts at a crossroads and ends on a veranda. Your guidance has been instrumental in bringing this vision to life.

To My Communities:
To the city of Greensboro, NC: thank you for the years of growth. My time serving the unsheltered and advocating for small businesses shaped my understanding of what it means to build a legacy of service. To my Negril community: thank you to my landlord, my neighbors, and the expat community for making this island feel like home. To the families we served during our food relief efforts: thank you for the privilege of being part of your lives. You taught me that "legacy" is what you leave in people, not just for them.

To the *Money Talk with Tiff* Audience:
To my 2,000+ newsletter subscribers, my podcast listeners, and my digital community: you are the reason I do this work. Your questions fueled the FAQ, your struggles inspired the Client Spotlights, and your victories are the fuel that keeps my "Umbrella" open. Thank you for trusting me with your stories.

To My Spiritual Foundation:
Thank you to God for the "Stewardship of the Soul" that guided my pen. This book is a testament to the fact that when you align your mindset with your purpose, the "Nirvana" of peace is possible even in the midst of a storm.

# HOW TO USE THIS BOOK

If you are holding this book, you are likely a Cycle-breaker. You are the one in your family or your community who has decided that "just getting by" is no longer an option. You are ready to move from survival to stewardship.

Because this journey involves both your heart and your bank account, I have designed this book to be a dual-track experience. It is part psychological deep-dive and part financial tactical manual. Here is how to get the most out of our time together:

## 1. THE MINDSET SHIFTS VS. THE MONEY MOVES

Each chapter is built around a mindset shift (the internal work) and a money move (the external action). Do not skip the mindset work to get to the math. As an AFC, I can tell you that the best financial systems in the world will fail if the money ghosts of your past are still driving the car.

# 2. THE ACTION GUIDES

At the end of each of the five parts of this book, you will find a Part Action Guide. These are not "homework"—they are your implementation blueprints. They contain the worksheets, checklists, and "Tiff's Takeaways" that translate the theory into your real-life architecture of flow.

# 3. THE APPENDICES: YOUR RESOURCE LIBRARY

The back of this book is a goldmine. From the Cycle-breaker's Glossary (Appendix A) to the Stewardship Stack (Appendix B), these resources are designed for you to return to long after you've finished the final chapter. If you hear a technical term like "EBITDA" or "amortization" and feel overwhelmed, flip to the back. I've translated the "alphabet soup" into plain English for you.

# 4. MOVE AT THE SPEED OF PEACE

Some of you will sprint through this book in a weekend; others will take a year to implement a single chapter. Both are correct. The goal is not speed; the goal is efficacy. Move at a pace that allows you to lower your biological tax and increase your peace.

Now, let's get to work.

# PART 1

# THE INTERNAL REVOLUTION

*"Don't copy the behavior and customs of this world, but let God transform you into a new person by changing the way you think ..."*

—Romans 12:2 NLT

Every revolution begins with a single, often quiet, decision. In the world of finance, we are taught to believe that the revolution starts with a spreadsheet, a stock pick, or a high-yield savings account. We are told that if we just get the math right, the rest will follow. But after years of navigating my own financial storms and guiding hundreds of clients through theirs, I have learned a hard truth: you cannot build a skyscraper on a swamp.

Before you can master the money moves—the tactical, practical steps of building wealth—you must first master the mindset shifts. You must address the ground you are standing on.

For me, that ground was in the bathroom at my boyfriend's house, staring at a positive pregnancy test at 17 years old. In that moment, the "math" of my life looked impossible. I was a high school student with dreams of culinary school, a newborn on the way, and zero dollars to my name. By every societal metric, my story was supposed to be one of statistics and struggle. The world looked at me and saw a "scarcity trap" personified.

But the courage to begin doesn't come from having a perfect plan; it comes from a fundamental shift in how you view your own agency.

In this first part of the book, we are going to explore the most critical asset you will ever own. It isn't your 401(k) or your home equity. It is your psychological capital or PsyCap. We are going to talk about the shift from an external locus of control—the belief that life is something that happens to you—to an internal locus of control, the unshakeable conviction that you are the driver of your own destiny, regardless of the obstacles in your path.

When I decided to enroll in community college with a baby on my hip, I wasn't making a financial move; I was making a mindset move. I was deciding that my "why" was bigger than my "how." I was choosing to believe that Hope, Efficacy, Resilience, and Optimism were not just "soft skills," but the very raw materials of wealth.

You might be at your own crossroads right now. Perhaps you are staring at a mountain of debt that feels insurmountable. Maybe you are recovering from a job loss, a divorce, or a business failure. Or perhaps you are simply tired of living paycheck to paycheck, feeling like you are running on a treadmill that never stops.

Whatever your "linoleum floor" moment is, the message of Part 1 is this: the struggle stops with you.

In the chapters that follow, we are going to dismantle the money ghosts of your past—the inherited fears and scarcity mindsets that have been holding you back. We are going to redefine budgeting as an act of self-love and permission, rather than restriction. We are going to find the emotional engine that will keep you moving when the initial excitement of a new goal wears off.

This section is about more than just "thinking positive." It is about the rigorous, scientific, and spiritual work of rebuilding your internal foundation. It is about finding the courage to look at your numbers without shame and your future without fear.

You have already taken the first step by opening this book. Now, it's time to decide that you are worth the investment. It's time to stop being a passenger in your financial life and start being the architect.

The math will come. The systems will follow. But first, we must find the courage to begin.

# CHAPTER ONE

# THE CROSSROADS

*"Financial freedom doesn't start in your bank account; it starts in the quiet moments when you decide you're worth the fight."*

—Tiffany Grant

The fluorescent lights of the doctor's office hummed, a sterile sound that did nothing to quiet the frantic beating in my chest. I had already taken three at-home tests, each one showing a faint but undeniable line that had rerouted my entire life. But I needed to be sure. When the doctor confirmed what I already knew to be true, the world outside her office door seemed to fall away.

I cried in my car. Not tears of regret for the child I was going to have, but tears of fear. Fear of shame. I was 17, raised in a heavily religious family where I wasn't supposed to be having sex, let alone getting pregnant. All I could think about were the two people who meant the most to me: my grandma and my mom. I knew they would be disappointed.

Just a few months earlier, we had walked the campus of Johnson & Wales University in Charlotte, the school I had dreamed of attending since I was five years old. My life's ambition was to be a chef, a passion kindled by watching Paula Deen and Emeril Lagasse on the Food Channel, cooking their recipes and adding my own spin. I had fought to get into culinary classes in high school. I loved it. The acceptance letter from Johnson & Wales, which had arrived just a couple of weeks prior, was supposed to be the first chapter of that dream. Now, sitting in my car with a confirmed pregnancy, I was at an unexpected, terrifying crossroads.

I called my mom first, unable to stop the tears. Her response was quiet, measured: "We'll talk about it when I get home from work."

In that silence, the other voices began to creep in. The whispers of what people would think, the low expectations, the quiet judgments. "Oh, you'll just be flipping burgers the rest of your life." In their eyes, my story was already written: another statistic, another dream deferred.

This is the first and most critical moment in any crisis: the moment you are surrounded by noise. The noise of other people's opinions, society's expectations, and your own inner critic. The first money move has nothing to do with money. It's the decision to silence the noise.

## THE ARCHITECTURE OF THE MASK

When I made the decision to silence the noise of the critics and the "burger-flipping" statistics, I didn't just build a plan for my education; I built a persona. I call it the Bulletproof Persona.

When you are a 17-year-old mother, you develop a specialized type of armor. You become the person who has all the answers. You become the one who never needs help. You become "the Expert," "the Provider," and "the Strong One." On the surface, this looks like the ultimate success story. But beneath the surface, the Bulletproof Persona is often a sophisticated trauma response known as Hyper-independence.

## The Hyper-independence Trap

Hyper-independence is the belief that *"if I don't do it, it won't get done,"* or more accurately, *"if I let anyone else help me, I am no longer safe."*

For years, I wore this armor with pride. It was the engine that drove me to get my MBA and build *Money Talk with Tiff.* I felt that if I was bulletproof—if my knowledge was indisputable and my success was visible—then no one could ever look down on me again. But armor is heavy. While it protects you from judgment, it also prevents you from receiving the support required to scale.

## High-functioning Survival Mode

Many of the entrepreneurs I counsel are living in High-functioning Survival Mode. You are achieving massive external results while your internal state is one of constant, low-grade panic. You are running on the fumes of the survival mindset you developed years ago.

I lived this to the extreme in 2021. I was the "Money Girl" by day and a dispatch operator in a personal crisis by night. I couldn't take the mask off because I was afraid that if I admitted I was struggling, the entire house of cards would fall. But true wealth requires the courage to say, "I am a manager of these resources, not the source of them."

Dismantling the persona doesn't make you weak; it makes you scalable. It moves you from High-functioning Survival to Sustainable Success.

**The Voice of Doubt: Common Obstacles and Mindset Shifts**

The fear of dismantling the Bulletproof Persona is a fear of identity. Let's address the voice that tells you that your strength is your only value.

**Obstacle:** "My family/clients/employees depend on me to have all the answers. If I show any weakness, I'll lose their respect."

**Your Mindset Shift:** You are confusing *invincibility* with *integrity*. People don't follow you because you're perfect; they follow you because you're consistent and honest. When I finally told my community about my struggle in 2021, I didn't lose their respect—I gained their trust. Your vulnerability is the bridge that allows others to connect with your expertise. You aren't a fraud for having struggles; you are a human being who is navigating them with strategy.

**Obstacle:** "Being hyper-independent is what got me here. It's my superpower. Why would I give it up?"

**Your Mindset Shift:** Hyper-independence was your survival skill, but it is not your growth skill. What got you out of the "Scarcity Trap" will not get you to the "Legacy Shift." To move to the next level, you must trade *control* for *collaboration*. You must move from being the "Solo Hero" to being the "Chief Steward."

# EXERCISE: THE PERSONA AUDIT

1. Identify the Mask: What is the one thing you are most afraid of people finding out about your business or finances? (e.g., "I'm actually in debt," or "I don't know how to read my P&L statement.")

2. The Cost of the Armor: How much time and energy are you spending every week trying to maintain the appearance of being "Bulletproof"?
3. The First Crack: What is one small thing you can delegate or one area where you can ask for help this week (e.g., hiring a bookkeeper, asking a mentor for a gut-check, or telling a partner you're overwhelmed)?

My decision to enroll in community college while caring for my newborn son wasn't just about getting a degree; it was an act of defiance against my circumstances. It was a declaration that my future would be determined by my choices, not by my challenges. I didn't have the language for it then, but I was fundamentally changing what psychologists call my "locus of control."

The concept, developed by psychologist Julian B. Rotter in the 1950s, is one of the most powerful predictors of success and well-being. It describes where you believe the power in your life resides.

An external locus of control is the belief that your life is dictated by outside forces. It's the voice of "things happen *to* me." You might blame fate, luck, other people, or systemic barriers for your situation. While these factors are undeniably real, residing in this mindset leaves you feeling powerless, like a ship without a rudder, tossed about by the waves of life. It's the mindset that keeps you stuck, waiting to be rescued.

A shift to an internal locus of control is the belief that you are the primary driver of your own life. It's the voice that says, "I make things happen." This doesn't mean you control everything—you don't. It means you believe your actions, your responses, and your efforts are the most powerful forces in shaping your outcomes. As Rotter's research and countless studies since have shown, individuals with a strong internal locus of control are more likely to achieve their goals, report higher levels of happiness, and demonstrate greater resilience in the face of setbacks.

## Client Spotlight: The Ostrich and the Visionary

I remember a client—let's call her Sarah—who was a brilliant business owner but was living in a state of constant, low-grade terror. The moment we got on our first discovery call, she broke down in tears.

"Tiff," she sobbed, "I really don't want to do this. I know I have to, but I'm scared."

Sarah was suffering from what I call the Ostrich Approach. She had her head buried so deep in the sand that she hadn't looked at her personal bank statements in months. To her, money wasn't just math; it was a source of deep, visceral trauma. She felt that if she faced the numbers, she would be forced to admit she was a failure.

Instead of jumping into spreadsheets or debt-payoff ratios, I stopped her. I realized that her PsyCap was depleted. She had no hope because she couldn't see a way out.

"Sarah," I said, "close your eyes. Forget the debt for a second. Envision your life if everything was perfect. Where are you living? What does your day look like? What are you driving?"

As she began to fantasize, the atmosphere shifted. She described a beautiful, sun-drenched house, a booming business that didn't require her 24/7 presence, and the feeling of being completely debt-free. As she spoke, I jotted down her words. I wasn't just listening to her dreams; I was drafting her strategic goals.

When she opened her eyes, she was calm. The anxiety had been replaced by a spark of efficacy. I read her dreams back to her, not as fantasies, but as a roadmap.

### *The Lesson*

Shame dies in the light of a vision. By moving from the Ostrich Approach to a Visionary Mindset, Sarah was finally able to face her numbers. Once we looked at the data, we realized the situation wasn't nearly as bad as the "Money Ghosts" in her head had led her to believe. Within that first call, her anxiety evaporated, and she was ready to do the work.

That decision to enroll in community college, for me, was the first step in building what we'll come to know as "psychological capital" or "PsyCap." It was the moment I took the helm of my own ship. This book is your invitation to do the same.

The dream of being a chef in Charlotte had to be put on hold. A newborn needed family, and my family was in Greensboro. I had to act fast. With the fall semester approaching, it was too late to apply to other local universities. My only option was the local community college.

I remember walking into the enrollment office, my transcript in hand. The woman behind the desk looked at my grades and then at me, her expression a mixture of confusion and disappointment. "What are you doing here?" she asked. I explained the situation, and though she said "Okay," her look confirmed what the world was thinking.

But in that moment, something inside me hardened. I refused to live a life I didn't want to live. I enrolled, choosing business as my major—my second love. I took most of my classes online, doing my schoolwork while my son slept, sometimes holding him in one arm while I typed with the other. It was difficult, but it was mine. I didn't let my circumstances dictate my outcomes. At 17 years old, I was learning that I was still in charge of my life's story.

Did I doubt myself? Absolutely. I questioned the choices that got me there. I doubted my ability to be a great mom when I was barely an adult myself. But then I would look at my son, and the resolve would return. I had to pull myself up by the proverbial bootstraps and keep going for him. I refused to give up. I had a whole new human being depending on me.

## Client Spotlight: The Brilliant Bottleneck

One of my favorite clients was a young mother who was, by all accounts, brilliant. She was organized, she was driven, and she had a deep desire to build a legacy for her children. When we looked at her life, she had all the raw materials for success, but she was stuck.

"Tiff," she told me, "I want to do the work. I'm ready to grind. I just … I don't know where the starting line is."

This is a common hurdle for Cycle-breakers. When you are the first in your family to build wealth, you don't have a blueprint. You have the resilience, but you lack the human capital—the specific, specialized knowledge of how to sequence your moves.

She was a "Brilliant Bottleneck." Her own lack of financial education was the only thing standing between her and her goals. My role wasn't to motivate her; it was to curate her education. We broke her journey down into a simple sequence:

1. Fix the foundation (The Three-bucket System).
2. Protect the builder (The Safety Net).
3. Attack the ghosts (Debt Payoff).

### *The Outcome*

Once she had a guide and a sequence, she moved with terrifying speed. Because she was already so organized, she hit her debt-payoff goals in record time—months faster than she thought possible.

### *The Lesson*

Focus without direction is just wasted energy. You don't need more "hustle"; you need a better syllabus. When you invest in the education of *how* to move, your results multiply.

This is the essence of what psychologists Richard Tedeschi and Lawrence Calhoun identify as post-traumatic growth (PTG)—the idea that profound struggle doesn't just have to be survived; it can be the very catalyst for a stronger, more meaningful life. My "test" was becoming my testimony.

Without knowing the academic term for it, I was building what organizational psychologist Fred Luthans and his colleagues call PsyCap—the inner resources of hope, confidence, resilience, and optimism that are often more valuable than financial capital (refer to Figure 1.1).

- Hope: I held on to the hope of a better future, even when the path was unclear.
- Efficacy: Every assignment I completed, every test I passed while rocking my son to sleep, built my confidence that I could do this.
- Resilience: Every time I wanted to quit but kept going, I was building the muscle of resilience.
- Optimism: I chose to believe that my future was not defined by my present circumstances.

**Figure 1.1 The HERO framework—your internal foundation for wealth.**

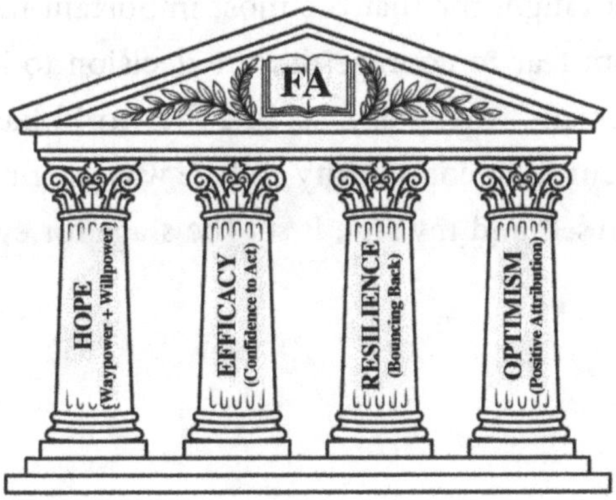

The term "psychological capital" isn't just a catchy phrase; it's a robust, evidence-based concept developed by management scholars Fred Luthans, Carolyn Youssef-Morgan, and Bruce Avolio. Their extensive research, published in numerous academic journals, has demonstrated that PsyCap is a measurable and developable resource that has a profound impact on performance, motivation, and success, not just in the workplace but in life.

Think of it like this: just as financial capital (money) allows you to invest in assets, PsyCap allows you to invest in yourself. It's the inner wealth that fuels your ability to navigate challenges and pursue opportunities. Unlike fixed personality traits, these four resources—Hope, Efficacy, Resilience, and Optimism—can be intentionally cultivated. Luthans and his colleagues proved that when people are trained to develop these capacities, they become more successful and satisfied.

So, as we break down each element, know that you are not just learning feel-good concepts; you are actively building a scientifically validated portfolio of psychological assets that will pay dividends for the rest of your life.

This chapter of my life, the one that felt like a detour, was actually the foundation. It taught me that the most important money move is the mindset shift from fear to courage. It's the decision to invest in yourself, even when—especially when—it feels like the world has written you off. That decision to enroll in community college was the first real investment I ever made in myself and my son. It set the stage for every money move that followed.

## The Voice of Doubt: Common Obstacles and Mindset Shifts

Making the decision to change is the first step, but it's often followed by a chorus of internal and external voices telling you it's impossible. They are the echoes of past failures, the fears of your family, and the anxieties of your present circumstances. Let's silence them, one by one.

**Obstacle:** "It's too late for me. I've made too many mistakes and I'm too far behind to ever catch up."

**Your Mindset Shift:** The past is a lesson, not a life sentence. My journey didn't truly begin in a classroom; it began in a moment of crisis with a newborn in my arms. Your story doesn't start when you're perfect; it starts the moment you decide you are worth the effort. The only time that matters is *now*. Every step you take from this moment forward is a step toward a new destination. You are not defined by where you've been, but by where you decide to go.

**Obstacle:** "I'm not smart enough for all this. Business, finance … it's just not how my brain works."

**Your Mindset Shift:** This isn't about becoming a Wall Street analyst. It's about becoming the chief financial officer of *your* life. You don't need a PhD in economics; you need the courage to look at your own numbers and the curiosity to ask questions. Remember, I was supposed to be a chef! I had to learn this language, and I promise you, it's a language you can learn too. We'll start with one word, one concept, one decision at a time.

**Obstacle:** "No one in my life supports this. My family thinks I'm crazy for wanting to start a business/go back to school/get serious about money."

(*Continued*)

(*Continued*)

**Your Mindset Shift:** You are the CEO of your dream, and sometimes the board of directors (your friends and family) will vote against you out of their own fear. Your responsibility is not to win their approval, but to honor your own vision. Find your support system elsewhere—in books, in podcasts, in communities (like the one I hope this book creates for you). Your success will be the only permission you ever needed.

# CHAPTER TWO

# CHOOSING EDUCATION

*"Education is the only asset that no market crash can take away and no creditor can repossess."*

—Tiffany Grant

We have established that the foundation of any true revolution is internal. You have identified your "Money Ghosts," committed to shifting your locus of control, and begun the work of building your psychological capital (PsyCap). But mindset without movement is just a dream. To turn your internal conviction into external reality, you must decide where to deploy your newly reclaimed agency. You must decide which "Money Move" will provide the highest return on your effort while you are still navigating the early stages of your journey.

For the Cycle-breaker, the most logical and high-leverage starting point isn't found in the stock market or a real estate portfolio. Those are external assets that require capital you may not yet have. Instead, the first move is an investment in the only asset that no one can ever repossess: your own mind. This is the shift from viewing yourself as a victim of your circumstances to viewing yourself as a high-value producer in the marketplace. By choosing to invest in your human capital through education, you are not just gaining a credential; you are building the engine that will drive every other financial success in this book.

# THE MOST POWERFUL INVESTMENT

The first money move isn't about stocks, real estate, or a savings account. It has nothing to do with money at all, at least not at first. The first and most crucial investment you will ever make is in yourself. It's the decision to choose education—formal or informal—as the bedrock upon which you will build your future. For me, that decision wasn't made in a classroom or a career counselor's office. It was made in the quiet, desperate hours of early motherhood, fueled by a fierce determination to break a cycle.

I didn't grow up with my mom. She had left me with my grandparents in New York when I was three years old to pursue her own college education in North Carolina. While I was loved, I carried the persistent ache of her absence. So, when I held my own son, I made a silent, unbreakable vow: I would not leave him. I would not force him to wonder where his mother was. That feeling, the one I knew all too well, was a future I was determined to fight against. He became my "why," the living, breathing reason for every sacrifice that was to come.

This vow reshaped my entire approach to education. The traditional path was no longer an option. Instead, I enrolled in online classes. It was a more challenging route, demanding a level of self-discipline I was only just beginning to discover. But the trade-off was priceless: I could be present for my son, raising him exactly how I wanted, and never letting him feel the void I had.

## THE HARSH REALITY AND THE HUSTLE

The world, however, doesn't always accommodate our plans. The job I had before my pregnancy, the one I'd held since I was 16, was my safety net. My manager had promised me my position was safe, that I could come back whenever I was ready. But while I was on maternity leave, a cold, formal letter arrived: I was terminated for exhausting my FMLA leave. The verbal promise meant nothing. I fought it, pleading my case with HR, but without anything in writing, it was a lost cause. I cried. It was more than just a job; it was the only professional world I had ever known, and the door had just been slammed shut.

Panic set in, but it was quickly replaced by resolve. I had a child to feed. I found a remote job at a call center, a lifeline that allowed me to work from home. Our life became a tightly choreographed dance of survival and ambition. His dad and I worked for the same company on opposite shifts. My day would start before dawn with schoolwork, followed by breastfeeding my son, and then logging into my shift. Between calls, I'd rush to feed him again. When my shift ended, his began, and I would switch back to mom and student, squeezing in study sessions during his precious nap times. It was a period of bone-deep exhaustion, a relentless cycle of duty, but my son's future was the only motivation I needed.

# RESOURCEFUL, NOT RESOURCED: BUILDING PSYCAP

Many people believe you need significant resources to get ahead. I learned you just need to be resourceful. My financial aid journey wasn't one of prestigious scholarships. It was about understanding the system. Because I was a single parent, I was considered an independent student on my FAFSA application. This meant my eligibility was based on my own meager income, not my mother's. The result was the Pell Grant, a federal program that became my financial key, fully funded my time at community college. It wasn't a lottery win; it was the result of research and understanding the rules.

This process is a real-world example of what researchers in the field of psychology refer to when they discuss the link between education and resilience. As Simon Cassidy noted in his research on the topic, successfully navigating academic challenges helps build academic self-efficacy—a person's belief in their ability to succeed in educational tasks. This isn't just about feeling smart; it's the confidence that comes from overcoming obstacles, whether it's a tough exam or a bureaucratic financial aid form. Each small win builds a foundation of resilience.

My entrepreneurial spark flickered too. Before the baby, I had a small side hustle selling cheesecakes. I tried to keep it going, but with a newborn and a full course load, the orders became few and far between. I didn't have the time or energy to market it, and once the call center job started, I had to let it go. It was a small failure, but a crucial lesson in capacity and focus.

# THE ROI OF YOU: TURNING CREDENTIALS INTO CASH FLOW

Every certificate, degree, and skill you acquire is a deposit into your own human capital, and the returns can be exponential. This isn't just a motivational platitude; it's a socioeconomic reality. Studies by researchers like Min Zhan and Shanta Pandey have shown that for single mothers, postsecondary education is one of the single most important factors in achieving long-term economic well-being. My own life is a testament to this principle.

My SHRM-CP (Society for Human Resource Management Certified Professional) certification was a direct catalyst for tripling my income. It elevated me from an HR Associate to an HR Business Partner, a role with far greater responsibility and compensation. The MBA added a layer of authority and respect that is hard to quantify but has been infinitely valuable in my business. When you have those three letters after your name, doors open.

The AFC® (Accredited Financial Counselor) credential gave me a new level of credibility. It wasn't just "Tiff's advice" anymore; it was advice from a certified professional. This allowed me to secure speaking engagements and get quoted in major publications, dramatically increasing my exposure and brand authority.

This transformation from credentials to cash flow is a textbook example of what economists call "human capital theory." First pioneered by economists like Gary Becker and Jacob Mincer, the theory posits that education and training are not expenses, but investments in an individual's own productivity and earning potential. Just like a business invests in better machinery to increase its output, you invest in your skills and knowledge to increase your personal economic output.

My story is a living testament to this. Each certification wasn't just a piece of paper; it was an upgrade to my personal "machinery," making me more valuable in the marketplace. Becker's Nobel Prize-winning work confirmed that higher levels of education are directly correlated with higher lifetime earnings. So, when you are debating whether to take that course, finish that degree, or learn that new skill, you are not just making a decision for today; you are making a strategic investment in your "human capital" that will pay dividends for decades to come.

And not all education comes with a price tag. I built my entire foundation in web development from the "University of YouTube" and countless blogs. That free education empowered me to build my first website, saving thousands in startup costs, and later blossomed into a full-fledged digital marketing company. The most powerful resource you have is your own curiosity.

# THE HUMAN CAPITAL ROI: CALCULATING THE VALUE OF YOUR BRAIN

In the first half of this chapter, I shared how choosing education over entertainment saved my life. But I don't want you to just take my word for it as a story of resilience. I want you to see the math. As an MBA and a financial wellness curator, I view every degree, every certification, and every new skill not as an expense, but as a capital investment.

In the world of business, we use return on investment (ROI) to decide if a project is worth the money. We should use the exact same rigor when deciding whether to invest in our own human capital. If you are going to spend your time and your money (or take on the "Debt Trap" we discuss in Chapter 3), you must ensure that the "Future You" is getting a fair deal.

Here is the technical framework for calculating your human capital ROI.

## The Payback Period: When Does the Investment Break Even?

The first metric to consider is the payback period. This is the amount of time it takes for the increase in your earnings to cover the total cost of the education.

**The Formula**

$$\textit{Payback Period} = \textit{Total Cost of Education} \div \textit{Annual Salary Increase}$$

- Total Cost of Education: This includes tuition, books, fees, and—crucially—the opportunity cost (the income you lose if you must stop working to study).
- Annual Salary Increase: The difference between what you earn now and the average starting salary for someone with that new credential.

**Example**
Imagine you are considering a data analytics certification that costs $5,000.

- Your current salary: $45,000.
- Average salary with the certification: $55,000.
- Annual Increase: $55,000 – $45,000 = $10,000

$$\textit{Payback Period} = \$5,000 \div \$10,000 = 0.5\,\textit{years}\ (6\,\textit{months})$$

In this scenario, the investment pays for itself in just six months. This is what we call a high-velocity asset. Compare this to a $100,000 degree that only nets you a $5,000 raise—that payback period is 20 years. That is a liability disguised as an asset.

# The Lifetime Value of a Skill

While the payback period tells you how fast you get your money back, the lifetime value (LTV) tells you how much wealth that skill will generate over your entire career. This is where the power of the "Education Move" truly reveals itself.

**The Formula**

$$LTV = (Annual\ Salary\ Increase \times Years\ Remaining\ in\ Career) - Total\ Cost\ of\ Education$$

Using our data analytics example again, if you are 30 years old and plan to work until 60 (30 years remaining):

- Annual Increase: $10,000
- Years: 30
- Cost: $5,000

$$LTV = (\$10,000 \times 30) - \$5,000 = \$295,000$$

By spending $5,000 today, you have added nearly $300,000 to your lifetime wealth. This is why I tell my clients: Your brain is the only asset you own that can't be repossessed and has an infinite ceiling for growth.

# The Strategic Education Audit

Before you sign a loan document or pay a deposit, you must perform a strategic education audit. This ensures that your human capital move is aligned with your Umbrella Method (Chapter 15) and your Expat Goal (Chapter 21).

Ask yourself these four "Curator Questions":

1. Is the Skill Portable? In 2025, a high-value skill should be location-independent. Does this credential allow you to work from a veranda in Jamaica, or does it tether you to a physical office in a high-cost city?
2. Is the Skill Scalable? Does this education teach you a service you can only perform one-on-one (trading time for money), or does it give you the knowledge to create a product or a system (the "Ribs" of your Umbrella)?
3. What Is the "Market Signal"? A degree from a prestigious university is a signal, but so is a portfolio of real-world projects. In many modern fields, a Google Career Certificate or a Lean Six Sigma Belt provides a stronger signal of competence than a general degree.
4. Can I "Micro-invest"? Before committing to a four-year degree, can you take a $50 Coursera course or a $500 certification? Use the "Micro-move" strategy to test the ROI before you commit to the "Macro-investment."

# The Tiff Takeaway: Don't Buy the Hype, Buy the ROI

The "Crossroads" I faced at 17 wasn't just about surviving; it was about calculating. I chose community college because the ROI was undeniable. It allowed me to gain the foundational business skills I needed while keeping my costs low and my "human capital" growing.

Your education is the engine of your growth. But like any engine, it needs to be efficient. Stop viewing school as a "rite of passage" and start viewing it as a wealth-building move. When you get the math right on your education, the math on your life becomes a whole lot easier.

## The Voice of Doubt: Common Obstacles and Mindset Shifts

Choosing to invest in yourself, especially when you're overwhelmed, can feel like a luxury you can't afford. Let's tackle the voices that tell you it's not for you.

**Obstacle:** "I can't afford to go back to school. I have no time and no money."

**Your Mindset Shift:** Redefine "education." It doesn't have to mean a four-year university. It can be a $10 online course, a free certification from Google, or borrowing a book from the library. As I learned building my web development skills from the "University of YouTube," the most valuable resource isn't money; it's your curiosity. Start with the time and money you do have. Can you find 15 minutes a day? Can you find $5 a month? Start there. The goal is momentum, not a mountain.

**Obstacle:** "I'm not a 'school' person. I was never good at it."

**Your Mindset Shift:** The traditional school system is only one path. Your education should follow your passion. If you love working with your hands, "education" might be an apprenticeship. If you love creating, it might be a graphic design course. Don't let a bad experience with algebra stop you from learning a skill that could change your life. The best education is the one you are excited to pursue.

**Obstacle:** "Is it even worth it? Will it really lead to a better job?"

**Your Mindset Shift:** You must be strategic. Don't just get a degree; solve a problem. Look at job postings for the roles you want. What skills are they asking for? What certifications are listed? Reverse-engineer your education from the outcome you desire. My SHRM-CP wasn't a random choice; it was a direct answer to the question, "How can I triple my income in the HR field?" Let the market tell you what education is worth.

Choosing to invest in yourself is the first, most courageous money move. It's the act of declaring that you are your own greatest asset. It's hard, it's often lonely, and it demands sacrifice. But as the research confirms, every late night, every dollar stretched, and every moment of self-doubt you push through is a down payment on a future of economic independence and profound personal resilience you are building, one skill at a time. But to unlock the doors that education had opened, I would have to conquer a ghost from my past—my deep-seated fear of credit.

# CHAPTER THREE

# THE BINDER OF CREDIT CARDS AND THE GHOST OF 2008

*"You cannot build a future on a foundation of ghosts; silence the past so you can hear the opportunities of the present."*

—Tiffany Grant

For most of my childhood, credit seemed like magic. My great-aunt had a thick, heavy binder, not for photos, but for credit cards. When she took my mom to go shopping, she'd flip through the plastic pages with a practiced ease, selecting the right card for the right store. My mom inherited this habit. Her collection wasn't in a binder, but it was just as impressive—a stack of cards three to five inches thick.

Her collection grew through a common retail trap. We'd be at the checkout counter, and the cashier would offer, "Would you like to save 20% on your purchase today by opening a store credit card?" My mom, thinking she'd be denied, would say yes. But then the words would come back: "You're approved!" In went another card, and often, a few more items into the shopping cart to make the most of the discount. It was a cycle, a behavior passed down through generations. To my young eyes, credit wasn't debt; it was a source of abundance, a tool that ensured we could get anything we wanted.

Then came 2008.

The world economy began to tremble, and the magic trick unraveled. I was in high school, straddling eleventh and twelfth grade, when the headlines about the financial crisis became personal. I saw the aftermath up close: bankruptcies, foreclosures, and the gut-wrenching stress that follows when the magic money runs out. The lesson I learned was swift and brutal: debt is a monster, and credit is the cage door you never, ever open. The abundance I had known was a mirage, and I wanted no part of it.

This sharp pivot from seeing credit as a tool of abundance to a tool of destruction is a classic response to financial trauma. My belief system was shattered, and in its place, a deep-seated fear took root. For years, I became a master of avoidance. I paid for everything in cash. I had no credit cards and wanted none. On the surface, I was being "responsible," but in reality, I was operating from a place of terror. I had developed what researchers call a scarcity mindset.

My experience wasn't just a personal quirk; it was a textbook example of how major economic shocks can create lasting psychological trauma. Researchers have found that economic scarcity can trigger a persistent "scarcity mindset" that fundamentally alters how we make decisions (Goldsmith et al., 2020). Events like the 2008 financial crisis exemplify this pattern. It's a state of mind where you believe there will never be enough, so you fixate on immediate threats and avoid perceived risks at all costs.

My wake-up call came when I was 22. I walked into the bank I had been using since I was 16, confident and prepared. I wasn't asking for a mortgage, just a simple, manageable $200 line of credit. It felt like a safe first step, a way to dip my toe into the world of credit without risk. I had a long history with the bank; surely, they could see my responsible cash habits.

"I'm sorry, you've been declined."

The words hit me like a physical blow. Declined? For $200? The loan officer explained why. First, at my $10-an-hour job, I simply wasn't making enough money. Second, and more shockingly, she said I had medical derogatory marks on my credit report. I was stunned. I had always been told that medical debt didn't really "count" against you. It was a myth I, and many others, believed. That day, I learned two hard truths: my income was insufficient, and medical debt absolutely mattered. I had no credit history to counteract these negatives. My strategy of avoidance had left me invisible and powerless in the financial system.

This is the paradox of a scarcity mindset. It creates a phenomenon called "tunneling" (Mullainathan and Shafir, 2013). Think of it like driving through a dark tunnel where your headlights only illuminate the 10 feet directly in front of you. Your brain becomes so focused on the immediate problem—for me, the perceived danger of any and all debt—that you can't see the bigger picture or the opportunities down the road. I was so focused on avoiding the monster that I couldn't see that credit, when used correctly, wasn't a monster at all. It was a necessary tool.

The constant worry and mental gymnastics of avoiding this perceived threat were also exhausting. This is what researchers refer to as a depleted "mental bandwidth." The constant stress of scarcity consumes so much of our cognitive energy that it impairs our ability to solve problems and think long-term (Haushofer and Fehr, 2014). It's not that we aren't smart enough to make good decisions; it's that our brains are simply too overloaded by the perceived crisis to function at their best. My fear was taking up so much space that I couldn't strategize for my future.

That rejection was the catalyst I needed. It lit a fire under me. I was tired of being afraid and tired of being powerless. I got a new job that paid more. I systematically started paying off the old medical debts. Then, armed with a better income and a cleaner history, I applied for a Capital One card. Approved.

I was still terrified. For months, I would swipe the card for a small purchase and then immediately log into the app and pay it off. I never carried a balance. On the surface, I was being "responsible," but in reality, I was operating from a place of terror. The same PsyCap—the hope, resilience, and optimism—that had carried me through my early motherhood was now being put to a new test. My fear of debt was preventing me from building the very future I was working so hard for. I was using the card not as a line of credit, but as a credit-building machine. A year later, I walked back into that same bank that had rejected me. I applied for their card. This time, I was approved for $1,000.

It's a wild reality of our financial system: you must have credit to build credit. My two cards, used carefully and intentionally, became my primary tools. All those small, disciplined steps—confronting my fear, cleaning up my past, and strategically building a positive history—were what led me to buy my first house at the age of 26.

This is the first and most crucial mindset shift: recognizing when fear has put you in a tunnel. Your past experiences are valid, but they don't have to be a life sentence. By understanding the psychology behind the fear, you can begin to dismantle it, take back your mental bandwidth, and start seeing the opportunities that lie just outside your headlights.

The girl who was once terrified of a credit card binder now held the keys to her own front door—all because she learned to see credit as a tool, not a monster.

## The Voice of Doubt: Common Obstacles and Mindset Shifts

For many of us, the word "credit" is loaded with fear, shame, and stories of disaster. It's the monster under the bed. If you're going to build wealth, you must turn on the light and see it for what it is: a tool.

**Obstacle:** "But what if I overspend and get into debt? I saw what happened to my family during the 2008 crash. Credit ruins lives."

**Your Mindset Shift:** You are right to be cautious. You saw firsthand how a tool, when misused, can cause immense damage. But a hammer can build a house, or it can break a window. You are not your family. Their story is a lesson, not your destiny. We are going to treat credit like a professional tool. You will start with a specific, controlled task: get a single, low-limit card, put one small recurring bill on it (like Netflix), and automate the payment in full every month. You will build a history of trust with yourself before you ever use it for anything more. This is about control, not consumption.

**Obstacle:** "My credit score is already terrible. It feels like a hopeless hole to dig out of."

**Your Mindset Shift:** A bad credit score is a temporary condition, not a character flaw. It's a snapshot of your past, not a verdict on your future. The most powerful thing you can do right now is get your credit report and look at it. Knowledge replaces fear. Once you see what's on there, you can make a plan. Do you have a late payment you can dispute? Do you have a small collection you can negotiate? We are looking for small wins that build momentum. The journey out of that hole starts with one single step.

# YOUR FIRST CREDIT ACTION PLAN: BUILDING TRUST WITH YOURSELF

Conquering your fear requires a plan that feels safe and puts you in complete control. We are not going to dive into the deep end. We are going to start by dipping a toe in the water, moving from fear to action with a clear, manageable strategy. Here is your step-by-step plan to start building or rebuilding your credit history safely, incorporating advice from the experts.

## Step 1: Pull Your Reports and Know Your Starting Point

Before you do anything else, you must know where you stand. As both my blog and experts emphasize, you cannot fix what you cannot see. You are entitled to a free credit report from each of the three major bureaus—Equifax, Experian, and TransUnion—every single week at the official government-mandated site: AnnualCreditReport.com. This is nonnegotiable. Download all three reports. Don't be afraid of what you'll find; knowledge is the antidote to fear. Review each report for errors, get a clear picture of any outstanding debts, and understand your current financial standing. If you find inaccuracies, use the dispute process on the bureau's website (e.g., Experian.com/dispute).

## Step 2: Choose Your "Training Wheels" Card

Your first goal is to get a single, positive payment history reporting to the bureaus. The safest way to do this is with a secured credit card. As I mention in my guide for beginners, a secured card is perfect for this. You provide a small, refundable security deposit (often $200–$500), and that amount becomes your credit limit. You are essentially borrowing against your own money, which makes it very low risk for the bank and, more importantly, for you.

## Step 3: Implement the "Set It and Forget It" Method

Once you have your secured card, do not think of it as a shopping card. Credit is a tool, and you don't need to accumulate debt to build a good score. Use this tool for a single job: choose one small, recurring monthly subscription you already pay for—like Netflix, Spotify, or your iCloud storage. Log into that service's website and set your new secured card as the automatic payment method.

## Step 4: Automate Your Success

This is the most critical step. Immediately log into your credit card's online portal and set up an automatic payment from your checking account to pay the statement balance in full every single month. Payment history is the most significant factor in your credit score, and even one late payment can have a severe impact. By automating this process, you guarantee a perfect payment history, and you will never pay a single penny of interest.

## Step 5: Keep Your Balances Low

While our "Set It and Forget It" method keeps your balance predictable, it's crucial to understand the principle of credit utilization—the ratio of your balance to your credit limit. As I cover in my podcast, you should aim to keep this ratio below 30%, but the lower, the better. Paying your balance in full each month ensures your utilization is effectively zero when it matters most. Avoid the myth that carrying a balance helps your score; it doesn't. It just costs you money.

This simple, five-step, automated system achieves the only goal that matters right now: it reports a positive payment history to the credit bureaus every month without you having to think about it and without any risk of overspending. You are using the card as a simple, powerful machine to build your credit score on autopilot, dismantling your fear with disciplined, decisive action.

# RESOURCES

**Free Credit Reports:** AnnualCreditReport.com

**Blog Post:** *A Comprehensive Guide to Credit for Millennials and Gen Z* can be found at moneytalkwitht.com/blog/guide-to-credit/

# CHAPTER FOUR

# MY GRANDFATHER'S LEGACY AND THE BILL YOU PAY FIRST

*"Paying yourself first isn't just a financial habit; it is a generational declaration that your future is a nonnegotiable priority, not a leftover."*

—Tiffany Grant

I was sitting in a church pew at my grandpa's funeral in 2016, listening to my uncle give a heartfelt eulogy, when a single sentence struck me like a lightning bolt. "My dad," he said, his voice thick with emotion, "always told me to pay myself first."

In that moment, a flood of memories came back to me. I could almost hear my grandpa's voice, the gentle lilt of his Jamaican accent, saying those exact same words to me during one of our conversations when I was a girl. It was a piece of advice I had heard but never fully understood until that day. Sitting there, reflecting on his life, the profound wisdom of that simple phrase finally clicked into place.

My grandfather was the patriarch of my dad's side of my family in the truest sense. He came to the United States from Jamaica with a singular, monumental goal: to bring his entire family over to what he saw as a land of opportunity. He started with nothing but his hands and his will. He worked as a carpenter and later a foreman, his skill helping to raise some of the iconic buildings that shape the New York City skyline.

From those humble beginnings, he built a life and then a legacy. He brought over his mom, his siblings, his wife, and his children. He even helped my great-grandmother get a job working for the Rockefellers, where she became their nanny and traveled the world. For nearly 50 years, he worked in the same industry, a testament to his consistency and dedication.

But his work didn't stop at his day job. With that "pay yourself first" mentality, he and my grandmother began to build a real estate empire. They bought multi-family houses, single-family homes, and apartment buildings across New York. They built so much that they were able to buy their dream retirement home in a gated golf community in Florida and another house for my great-grandmother on the very same street. They financed homes for other family members. All of this grew from the seed of that one idea: before you pay the landlord, the grocer, or the electric company, you pay your future self.

It's not lost on me that my own story is now echoing his, as I build a new construction business in Negril, Jamaica. It feels like a full-circle moment, carrying on his legacy of building from the ground up.

My grandfather's advice to "pay yourself first" wasn't just timeless family wisdom; it's a principle deeply supported by modern behavioral science. The power of this habit goes far beyond the dollars and cents in your account; it fundamentally rewires your brain's response to financial stress.

Financial insecurity is a significant source of chronic stress, which impairs cognitive function, fuels anxiety, and leads to poor decision-making. It's hard to plan for the future when your brain is stuck in a present-day panic.

This is where even a small, consistent act of saving becomes a powerful psychological intervention. While large-scale studies often focus on disaster recovery, the underlying principle is the same: having a financial buffer, no matter the size, provides immediate stress-reducing benefits. Research from institutions like the Australian Psychological Society and articles in journals such as *Disaster Prevention and Management* highlight that financial preparedness is directly linked to improved mental health and reduced trauma during crises.

Think of it this way: your brain doesn't just see a $100 emergency fund. It sees options. It sees a safety net. That small cushion creates what scientists call "cognitive slack" or "mental bandwidth." Instead of your mind being consumed by the fear of a flat tire, it is freed up to think more clearly, solve problems more creatively, and focus on long-term goals.

My grandfather knew this intuitively. He knew that the feeling of having something set aside—of knowing you've prioritized your own security—was the true treasure. That $1, $10, or $100 you save isn't just money. It's a deposit of peace of mind. It's a tangible signal to your nervous system that you are secure, you are capable, and you are in control.

My grandfather didn't have a PhD in behavioral economics, as a matter of fact, he only had a grade school level of education, but his advice to "pay yourself first" is a perfect real-world application of what Nobel laureate Richard Thaler calls "choice architecture" (Thaler and

Benartzi, 2004). The simple genius of this strategy is that it makes your future self the first and most important "bill" you pay, not the last. It redesigns your financial environment so that saving becomes the default, not an afterthought.

Most people do the opposite. They pay their bills, buy their groceries, spend on entertainment, and then hope to save whatever is left. The problem is, there's rarely anything left. This is a natural human tendency called "present bias"—we are wired to prioritize the needs and wants of today over the needs of our future selves (Xiao and Porto, 2019). "Paying yourself first" is the ultimate hack for this bias. It treats your savings and investments as a nonnegotiable expense.

The most effective way to do this is to make it invisible. When I say this has become a critical aspect of my life, it's because I've automated it. The money comes out of my income before it even hits my main checking account. You don't miss the money because you never see it. It works just like your healthcare deductions or retirement contributions from a 9-to-5 job; you adjust your life to the net amount you receive. You're only used to what you see in your bank account, so the money you've siphoned off for your future grows quietly in the background without causing you any pain or requiring any willpower.

This isn't just about accumulating wealth; it's about buying peace of mind. Research has shown a direct link between having savings and improved psychological well-being (Hall, 2021). By automating your savings, you reduce your "cognitive load." You no longer have to wrestle with the decision of how much to save each month. You've already made the decision once, and the system takes care of the rest. This frees up your mental energy and reduces the constant, low-grade anxiety that so many people feel about their finances.

My grandfather's legacy is more than the buildings he built or the houses he owned. His legacy is this powerful, generational wisdom: build the life you want by paying for it first.

## The Voice of Doubt: Common Obstacles and Mindset Shifts

"Pay yourself first." It sounds so simple, so wise. But when you're living paycheck to paycheck, it can also sound completely impossible. It can feel like a slap in the face. Let's dismantle that feeling.

**Obstacle:** "You don't get it. I literally have nothing left over. After rent, food, and bills, there is zero. How can I pay myself first?"

**Your Mindset Shift:** I hear you, and I have been there. This is the single most important obstacle to understand. If, after covering your absolute essentials, there is no money left, you do not have a spending problem—you have an income problem. But the principle of "pay yourself first" is not about the *amount*; it is about the *habit* and the *priority*.

The shift is to start ridiculously small. Can you save $1? Open your banking app right now and transfer $1 from your checking to your savings. That's it. You've done it. You have just told yourself, your money, and the universe that *you come first*. You have started to build the muscle. The goal right now isn't to build a massive fund; it's to prove to yourself that you are a person who saves. The amount will grow when your income does, but the identity starts now.

**Obstacle:** "What's the point of saving $5 or $10? It won't make a difference when I need thousands for a real emergency."

**Your Mindset Shift:** You are building what I call a "crisis buffer." That $10 may not replace your transmission, but it might be the difference between putting gas in your car to get to a job interview or staying home. It might be the co-pay for a doctor's visit that prevents a bigger health issue. It stops small problems from cascading into life-altering disasters. More importantly, it breaks the cycle of dependence on debt for minor inconveniences. It's your first layer of financial freedom.

# PART 1 ACTION GUIDE

You have completed the first stage of your journey. You've explored the crossroads of decision-making, learned to build your PsyCap, confronted the "ghosts" of your financial past, and committed to the principle of paying yourself first.

But transformation doesn't happen through reading; it happens through doing. This Action Guide is designed to help you excavate the beliefs and habits that have been holding you back so you can clear the ground for the systems we will build in Part 2.

## EXERCISE 1: THE LOCUS OF CONTROL INVENTORY

In Chapter 1, we discussed Julian B. Rotter's concept of the locus of control. Use this exercise to identify where you are currently ceding your power to external circumstances.

1. Identify the "They": List three financial frustrations you currently have (e.g., "I can't save because inflation is too high," or "I'll never get a raise because my boss is unfair").
2. The Pivot: For each item, rewrite the sentence to focus on your internal agency.
   - *Example:* "Inflation is high, so I will audit my subscriptions to find $50 of 'leaked' money to protect my savings."

3. The Commitment: What is one area of your financial life where you have been acting as a "passenger"? What is the first move you will take this week to get back into the driver's seat?

# EXERCISE 2: THE PSYCAP HERO AUDIT

Rate yourself on a scale of 1–10 for each of the four pillars of PsyCap. Be honest—this is your baseline.

- Hope (Waypower and Willpower): Do you have a clear goal and a belief that there is a path to reach it? [ ]
- Efficacy (Confidence): Do you believe you have the skills (or the ability to learn them) to manage your money? [ ]
- Resilience (Bouncing Back): When a financial setback happens, how quickly do you move from panic to a plan? [ ]
- Optimism (Positive Outlook): Do you believe your financial future will be better than your past? [ ]

**Action Step:** Choose your lowest scoring pillar. What is one small "win" you can engineer this week to boost that score? For example, if you scored low on Efficacy, watch one 10-minute tutorial on how to read a credit report.

# EXERCISE 3: IDENTIFYING YOUR MONEY GHOSTS

In Chapter 3, we talked about the "Ghost of 2008." We all have financial stories we've inherited. It's time to bring yours into the light.

- The Memory: What is your earliest memory of money? Was it a source of joy, or a source of tension?
- The Inherited Rule: Complete this sentence: "In my family, people like us [________] with money." (e.g., " … always struggle," " … don't talk about," " … spend it as soon as we get it.")
- The Exorcism: Is that rule serving your "Why"? If not, write a new rule for your own household.

# EXERCISE 4: THE "PAY YOURSELF FIRST" COMMITMENT CONTRACT

Chapter 4 introduced the most important bill you will ever pay. Use this space to make it official.

I, [Your Name], commit to paying myself first starting on [Date].

My Starting Amount: $__________ (Remember: even $1 counts as a win!)

My "Why": I am saving this money because I want to feel [Emotion, e.g., Secure/Free/Powerful] so that I can [Goal, e.g., take my kids to the beach/quit my second job].

Signature: ______________________________________

**Client Spotlight:**
**Maya's Internal Revolution**

When Maya first sat down with me for a financial counseling session, she didn't bring a spreadsheet. She brought a stack of unopened envelopes and a heavy sense of shame. Maya was a 34-year-old marketing professional earning a respectable salary, yet she was living in a state of perpetual "financial vertigo." No matter how much she earned, she felt like she was falling.

### *The Money Ghost*

As we began the work of identifying her money ghosts, Maya realized that her relationship with money was haunted by her childhood. She grew up in a household where money was a weapon. Her parents' divorce was a decade-long battle of financial withholding and "scarcity as control." For Maya, looking at a bank balance triggered the same physical anxiety she felt as a child listening to her parents argue over child support.

Her "Ghost" told her: "Money is a source of pain and conflict. If you don't look at it, it can't hurt you."

This had led Maya to a profound external locus of control. She viewed her debt as something that had "happened" to her—the result of bad luck, a predatory car loan, and an expensive city. She felt like a passenger in a car with no brakes, waiting for the inevitable crash.

### *The Shift to PsyCap*

Our first three sessions weren't about her interest rates; they were about her PsyCap. We had to rebuild her internal accounts before we could touch her external ones.

1. Building Efficacy: We started with a "micro-move." I asked Maya to open just one envelope per day. Not to pay the bill, not to solve the problem—just to look at the number. When she realized the world didn't end when she saw a balance, her Efficacy (the belief in her ability to handle a task) began to grow.

(*Continued*)

(*Continued*)

2. Cultivating Hope: We moved from "How do I pay this?" to "Why do I want to be free?" Maya's "why" was her 10-year-old daughter. She wanted her daughter to grow up in a house where money was a tool for peace, not a weapon of war. This gave her Hope—the "way-power" to see a path through the debt.
3. Practicing Resilience: Maya had a setback in month two—an unexpected medical bill that felt like a punch in the gut. In the past, this would have caused her to give up entirely. Instead, we used the Resilience framework. We acknowledged the setback, analyzed the "Four Walls" to find a temporary adjustment, and she got back on track within 48 hours.

### *The Result: From Passenger to Architect*

The turning point came when Maya stopped saying, "I can't afford this," and started saying, "I am choosing not to spend on this because I am prioritizing my daughter's college fund."

That shift in language was the sound of her internal locus of control clicking into place. She was no longer a victim of her circumstances; she was the architect of her flow.

Six months later, Maya had not only paid off $4,500 in high-interest debt, but she had also negotiated a $7,000 raise at work using the "Art of the Ask" techniques we will discuss in later chapters. But the real victory wasn't the money. It was the fact that Maya now checks her banking app every morning while drinking her coffee. The vertigo is gone. She is no longer falling; she is building.

**Tiff's Takeaway:** Maya didn't need a better math teacher; she needed to reclaim her agency. Her story reminds us that the biggest obstacle to wealth isn't the number on the screen—it's the story in your head.

Ready to put these shifts into motion? Scan the code below to access the **Cycle-Breaker's Resource Vault**, where I've provided downloadable worksheets, budget templates, and video deep-dives for every move in this section.

**Link:** moneytalkwitht.com/moves

# PART 2

# THE ARCHITECTURE OF FLOW

*"Know the state of your flocks, and put your heart into caring for your herds."*

—Proverbs 27:23 NLT

If Part 1 was about the ground you stand on, Part 2 is about the house you build.

We have done the hard work of shifting your mindset. You have looked your money ghosts in the eye, reclaimed your internal locus of control, and committed to paying yourself first. But as any architect will tell you, a vision without a blueprint is just a dream. To turn your new mindset into a lasting reality, you need a system that works for you, not against you.

For years, the financial industry has sold us the idea that budgeting is about restriction. We've been told that to be "good" with money, we must live a life of "no." No lattes, no dinners out, no spontaneous trips, no joy. We've been taught to view our money as a finite, shrinking pool that we must guard with a spirit of deprivation.

In this section, we are going to flip that script entirely.

We are moving away from the "Starvation Budget" and toward the architecture of flow. We are going to design a system where your money doesn't just sit in a stagnant pile—it moves with purpose. We are going to build a money flow system that reflects your values, supports your "why," and, most importantly, gives you permission to spend.

This is the section where the theory gets its hands dirty.

We will start by reframing the very concept of a budget. You'll learn why your past attempts at tracking probably failed (hint: it wasn't a lack of willpower; it was a lack of awareness) and how to use your first 30 days of data to perform an autopilot reset.

We will explore the "Do More, Do Less, Stop" framework—a tool designed to help you prune away the "empty calories" of your spending so you can nourish the things that actually bring you joy. We will walk through the technical mechanics of different pay cycles, ensuring that whether you get paid weekly, bi-weekly, or irregularly, your system remains steady.

Finally, we will build your Four Walls. We'll establish the "Emergency Buffer" that protects your peace of mind and the triage system that ensures your survival is never at risk, even when the storms of life—like a job loss or a global pandemic—hit your front door.

Building this architecture requires a different kind of courage than Part 1. It requires the courage to be honest with your numbers. It requires the discipline to track your flow without judgment. But the reward is something few people ever truly experience: financial clarity.

When you have a system, you stop wondering where your money went and start telling it where to go. You move from being a passenger in your financial life to being the CEO.

It's time to stop fighting against your money and start designing a flow that carries you toward your dreams. Let's start building.

# CHAPTER FIVE

# BUDGETING IS PERMISSION

*"A budget isn't a cage; it's the key that gives you permission to spend on the things that actually matter."*

—Tiffany Grant

In the previous chapter, we established the most important "Money Move" in your arsenal: the nonnegotiable commitment to pay yourself first. It is a declaration of your worth and a down payment on your future freedom. However, once that first dollar is swept into your savings or investment account, a new challenge arises. You are left with the remaining balance of your income and a lifetime of ingrained habits, cultural pressures, and emotional triggers telling you how to spend it.

This is where most financial plans fail. We treat the remaining money like a battlefield where we must constantly fight against our own desires. We view the act of managing those funds—budgeting—as a form of self-punishment. But if we are going to sustain the revolution we started in Part 1, we must change the definition of the word itself. We must move from a mindset of restriction to a mindset of empowerment.

The following pages are designed to flip the script on how you view your monthly plan. We aren't going to talk about what you *can't* do; we are going to talk about how to give yourself the ultimate gift: the permission to spend your resources on the things that actually nourish your soul, without a single ounce of guilt.

## THE BUDGETING HANG-UP

Let's be honest. When you hear the word "budget," what's the first thing that pops into your head? For most people, it's a four-letter word. It conjures up images of deprivation, restriction, and constantly saying "no" to yourself. It feels like a financial straitjacket designed to suck the joy out of life.

I know this feeling well. For years, I approached budgeting like a punishment. Every time I looked at my spreadsheet, I felt a familiar pang of guilt and shame, usually tied to a past financial mistake or a purchase I couldn't truly afford. I was constantly battling the emotional weight of my money history.

The truth is, many of us carry financial trauma—the emotional scars left by past crises, family scarcity, or unexpected setbacks. When we try to budget, we aren't just dealing with numbers; we are dealing with those deep-seated feelings. If budgeting feels like a fight, you're never going to stick with it.

## THE MINDSET SHIFT

What if I told you that a budget is the exact opposite of a straitjacket?

A budget is, fundamentally, permission to spend.

Think about that for a moment. When you intentionally decide where your money is going to go before you spend it, you are giving yourself permission to enjoy the things you've planned for, without the crushing guilt that follows impulse buys.

This shift—from viewing a budget as a restriction to seeing it as a plan—is more than just a mental trick; it's a powerful strategy to combat a well-documented psychological phenomenon known as **decision fatigue**.

Every day, you make hundreds of small decisions, and your capacity for making rational, thoughtful choices is a finite resource. As numerous studies in psychology and behavioral economics have shown, the more decisions you make, the more your cognitive resources are depleted. This leads to decision fatigue, where your brain, seeking to conserve energy, starts to look for shortcuts. These shortcuts often manifest as impulsive choices (like ordering expensive takeout after a long day) or avoidance (refusing to think about money at all).

This is where your budget becomes your greatest ally. By deciding ahead of time what your money's jobs are, you automate dozens of daily financial decisions. You are no longer debating whether you can afford a coffee, wondering if you should buy that book, or feeling guilty about a purchase. The decision has already been made. Your plan has already given you the answer.

As research from fields like health psychology and finance has shown, having a clear plan reduces cognitive load and preserves your mental energy for more important choices. It creates a sense of control and predictability that is directly linked to lower financial stress and improved psychological well-being. By giving your money a mission, you are freeing your mind from the constant, draining cycle of financial uncertainty. You are not just creating a budget; you are designing a system to protect your most valuable asset: your peace of mind.

I learned this lesson firsthand. A few years ago, my singular focus was to be completely debt-free by the time I turned 30. I was laser-focused on this goal, and every dollar I spent on something other than debt felt like a step backward. One day, I looked down at my shoes and realized they were literally falling apart at the seams. I clearly needed a new pair, but the thought of spending money on them filled me with anxiety. In my mind, buying shoes meant taking money away from my debt-free goal.

Something told me to go back and look at my budget. I pulled it up, and as I scanned the line items, I saw it: a category for "Clothing" that I had funded at the beginning of the month but had completely forgotten about.

In that instant, everything clicked. The money was already there, waiting for its assigned job. I wasn't stealing from my goal; I was using my plan exactly as I had designed it. It was a profound realization: my budget wasn't restricting me—it was giving me explicit, guilt-free permission to spend on something I needed.

Not only did I go out and buy a new pair of shoes, but I also found a coupon and was able to get two pairs for the price I had originally budgeted. That day, my budget transformed from a source of restriction into a source of freedom.

This is the core mindset shift that takes you from budget purgatory to Budget Nirvana. You are the CEO of your money, and your budget is your strategic plan. It's not about cutting everything; it's about aligning your spending with your values and your goals.

## The Voice of Doubt: Common Budgeting Obstacles

Even after this mindset shift, the old feelings about budgeting can die hard. The word itself is heavy with past failures and anxieties. Let's confront the most common thoughts that can derail your progress before you even begin.

**Obstacle:** "This feels overwhelming. I don't even know where to start. Looking at my finances gives me anxiety."

**Your Mindset Shift:** You don't have to boil the ocean. Your only job right now is to embrace one single idea: **a budget is permission to spend.** That's it. You don't need a perfect spreadsheet or a complex app today. For now, just let this new definition sink in. My story about the shoes wasn't about being a perfect budgeter; it was about realizing my plan could give me freedom, not just restriction. We will get to the "how" in the next chapters. For now, your only task is to believe a new way is possible.

**Obstacle:** "What's the point? Something unexpected always comes up and blows my budget anyway."

**Your Mindset Shift:** You are 100% correct. Life is unpredictable. A traditional, rigid budget fails because it doesn't account for reality. A *successful* budget, however, anticipates the unexpected. It's not a fragile plan that shatters on impact; it's a flexible guide. When an unexpected expense arises, your budget doesn't fail—it simply gives you the clear information you need to make a new decision. It helps you ask, "Okay, this happened. To cover it, what other 'job' do I need to reassign my money from?" It turns panic into a calm, strategic choice.

**Obstacle:** "I'm just not a 'details' person. I'll never be able to keep track of every single dollar."

**Your Mindset Shift:** You don't have to. The goal isn't to become a meticulous accountant; it's to become a conscious spender. You don't need to track every penny for the rest of your life. You need to track your spending for a short, defined period (which we'll cover in later chapters) to get the crucial data. Think of it like a doctor taking your vitals. You don't wear a heart rate monitor 24/7, but you need that initial check-up to understand your health. This is your financial check-up. It's a temporary diagnostic tool, not a permanent life sentence of tracking.

# CHAPTER SIX

# FINDING YOUR "WHY"

*"If your 'why' doesn't make you move when you're tired, it isn't big enough yet."*

—Tiffany Grant

In the first part of this book, we focused on the internal revolution. You've addressed your "Money Ghosts," reclaimed your internal locus of control, and begun building your psychological capital. You have the mindset of a Cycle-breaker, and you are ready to build. But as we move into the **architecture of flow**, we must answer a critical question: What is the fuel for your engine?

A budget is a mechanical system, but humans are not machines. You can have the most sophisticated spreadsheet or the best automation tools in the world, but if you don't have a deep, emotional anchor, you will eventually drift. When the "new car smell" of your financial goals wears off and the reality of daily discipline sets in, your logic will fail you. In those moments, you don't need more math; you need a "why" that is bigger than your "how."

This chapter is about finding the emotional heartbeat of your financial plan. We are going to move beyond surface-level desires and tap into the core motivations that will sustain you through the "boring middle" of your journey. Before we build the walls of your financial house, we must identify the reason you are building it in the first place.

# THE DAY THE "WHY" BECAME EVERYTHING

In 2014, I hit my financial rock bottom. I was a single mother to two boys, and I was struggling. I was trying to do everything right—working, going to school, and balancing the books—but I felt like I was constantly failing. The stress was crushing, and the shame was isolating.

It's easy to set a goal like "I want to be debt-free" or "I want to save $10,000." But when the inevitable challenges hit—when the car breaks down, when a surprise bill arrives, or when you simply feel tired—those surface-level goals crumble. They don't have the emotional weight to keep you fighting.

For me, the shift came when I stopped focusing on the what (the debt, the savings goal) and started focusing on the why. My "why" was not a number on a spreadsheet; it was the two little faces looking up at me. It was the fierce determination that my children would not have to inherit my financial stress. It was the desire to build a life where I could be present, not constantly worried about the next paycheck.

That deep, emotional connection to my goal was the engine that powered every single financial decision I made afterward. It allowed me to say "no" to things that didn't serve me and "yes" to the hard work that would lead to lasting change.

# THE POWER OF THE DEEP WHY

Your "why" is the foundation of your financial house. If the foundation is weak, the whole structure will collapse under pressure.

This isn't just a motivational platitude; it's a core principle of human psychology. Researchers who study goal attainment, like psychologist Edwin Locke, have consistently found that the most powerful goals are those with high personal significance which creates strong **goal commitment (Locke and Latham, 2002)**.

A surface-level goal, like "I want to save money," has low commitment because it lacks an emotional anchor. It's abstract. But a deep "why"—"I want to save money so I can give my children a life free from the financial stress I experienced"—creates a powerful emotional connection.

This connection transforms the goal from a "should" into a "must." It taps into what's called **intrinsic motivation**—the drive that comes from within, rather than from external rewards or pressures. Studies have repeatedly shown that people who are intrinsically motivated are more persistent, more resilient in the face of setbacks, and ultimately more successful in achieving their long-term objectives. When you uncover your deep "why," you are not just finding a reason; you are unlocking your most powerful and sustainable source of fuel.

The problem is that most people stop at the first, most obvious "why." They say, "I want to save money to buy a house." That's a good goal, but it's not a deep "why." We need to dig past the surface to find the core motivation—the emotional root that will sustain you when the journey gets tough.

To find your deep "why," we are going to use a simple but profound exercise called the Five Whys. This technique, borrowed from problem-solving methodologies, forces you to peel back the layers of your motivation until you reach the emotional core.

## Exercise: Ask Why Five Times

Take a financial goal you have right now. Write it down and then ask yourself, "Why?" at least five times, using the answer from the previous question as the starting point for the next.

**Example Goal:** I want to save $10,000 this year.
Why do I want to save $10,000 this year?
*Answer:* So, I can finally have a down payment for a house.

Why do I want a house?
*Answer:* Because I want a safe, stable place for my family to grow up.

Why is a safe, stable place important to me?
*Answer:* Because I grew up moving around a lot, and I want my children to have the security and peace of mind I didn't have.
Why is that security and peace of mind so important?
*Answer:* Because it will allow me to focus on my business and my purpose, knowing that the most important people in my life are protected.

Why is focusing on my purpose so important?
*Answer:* Because my purpose is to help others achieve financial freedom, and I can't be an effective leader if I am constantly distracted by my own financial instability.

The surface goal was $10,000. The deep "why" is the desire for security, purpose, and the ability to lead by example.

When you are tempted to skip a savings contribution or make an impulse purchase, you won't be fighting against a number on a spreadsheet; you will be fighting for the security of your family and the fulfillment of your life's purpose. That is a fight you can win.

## The Voice of Doubt: When Your "Why" Feels Distant

The process of finding your "why" can feel emotional and even a little strange, especially if you're not used to this kind of self-reflection. It's common for voices of doubt to creep in, telling you this "fluffy stuff" doesn't matter. Let's silence them now.

**Obstacle:** "This feels silly. How is thinking about my 'feelings' going to pay my bills?"

**Your Mindset Shift:** You are right to be skeptical. Feelings alone don't pay bills. But what does? *Consistent action.* And what drives consistent action when you're tired, discouraged, and tempted to give up? Your feelings. Your deep emotional connection to your goal is the fuel that makes you choose to pack a lunch instead of buying it, to work on your side hustle instead of watching TV, or to stick to your debt payoff plan. We are not just "thinking about feelings"; we are strategically identifying the most powerful fuel source you have to ensure you follow through on the practical steps.

**Obstacle:** "My 'why' just seems to be 'not being broke.' It doesn't feel very deep or inspiring."

**Your Mindset Shift:** "Not being broke" is a perfectly valid starting point. Now, let's go one level deeper. What will *not being broke* give you? What is the feeling you are truly chasing? Is it peace? Security? Freedom? The ability to sleep through the night without a knot of anxiety in your stomach? "Not being broke" is the absence of a negative. Your true "why" is the presence of a positive. Focus on the feeling of peace you want to gain, not just the feeling of panic you want to lose.

**Obstacle:** "I did the exercise, but I still don't have a clear 'why.' I just feel numb or confused."

**Your Mindset Shift:** That's okay. Sometimes, when you've been in survival mode for a long time, the connection to your deeper desires can

(*Continued*)

(*Continued*)

feel faint. Don't force it. Your "why" doesn't have to be a lightning bolt from the sky. For now, your "why" can simply be: "To discover what I truly want." It can be a goal of exploration. Start with a small, tangible goal (like saving your first $100) and pay close attention to how it makes you feel. Sometimes, the "why" isn't found by thinking; it's revealed through doing.

# CHAPTER SEVEN

# YOUR FIRST 30 DAYS

*"You cannot manage what you do not measure; data is the bridge between where you are and where you want to be."*
—Tiffany Grant

Finding your "why" is the emotional spark that ignites your journey, but even the most powerful engine needs a dashboard to tell you where you are going. You have done the hard work of excavating your mindset and identifying the faces and futures that drive you. Now, it is time to pair that passion with precision. To move from the "internal revolution" to the **architecture of flow**, we must transition from the abstract to the actual. We need to stop guessing how we feel about our money and start knowing exactly what it is doing.

This chapter represents your first true "money move" in the physical world. It is the bridge between your intentions and your reality. For the next 30 days, we are going to set aside our assumptions and our aspirations to focus on one thing: data. Before we can build the life you designed on your "Veranda," we must understand the current state of your foundation. This process isn't about restriction; it's about awareness. It's about taking a clear-eyed look at your financial vitals so that we can begin to direct your resources toward the "why" you've just defined.

## THE FINANCIAL PULSE CHECK

When you go to the doctor for a physical, they don't immediately prescribe medication or surgery. They take your vital signs—your temperature, your blood pressure, your pulse. They are gathering data to understand your current state of health.

We need to do the exact same thing with your money.

Before you can create a budget, before you can cut expenses, and before you can save a single dollar, you must know where your money is going right now. This is your financial pulse check.

The biggest mistake people make is trying to budget based on what they think they spend, or worse, based on what they wish they spent. You need facts, not feelings.

## THE 30-DAY NO-JUDGMENT RULE

For the next 30 days, your only job is to track every dollar that comes in and every dollar that goes out. This is not a time for judgment or shame. This is a time for awareness. You are simply gathering data. Think of yourself as a detective, not a judge.

The principle of "track, don't judge" is rooted in decades of psychological research on **behavioral self-monitoring**. This concept, a cornerstone of cognitive-behavioral therapy, is one of the most effective strategies for initiating change, whether the goal is to improve health, break a bad habit, or, in our case, transform your financial life.

The power of self-monitoring lies in its ability to create **awareness**. As numerous studies, such as the review by Chen, Fearey, and Smith in the *Journal of Behavior Therapy and Mental Health*, have shown, the simple act of systematically observing and recording your own behavior brings unconscious patterns into conscious view. You cannot change what you do not see. By tracking where your money goes, you are simply turning on the lights.

This process does two critical things. First, it breaks the cycle of mindless spending. When you know you will be writing down that purchase later, you are forced into a moment of mindfulness. That brief pause is often all it takes to interrupt an impulsive habit. Second, it increases your sense of **self-efficacy**—your belief in your own ability to manage your life. As you gather data and see a clear picture emerge, you move from a place of powerless anxiety to one of informed control. You begin to see that your financial situation isn't a mysterious force acting upon you, but the result of a series of small, understandable, and—most importantly—*changeable* decisions.

So, as you begin this 30-day challenge, know that you are not just making a list of transactions. You are engaging in a scientifically validated process of self-discovery that is the essential first step toward lasting financial well-being.

If you spend $20 on a fancy coffee, write it down. If you spend $500 on a last-minute flight, write it down. The goal is not to change your behavior yet; the goal is to see your behavior clearly.

I once had a client come to me because she was drowning in about $10,000 of credit card debt. It was the thing that kept her up at night, a constant source of stress and anxiety. The first thing we did was implement this 30-day tracking rule. She committed to writing everything down without judgment.

When we reviewed her spending at the end of the month, the culprit wasn't one big, catastrophic expense. It was a slow, consistent leak. She was spending nearly $500 every month on going out with friends for drinks and meals. It was a complete shock to her. While the experiences were fun in the moment, she had never connected that spending to the long-term pain her debt was causing her.

That single piece of data was the eye-opening moment she needed. It gave her the clarity to make a change. We didn't cut her social life entirely; that's not realistic. We simply started by cutting that spending in half, redirecting the other $250 each month directly to her credit card debt. It was a manageable change that put her back in control, all because she took the time to track the facts.

## HOW TO TRACK: CHOOSE YOUR WEAPON

The best tracking method is the one you will actually use. Don't overcomplicate this step. You have several options, and you should choose the one that fits your personality and lifestyle:

**The Digital Tracker (Apps):** Apps like YNAB (which I personally use and love) or Monarch Money are excellent because they can connect directly to your bank accounts and automatically categorize transactions. This is the fastest, most comprehensive method, but it requires a comfort level with technology.

**The Spreadsheet:** A simple Google Sheet or Excel file can work perfectly. You manually enter the date, the amount, the vendor, and the category for every transaction. This method forces you to be highly engaged with your spending.

**The Notebook:** For those who prefer analog, a small notebook or journal where you jot down every purchase immediately after you make it is a powerful tool. At the end of the week, you can transfer these notes to a simple ledger.

The key is consistency. For 30 days, you are committed to capturing 100% of your transactions. If you miss even one, the data are incomplete, and your "pulse check" will be inaccurate.

# PLUGGING THE LEAKS IN YOUR BOAT

After 30 days, you will have a complete picture of your money flow. Now, you can start to analyze the data.

I want you to think of your financial life like a boat you are rowing toward a destination—your deep "why." You can be rowing as hard as you can, but if your boat has holes in it and is taking on water, you're going to feel like you're sinking no matter how much effort you put in. You might even drown before you reach the shore.

This 30-day tracking exercise is how we find those holes. The goal of a budget is to plug those leaks so you can row efficiently and actually make progress toward your destination.

When you analyze your spending data, look for these three types of leaks:

**The Big Three:** Housing, transportation, and food. These are typically the largest expenses and offer the biggest opportunities for savings.

**The "Bleeders":** These are the small, frequent purchases that drain your account without you noticing. The daily coffee, the forgotten subscriptions, the impulse buys. These are the tiny, almost invisible holes that can collectively sink your boat.

**The Values Gap:** Compare your spending to your deep "why" (from Chapter 6). Are you spending heavily on things that align with your core values? Or are you spending on things that don't matter to you at all?

To close this gap, use the "Do More, Do Less, Stop" framework. Go through your spending categories and make a conscious decision for each one:

**Do More:** "I see I only spent $50 on books last month, but lifelong learning is my 'why.' I want to intentionally spend more in this area."

**Do Less:** "I spent $500 on dining out, which was fun, but it's not aligned with my goal of buying a house. I will consciously do less and cut this back to $250."

**Stop:** "I am paying for three streaming services I never use. I will stop this spending completely and cancel those subscriptions."

This simple exercise gives you the blueprint for your budget. You are no longer guessing. You have the facts and you've made the decisions. You are ready to move on to the next phase: taking this raw data and turning it into a strategic, empowering budget.

## The Voice of Doubt: Overcoming the Fear of Tracking

I'm asking you to look your finances square in the eye, and that can be terrifying. For many of us, it's easier to live with the vague, low-grade anxiety of not knowing than it is to face the hard, cold numbers. Before you track a single dollar, let's address the fears that are probably screaming in your head right now.

**Obstacle:** "I'm scared of what I'll find. I'd rather not know how bad it really is."

**Your Mindset Shift:** This is the most common fear, and it's completely valid. But let me ask you this: does not knowing make the situation any better? The truth is, the uncertainty is often more stressful than the reality. Facing the numbers isn't about judgment; it's about trading vague anxiety for clear information. Think of it like turning on a light in a dark room. It might be messy, but at least you can see where you're going and what to do next. Clarity is the first step to control.

**Obstacle:** "This sounds like so much work. I'm too busy to write down every single thing I buy."

**Your Mindset Shift:** Reframe this from a lifelong chore to a short-term project. You are not signing up to do this forever. This is a 30-day diagnostic period—a data-gathering mission. You are a detective on a 30-day assignment to uncover where your money is going. That's it. At the end of the 30 days, the mission is complete. You can use an app, a notebook, or even just take pictures of your receipts. The method doesn't matter. The commitment to a short, defined period of awareness is what counts.

**Obstacle:** "I already know I spend too much on things like coffee and takeout. What's the point of tracking it just to feel guilty?"

**Your Mindset Shift:** This is the most important rule of the 30-day challenge: **Track, don't judge.** I'll repeat that. Track, don't judge. This is not a moral inventory. The goal is not to make you feel bad about your spending. The goal is simply to gather data. You are a scientist observing patterns, not a judge handing down a verdict. That $5 coffee isn't "good" or "bad." It's just data. It's a number that will later help you make conscious decisions that align with your "why." For these 30 days, your only job is to be a curious, nonjudgmental observer of your own life.

# CHAPTER EIGHT

# THE AUTOPILOT RESET

*"The right automation is the highest form of self-care for your future self."*

—Tiffany Grant

Have you ever gotten to the end of the month, looked at your bank account, and wondered, "Where did all my money go?" It feels like it just … disappears. A little here, a little there, and suddenly a significant chunk of your income has vanished into thin air.

If this feels familiar, you're not alone. You're experiencing a phenomenon I call "spending on autopilot." And it's not your fault. Our entire society is designed to encourage it. Think about it: Amazon saves your credit card so you can buy with a single click. Your phone lets you pay without ever pulling out a wallet. The very act of swiping a card disconnects you from the psychological feeling of money leaving your hand. This isn't an accident; it's a feature. Marketers and advertisers work relentlessly to remove every possible friction point between you and a purchase.

Add to that the constant pressure from social media, where curated vacation photos and "hauls" create a powerful sense of FOMO (Fear Of Missing Out). Friends and family have their own expectations too. We are bombarded daily by messages telling us what to buy, where to go, and who to be. As I always say, we must consciously fight against this system every single day and make decisions that best suit us, not what society wants or tells us to do.

This is where we take back control. This is where we turn off the autopilot.

# FINANCIAL STARVATION VS. FINANCIAL NOURISHMENT

Long before I was a financial wellness curator, I was a student with a dream of becoming a chef. I loved the idea of taking raw ingredients and transforming them into something that provided energy, joy, and comfort. Even though my career path shifted, I still view the world through that lens.

When most people hear the word "budget," they think of a starvation diet. They think of restriction, blandness, and the pain of going without. And just like a crash diet, a "starvation budget" is destined to fail. You can white-knuckle your way through a week of eating nothing but rice and beans, but eventually, you're going to binge. You'll get frustrated, feel deprived, and end up spending more than you saved just to soothe the "hunger."

I want you to throw that "starvation" mindset away.

An intentional spending plan isn't a diet; it is financial nourishment. When you create a meal plan for your body, you aren't trying to see how little you can eat; you are trying to ensure you have the right nutrients to fuel your goals. You're making sure you have the energy to work, the strength to play, and the health to enjoy your life.

Your budget is the "meal plan" for your dreams. It's about looking at your raw ingredients—your income—and deciding how to combine them to create the most fulfilling life possible. If you spend all your "nutrients" on empty-calorie habits that don't satisfy you, you'll end up financially malnourished. But when you give every dollar a job that aligns with your "why," you are feeding your future. You are choosing the ingredients that will help you build the life you actually want to live.

In the last chapter, you completed the crucial first step: tracking your spending for 30 days. You now have the raw, judgment-free data. Now, we're going to use that data to perform a powerful diagnostic on your financial life using a simple but transformative framework: Do More, Do Less, Stop.

This simple exercise is more than just a list; it's a practical application of what researchers call "values-based budgeting." The goal isn't to shame you for your spending; it's to consciously align your financial decisions with what truly matters to you. You are taking control of your unconscious "mental budgets" and making them work for you, not against you (Thaler, 1999).

Let's get started. Grab your spending tracker and a blank sheet of paper. We're going to make three columns.

## COLUMN 1: STOP

This is the most ruthless and liberating category. Look through your spending tracker and identify every single expense that brought you zero joy, value, or progress toward your goals. These are the things you wouldn't even miss.

**Examples:** Forgotten subscriptions, bank fees, late fees, impulse buys that are now collecting dust.

*Your Action:* Cut these immediately. Cancel the subscriptions. Set up alerts to avoid fees. This is found money.

## COLUMN 2: DO LESS

This category is for spending that you enjoy, but that might be happening more often than your goals can afford. This isn't about deprivation; it's about mindful reduction.

**Examples:** Eating out for lunch daily, frequent happy hours, multiple streaming services, daily coffee shop runs.

*Your Action:* Find the right balance. Could you buy lunch three days a week instead of five? Could you host friends at home once a month instead of going out? The goal is to reduce the frequency or cost, not eliminate the joy.

## COLUMN 3: DO MORE

This is the most exciting category. Look at your spending and identify the purchases that brought you genuine happiness, peace, or moved you closer to a major life goal.

**Examples:** A dinner with a loved one you'll always remember, a book that changed your perspective, an extra payment toward high-interest debt, a contribution to your travel fund.

*Your Action:* This is where you want to redirect the money you saved from the "Stop" and "Do Less" columns. This is you actively funding the life you want.

Let's go back to my previous client example of the woman who came to me with five figures of credit card debt that was literally keeping her up at night. After tracking her spending, she was shocked to discover she was spending nearly $500 a month on going out with friends for drinks. The debt was her biggest stressor, but the social time was her main source of joy.

She didn't want to "Stop" seeing her friends, so we put "going out" in the "Do Less" column. She decided to cut back, suggesting more affordable hangouts. The $250 she saved each month was then moved to the "Do More" column, specifically labeled "Aggressive Debt Payoff." By aligning her spending with her primary value—getting a good night's sleep, free from debt anxiety—she created a plan that worked for her.

This brings up a critical point about the zero-based budget we discussed earlier. Money is finite. If you spend money in one area, it must come from another. The "Do More, Do Less, Stop" framework makes these trade-offs conscious and clear.

I had another client who loved watching TV. It was her primary form of relaxation. Typical financial advice screams, "Cut the cable bill!" But for her, cable was a high-value item. At the same time, she was in the negative each month and desperately wanted to travel and get her hair and nails done. We had to look at the trade-offs. I asked her, "If we keep cable, which is important to you, does that mean we have to 'Do Less' on self-care for a while, or 'Do Less' on saving for that vacation?"

When you see it laid out like that, the choice becomes yours. You are the one in control. When your money aligns with what you feel is important, regardless of what typical financial advice says, you will live a much happier and more authentic life. This framework is your tool to ignore the noise and design a financial life that is truly your own.

This "Do More, Do Less, Stop" framework is a practical application of a core principle in positive psychology: **value-congruent living**. The idea is simple but profound: life satisfaction and happiness increase dramatically when our daily actions are aligned with our core values.

When your spending is on autopilot, it's often driven by convenience, marketing, or habit—not your values. This creates a disconnect, or "value incongruence," which can lead to feelings of guilt, anxiety, and a sense that you're working hard but not getting anywhere. Research on self-determination theory shows that autonomous, values-based choices enhance well-being (Ryan and Deci, 2000), while Sonja Lyubomirsky's work demonstrates that intentional activity—deliberate practices we choose—drives sustainable happiness (Lyubomirsky, 2008).

By analyzing your spending through the "Do More, Do Less, Stop" lens, you are not just cutting costs. You are consciously redirecting your financial resources away from low-value, unintentional habits and toward high-value, intentional goals that reflect your "why." You are closing the gap between what you *say* you value and what your bank statement *shows* you value. This alignment is what transforms budgeting from an act of deprivation into an act of profound self-care.

## THE RANKING STRATEGY: HOW TO DECIDE WHAT STAYS

Once you have your 30 days of data in front of you, the "Do More, Do Less, Stop" framework helps you categorize it. But what happens when everything feels like it belongs in the "Keep" pile? What if the math doesn't work, and you must make a cut, but you're emotionally attached to every line item?

This is where we use the ranking strategy.

Beyond your "four walls" (the absolute essentials of food, shelter, utilities, and transportation), every other expense in your life has a different "value score." To find yours, I want you to look at your nonessential spending and rank each item on a scale of 1 to 10 based on two criteria:

1. Alignment with your "why": Does this expense move you closer to the "feeling" you identified in Chapter 6?

2. The "joy-to-cost" ratio: Does the amount of happiness or utility this provides justify the amount of work-hours it took to pay for it?

The Ranking Exercise:

- Rank 8–10 (The Essentials of Joy): These stay. These are the things that nourish you. If your "why" is family connection, and that $50 monthly board game night is the highlight of your kids' week, that is a 10. We don't cut 10s.
- Rank 5–7 (The "Do Less" Zone): These are candidates for optimization. You enjoy them, but they aren't critical to your soul. This is where you look for ways to get the same joy for less cost—switching to a cheaper streaming plan or finding a "happy hour" version of your favorite outing.
- Rank 1–4 (The "Stop" Zone): These are the "empty calories." These are the subscriptions you forgot you had, the convenience purchases made out of stress, and the habits you've outgrown. These are the first things to go.

By ranking your spending, you remove the "all or nothing" pressure of budgeting. You aren't cutting your life to the bone; you are simply clearing away the Rank 2 clutter so you have more room for the Rank 10 experiences.

## The Voice of Doubt: Navigating the Analysis Paralysis

You have the data. You have the framework. Now comes the hardest part: making decisions. This is where guilt, shame, and conflict can surface. Let's get ahead of the voices that can stop you from turning your data into a plan.

**Obstacle:** "I feel so much shame looking at this. I can't believe I spent so much on [fast food, online shopping, etc.]. I don't even want to think about it."

*(Continued)*

(*Continued*)

**Your Mindset Shift:** Acknowledge the feeling and then let it go. Remember the rule from the last chapter: Track, don't judge. That rule still applies here. Shame is a backward-looking emotion that keeps you stuck. We are forward-looking strategists now. That spending wasn't "bad"; it was simply "unintentional." It was the result of being on autopilot. Your only job now is to look at that number and ask a simple, neutral question: "Does this align with my 'why'?" If the answer is no, you now have the power to give that money a new, more fulfilling job next month.

**Obstacle:** "My partner and I are not on the same page. Their 'Do More' is my 'Stop,' and this is just causing fights."

**Your Mindset Shift:** This is incredibly common. You and your partner are two different people with different values. The goal is not to force agreement on every line item, but to find alignment on your shared "why." Sit down together, away from the spreadsheet, and revisit your big-picture goals. Are you trying to buy a house? Travel more? Feel more secure? Once you are realigned on the shared destination, you can approach the spending analysis as a team of problem-solvers. The question isn't, "Why did you spend so much on video games?" but rather, "If we want to save for our trip to Italy, what can we *both* agree to 'Do Less' of to make that happen?"

**Obstacle:** "There's nothing to cut! Everything in the 'Stop' or 'Do Less' category feels essential. I'm already stretched thin."

**Your Mindset Shift:** If you've gone through your spending and truly can't find anything to cut, then you have not discovered a spending problem; you have confirmed an **income problem**. This is incredibly valuable information. It means that no amount of budgeting or cutting will solve your core issue. The "Autopilot Reset" has done its job: it has given you a clear diagnosis. Your focus must now shift from cutting expenses to increasing your income. It's time to start exploring side hustles, asking for a raise, or looking for a higher-paying job. This clarity, while daunting, is a gift.

# CHAPTER NINE

# CREATING YOUR MONEY FLOW SYSTEM

*"Your money flow system should serve your life, not consume it."*
—Tiffany Grant

In the previous chapter, you performed a vital act of financial surgery. By applying the "Do More, Do Less, Stop" framework, you identified the leaks in your boat and cleared away the unintentional spending that was draining your resources. You have successfully moved through the "Pulse Check" and the "Autopilot Reset," and for the first time, you are looking at your financial reality without the fog of "Money Ghosts" or the weight of judgment. You have the data, you have the clarity, and you have the desire to build something better.

But data alone is not a strategy. Knowing where your money *went* is only half the battle; the real power lies in deciding where it *will go*. To sustain your legacy, you must move from being a passive observer of your

**Figure 9.1 The architecture of flow—directing income to survival, stability, and growth.**

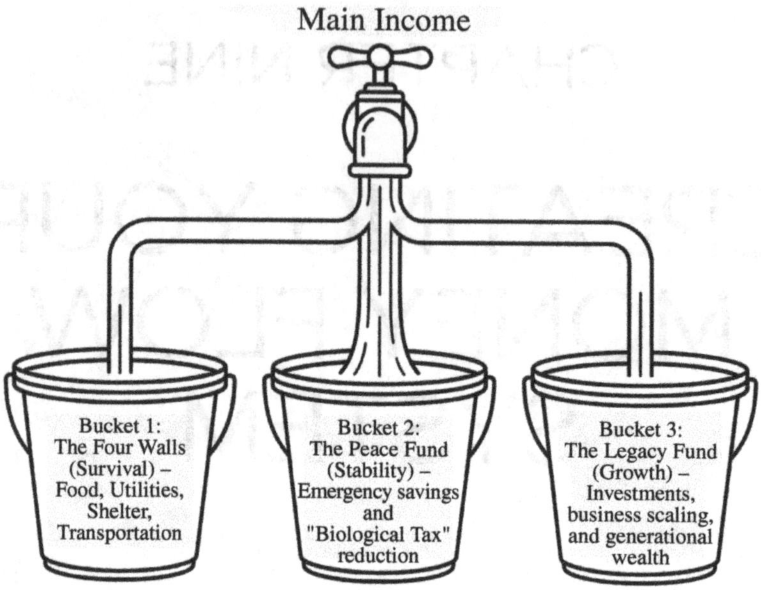


bank statement to being the active architect of your flow (Figure 9.1). This is the moment where we stop playing defense and start playing offense. We are going to take the raw materials of your income and the insights from your tracking and use them to build a "Money Flow System"—a strategic blueprint that ensures every single dollar you earn is working toward the "why" you defined in Chapter 6.

# FROM DATA TO DECISIONS

In the last chapter, you did the hard work of tracking your spending and identifying the leaks in your financial boat. You now have a clear picture of where your money is going, and you've made conscious decisions about what you want to do more of, do less of, or stop completely.

Now, we will turn that data into your strategic plan—your money flow system. This is where you move from being a passenger in your financial life to being the pilot. You are going to tell your money where to go, instead of wondering where it went.

## THE ZERO-BASED BUDGET: GIVE EVERY DOLLAR A JOB

The most effective method for taking control of your finances is called zero-based budgeting. This doesn't mean you have to have zero dollars in your bank account. It simply means that your income minus your expenses equals zero.

Every single dollar that comes into your life is assigned a specific job before the month begins. Some dollars will have the job of paying rent. Others will have the job of buying groceries. Some will be assigned to debt repayment, some to long-term savings, and—crucially—some will have the job of being your "fun money."

When every dollar has a job, there are no "leftover" funds to be spent impulsively. You are in complete control.

## BUILDING YOUR BUDGET: A STEP-BY-STEP GUIDE

Grab your spending data from the last 30 days and your "Do More, Do Less, Stop" list. Let's build your first zero-based budget.

## Step 1: List Your Total Monthly Income

This step is critical. You must list every single dollar that comes into your life. This includes your primary paychecks, any income from side hustles, rental income, child support, affiliate earnings, or any other money deposited into your bank account or received in cash. If your income is variable, use a conservative average or the lowest amount you've earned in the last six months. You can always adjust if you earn more, but it's safer to budget from a baseline.

## Step 2: Pay Yourself First

This may go against conventional financial advice, but it is the most important step you can take. Before you pay your landlord, before you pay the electric company, you must pay yourself first. My late grandfather always told me this, and it is the foundation of building wealth.

"Paying yourself first" means treating your savings and investments as the most critical bill you have. This is nonnegotiable. Whether it's contributing to a retirement account or putting money into a savings account for a future goal, this comes off the top. The amount doesn't have to be large—it could be as little as a dollar—but it must be something. Consistency is more important than volume when you are building the habit. Most people can have this automated directly from their paycheck, but if you can't, this is the very first transfer you make on payday.

The system we are building here—automating your savings, your investments, and your bill payments—is not just a time-saving convenience. It is a deliberate and powerful application of what behavioral scientists call **choice architecture**. The term, popularized by Nobel laureate Richard Thaler and his colleague Cass Sunstein, refers to the practice of designing the environments in which we make decisions to "nudge" us toward better outcomes (Thaler and Sunstein, 2018).

You are acting as the choice architect of your own financial life. Instead of relying on willpower, which is a finite and unreliable resource, you are designing a system where the best choice is the easiest choice—in fact, it's the *automatic* choice.

By automating your savings, you remove the daily decision of whether to save or to spend. The money is moved before you even have a chance to miss it, perfectly executing the "Pay Yourself First" principle. This leverages the power of inertia and the status quo bias; once the system is set up, it takes more effort to *stop* saving than to continue.

As research in behavioral finance has repeatedly shown, automating financial decisions is one of the single most effective strategies for improving long-term outcomes, from increasing retirement savings through automatic 401(k) contributions to reducing debt by setting up automatic bill payments. You are taking your flawed, emotional, and easily fatigued human brain out of the driver's seat for these critical, repetitive decisions and letting a simple, unemotional system do the heavy lifting. This doesn't just build wealth; it frees up your mental energy and reduces financial anxiety, allowing you to focus on the bigger picture.

## Step 3: Secure Your Four Walls

After you have paid yourself, you must cover your core needs. I call these "the four walls"—the absolute necessities that keep you safe and secure. List them in this order of priority:

**Housing:** Rent/Mortgage, utilities, insurance.

**Food:** Groceries (not dining out).

**Transportation:** Car payments, gas, insurance, public transit costs.

**Basic Clothing and Utilities:** Anything essential to keep your household running.

These are nonnegotiable. Fund these categories first. If you have a variable income, this list is your roadmap. After you've paid yourself first, you start at the top of the four walls and fund these categories in order as money comes in. You cover housing first, then food, and so on, until your essentials are secure for the month.

## Step 4: List All Other Monthly Expenses

Now, go through the rest of your spending data. List every other category of spending:

- Debt payments (student loans, credit cards)
- Insurance (health, life)
- Childcare
- Subscriptions (streaming services, gym memberships)
- Personal care (haircuts, toiletries)
- Giving/charity
- Dining out
- Entertainment

## Step 5: Assign Budget Amounts Using Your "Do More, Do Less, Stop" List

This is where your decisions become reality. Look at each category and assign a dollar amount based on your goals.

For categories you decided to "Stop," the budget amount is $0.

For categories you decided to "Do Less," assign the new, lower amount (e.g., $250 for dining out instead of $500).

For categories you decided to "Do More," assign the new, higher amount.

## Step 6: Don't Forget the Fun Money!

A budget that doesn't allow for joy is a budget that is destined to fail. You must, and I repeat, must have a line item for guilt-free spending. This is your "Fun Money" category. This is the pressure-release valve that makes your budget sustainable.

Use this money for those minor, unbudgeted impulse buys. For example, if you are in a store and see something you really want that you didn't account for in any of your other categories, and you have money left in your Fun Money budget, you can use it—guilt-free! A warning, however: do not try to make your Fun Money budget too big. Everything should have a category. This is just for those little one-off things that may happen over the course of a month, acting as a safety net for minor impulses, not a replacement for proper planning.

## Step 7: Do the Math: Income – Expenses = Zero (or Better)

Subtract all of your budgeted expense amounts from your monthly income.

If you have money left over: Great! Assign those extra dollars to a goal, like extra debt repayment or boosting your savings. Don't leave it unassigned!

If you have a negative number: This is a flashing red light. Your expenses are higher than your income. You must go back to your "Do Less" and "Stop" categories and make more cuts until your budget balances to zero.

What if you can't cut anymore?

If you have gone through every category, cut all the "Do Less" and "Stop" items, and your expenses are still higher than your income, you have reached a crucial realization: You have an income issue, not a spending issue.

Having your budget laid out in black and white is a gift because it tells you exactly how much you need to increase your income to make the numbers work. You are no longer guessing. You know the exact deficit you need to fill.

Your next step is to strategize on increasing your income, whether that means doing one or more of the following:

Asking for a raise: You know the precise number you need to make your budget balance.

Finding a new job: You know the minimum salary required to live comfortably.

Starting a side hustle: You know the exact amount you need to earn each month to stop operating in the negative.

This process might take a few tries, but once you get it to zero, you have your first workable budget. You have a plan.

# SYNCING THE FLOW: HOW TO BUDGET FOR YOUR SPECIFIC PAY CYCLE

A common frustration I hear is: "Tiff, a monthly budget sounds great, but I get paid every Friday. How do I make the math work?"

Your money flow system must be tailored to the rhythm of your income. If you try to force a weekly paycheck into a monthly box without a plan, you'll end up with "too much month at the end of the money." Here is your guide to syncing your budget with your pay cycle.

## The Weekly Paycheck (The "Micro-flow" Strategy)

If you get paid every week, you have the advantage of frequent "re-ups," but the challenge of managing large monthly bills like rent or mortgage.

- The Move: Divide your largest bills by four. If your rent is $1,200, set aside $300 from every single paycheck into a separate "bills" account. By the time the first of the month rolls around, the money is already there, waiting. This prevents the "rent week" from being a week of starvation.

## The Bi-weekly Paycheck (The "Two-check" Rhythm)

This is the most common cycle (26 paychecks a year). Most months you get two checks, but twice a year, you get a "magic" third check.

- The Move: Build your "four walls" and essential spending based on two paychecks per month. This ensures you can always cover your needs.
- The Bonus: When those "magic third check" months happen, treat that entire third check as a massive leap toward your current goal—whether that's padding your emergency fund (Chapter 10) or a debt snowball payment (Chapter 13).

## The Semi-monthly Paycheck (The "Fixed Date" Strategy)

Getting paid on specific dates (usually the 1st and 15th) makes it easy to map out which bills belong to which check.

- The Move: Create a "First Half" and "Second Half" budget. Check one covers the mortgage and early-month utilities. Check two covers the car payment and savings goals. Because the dates are fixed, you can automate your transfers to happen on the 2nd and 16th with total confidence.

## The Monthly Paycheck (The "CEO" Method)

Getting paid once a month requires the highest level of discipline but offers the clearest "CEO" view of your finances.

- The Move: You must use the "envelope method" (either physical or digital). Since all your money hits at once, it's easy to feel wealthy on the 2nd and broke by the 20th. Allocate your "giving" and "saving" immediately, then "drip" your spending money into your checking account weekly to prevent overspending early in the month.

## The Irregular Income (The "Baseline" Approach)

If you are a freelancer, entrepreneur, or work on commission, your income is a series of "hills and valleys."

- The Move: Budget based on your "baseline"—the lowest amount you reasonably expect to make in a bad month. Use that baseline to cover your four walls.
- The Hill Strategy: When you have a "hill" month (a big commission or a high-sales month), don't increase your lifestyle. Instead, use the surplus to build a "hills and valleys" buffer account. This account

sits in your savings and "tops off" your income during the "valley" months, giving you a steady, predictable salary regardless of what the business does.

# THE STEWARD'S HEART: SCRIPTURAL AFFIRMATIONS FOR YOUR JOURNEY

In the original vision for this book, I had sections on using crystals to attract abundance. But as my journey has evolved, I've realized that the most powerful "energy" we can tap into isn't found in a stone; it's found in the promises of God.

Budgeting is an act of stewardship. It is the process of managing what has been entrusted to you with wisdom and intention. When the "voice of doubt" gets loud, or when the math in your money flow system doesn't seem to add up, use these scriptural affirmations to realign your mindset.

## When You Feel Fear About the Future

- The Word: "For God has not given us a spirit of fear, but of power and of love and of a sound mind." (2 Timothy 1:7)
- The Affirmation: "I do not operate from a place of panic. I have been given a sound mind to make wise decisions, and I have the power to change my financial story."

## When You Are Facing a Scarcity Trap

- The Word: "And my God shall supply all your need according to His riches in glory by Christ Jesus." (Philippians 4:19)
- The Affirmation: "I move from a mindset of lack to a mindset of abundance. I trust that my needs are covered, which gives me the freedom to plan for my future with hope."

## When You Are Doing the Hard Work of Tracking and Planning

- The Word: "Be diligent to know the state of your flocks, and attend to your herds." (Proverbs 27:23)
- The Affirmation: "I am a diligent steward of my resources. By knowing the condition of my 'flocks'—my accounts and my spending—I am honoring the life I am building."

## When You Are Building for the Next Generation

- The Word: "A good man leaves an inheritance to his children's children ..." (Proverbs 13:22)
- The Affirmation: "My 'Money Moves' today are building a bridge for tomorrow. I am a Cycle-breaker, and the financial wisdom I am gaining will bless my family for generations to come."

# When You Need Discipline to Stick to the Plan

- The Word: "For which of you, intending to build a tower, does not sit down first and count the cost ...." (Luke 14:28)
- The Affirmation: "My budget is not a restriction; it is my blueprint. I count the cost today so that I can live in the 'tower' of my dreams tomorrow."

## The Voice of Doubt: When the Plan Meets Reality

You've done the work, and now you have a plan on paper. But the space between the spreadsheet and your real life is where the real challenges begin. It's normal to feel a mix of excitement and anxiety. Let's tackle the obstacles that can pop up as you try to implement your new money flow system.

**Obstacle:** "My numbers don't work. After I budget for everything, I'm in the negative. This is impossible."

**Your Mindset Shift:** This is not a failure; it is a mathematical certainty that you cannot solve with this budget alone. Your plan has done its job perfectly: it has given you undeniable proof that you have an income problem, not a spending problem. The immediate next step is to go back to your "Do Less" and "Stop" lists and be even more ruthless. What can be cut, even temporarily? The long-term solution, however, is to focus all your energy on the income side of the equation. Your budget has given you the clarity and the motivation you need to pursue that raise, find that higher-paying job, or start that side hustle.

**Obstacle:** "This feels way too restrictive. I feel like I have no freedom or flexibility for fun."

(*Continued*)

(*Continued*)

**Your Mindset Shift:** If your budget feels like a cage, you've built it wrong. Go back and look at your "why" and your "Do More" list. Did you budget for the things that bring you joy? A successful budget isn't about eliminating fun; it's about *planning* for it. It's about giving yourself guilt-free permission to spend on the things you love by consciously spending less on the things you don't. If you need more room for "fun money," revisit your other categories. The goal is to create a plan you can stick with, and a plan with no room for joy is a plan that is destined to fail.

**Obstacle:** "I tried to stick to it, but I already messed up. I overspent in one category. I might as well just give up."

**Your Mindset Shift:** A budget is not a fragile, perfect object; it's a living document. You did not "mess up"; you simply generated new data. Life happens. The goal isn't to be perfect; the goal is to be intentional. When you overspend in one area, you must simply "reassign" money from another. It's a simple, nonemotional choice. Did you overspend on groceries? Okay, maybe the "eating out" budget for the rest of the month needs to cover the difference. This isn't a failure; it's you actively managing your money, which is the entire point of the system. Every time you adjust, you are strengthening your financial muscles.

# THE 90-DAY GRACE PERIOD: WHY YOUR FIRST BUDGET WILL "FAIL"

If you've ever tried to start a new workout routine, you know that the first week is nothing but sore muscles and a desire to quit. Budgeting is no different. One of the biggest reasons people abandon their money flow system is that they expect it to work perfectly in the first 30 days.

I want to give you a three-month grace rule.

In my years of financial counseling, I have seen a consistent pattern: it takes exactly 90 days for a budget to move from a "chore" to a "rhythm." If you can commit to the first three months, you will succeed. Here is what to expect during that 90-day window:

- Month 1: The Messy Discovery. You will forget things. You'll realize you didn't account for that quarterly subscription, or you'll vastly underestimate how much you spend on household supplies. Your numbers won't balance, and you'll feel a surge of that old "scarcity anxiety." This is not failure. This is the data-gathering phase. You are simply shining a light on the corners of your financial life that have been in the dark for years.
- Month 2: The Adjustment. You'll take the lessons from Month 1 and tweak your categories. You'll be more realistic about your spending, but "life" will still happen. An unexpected car repair or a last-minute birthday gift will pop up. In Month 2, you learn how to pivot. You'll practice moving money from one category to another without the emotional guilt.
- Month 3: The Click. This is the month where the system starts to feel like "permission" rather than "restriction." You'll anticipate your expenses before they happen. You'll stop checking your bank balance with a pit in your stomach because you already know what's in there. You aren't just "doing a budget" anymore; you are managing a system.

Give yourself the grace to be a "beginner" for 90 days. Don't judge the system by the first month; judge it by the peace it brings you by the third.

# CHAPTER TEN

# BUILDING YOUR FINANCIAL SAFETY NET

*"A $1,000 buffer is the difference between an emergency and a mere inconvenience."*

—Tiffany Grant

Creating your money flow system was a pivotal moment in your journey. By giving every dollar a job, you have moved from the chaos of reactive spending to the clarity of proactive stewardship. You have built the architecture of your flow, and for the first time, your resources are aligned with your values. However, as any seasoned traveler knows, having a map and a full tank of gas does not prevent the road from occasionally being blocked. Even the most perfectly designed budget can be disrupted by the unpredictable nature of life.

To sustain your progress and protect the legacy you are building, you must move from simply managing your flow to securing it. This requires a shift in focus from the "known" expenses of your daily life to the "unknown" risks of the future. Before we begin the long-term work of investing and wealth creation, we must install the guardrails that will keep you from falling back into the cycle of debt when a crisis occurs. This chapter is about building your first line of defense—a financial buffer that ensures that when life happens, it remains an inconvenience rather than a catastrophe.

# THE FINANCIAL FIRE EXTINGUISHER

You've done the hard work. You've found your "why," you've tracked your money, and you've built your zero-based budget. You are now the pilot of your financial life, not a passenger. But even the best pilots need a safety net.

Imagine you are sailing your newly plugged boat toward your destination. Suddenly, a rogue wave hits—a flat tire, a surprise medical bill, or an unexpected plane ticket. If you don't have a financial safety net, that rogue wave will sink your boat and force you to reach for the credit card, immediately undoing all the progress you've made.

This is why the very first financial goal we pursue is the Baby Emergency Fund: $1,000 in cash, stored in a separate, easily accessible savings account.

Why $1,000?

Why not $500? Why not three months of expenses?

We start with $1,000 because it is the single most powerful deterrent against small financial disasters. Most unexpected expenses that derail a budget—a car repair, an insurance deductible, a trip to the emergency room—fall under this amount.

Achieving this goal quickly is a massive psychological win. It proves that you can set a goal and hit it. It gives you confidence and momentum.

# THE POWER OF THE BUFFER

The Baby Emergency Fund acts as a buffer between life's inevitable surprises and your debt and savings goals.

**The Flat Tire Scenario:** Your tire blows out, costing $250.

**Without the Fund:** You put it on a credit card, adding to your debt, paying interest, and feeling like a failure.

**With the Fund:** You transfer $250 from your Baby Emergency Fund, pay the bill in cash, and immediately adjust your budget to replenish the $250 next month. You stay on track and maintain your momentum.

# THE PSYCHOLOGY OF THE BUFFER: WHY $1,000 MAKES YOU SMARTER

While we've discussed the practical safety of the Baby Emergency Fund, there is a much deeper, biological reason why this $1,000 is your most important money move. It isn't just about paying for a car repair; it's about reclaiming your brain.

To understand this, we must look at scarcity theory, a landmark field of study pioneered by behavioral economist Sendhil Mullainathan and psychologist Eldar Shafir. In their research, they discovered that scarcity—whether it's a lack of time, food, or money—captures the mind. It creates a "bandwidth tax" that physically and mentally impairs your ability to function.

## The Bandwidth Tax

Imagine your brain is like a computer. You have a certain amount of "RAM" (random access memory) available to process information, make decisions, and control your impulses. When you are living without a financial buffer, a significant portion of your RAM is constantly running a background program called "survival."

You are subconsciously calculating: Do I have enough for gas? Will the check clear? What if the kids need shoes?

This background program is heavy. It creates what Mullainathan and Shafir call tunneling. When you are in the tunnel of scarcity, you lose the ability to see the big picture. You focus only on the immediate fire in front of you. This is why people in financial stress often make decisions that seem "irrational" to outsiders—like taking out a payday loan or skipping a utility bill to buy a small luxury. They aren't being "bad" with money; they are suffering from a depleted brain.

## The IQ Drop

One of the most startling findings in scarcity theory came from a study of sugarcane farmers in India. These farmers receive their entire year's income all at once after the harvest. This means they experience a cycle of "abundance" right after the harvest and "scarcity" right before the next one.

The researchers gave the farmers cognitive tests at both points in the cycle. They found that the same farmers scored significantly lower during the period of scarcity—by as much as 9 to 10 IQ points on intelligence tests and 13 to 14 points on tests of cognitive control. To put that in perspective, a 10-point drop is the equivalent of losing an entire night's sleep or the difference between an average IQ and a "gifted" one (Mani et al., 2013).

Scarcity doesn't just make you stressed; it literally makes you less capable of solving the problems that would get you out of scarcity.

## The $1,000 Reset

This is where your Baby Emergency Fund comes in. That $1,000 is not just cash; it is cognitive slack.

When you have a buffer, you give your brain permission to shut down the "survival" program. When the tire blows out, you don't enter the tunnel of panic. You don't lose those 10 IQ points. You simply think, "I have the money for this," and you move on.

By protecting your four walls with a $1,000 buffer, you are buying back your mental bandwidth. You are freeing up the RAM you need to focus on Part 3 of this book: building your Engine of Growth. You cannot be a visionary entrepreneur or a strategic "financial wellness curator" if your brain is stuck in the tunnel of survival. The buffer is the light at the end of that tunnel.

## The Cortisol Connection

Beyond your IQ, the buffer changes your biology. Chronic financial stress keeps your body in a state of "high allostatic load," constantly pumping out cortisol—the stress hormone. Over time, high cortisol levels lead to the very health issues I faced before moving to Jamaica: high blood pressure, inflammation, and exhaustion.

Having $1,000 in a separate account is a biological signal to your nervous system that you are safe. It lowers your baseline cortisol, allowing your body to move from "fight or flight" to "rest and digest."

As you build this fund, I want you to stop thinking of it as "just in case" money. Start thinking of it as your intelligence and health insurance. It is the foundation upon which your entire life by design is built.

This fund is not for a vacation, a down payment, or a new pair of shoes. It is a financial fire extinguisher. You hope you never have to use it, but when a fire breaks out, you are ready.

The peace of mind that comes from having an emergency fund isn't just a feeling; it's a well-documented psychological phenomenon. The simple presence of liquid savings—accessible cash—acts as a powerful buffer against financial stress, which in turn has a profound impact on your mental health and decision-making abilities.

Research has consistently shown a strong link between financial security and psychological well-being. A 2019 study published in the *Proceedings of the National Academy of Sciences* found that when people were relieved of debt, their psychological functioning improved and their decision-making became more forward-thinking (Ong et al., 2019). This is because financial scarcity, or the constant worry about money, consumes significant mental resources. Your brain gets stuck in a state of chronic stress, making it difficult to think clearly and to plan.

Your emergency fund directly counteracts this. It creates what economists call **financial resilience**. Instead of panicking when a crisis hits, your brain can remain in a calmer, more rational state, allowing you to assess the situation and make better decisions. You move from a reactive, short-term survival mode to a proactive, long-term planning mode.

In essence, your emergency fund is a deposit into your own mental health. It's an investment in resilience, a tool that reduces the corrosive effects of financial anxiety, and a system that allows your best, most rational self to stay in control, even when life is unpredictable.

# HOW TO GET THERE FAST

Remember Step 2 from Chapter 6: Pay Yourself First. This $1,000 is the first thing you are paying yourself for.

**Prioritize:** Every extra dollar you find in your budget (from the "Do Less" and "Stop" categories) should be directed here.

**Start a Savings Challenge:** A great way to make saving feel fun is to gamify it. I have a popular savings challenge on my website that you can download. The premise is simple:

Get 50 envelopes and label them from 1 to 50.

Each week (or each payday), you pick an envelope and stuff it with the dollar amount written on it.

By the time you've filled all 50 envelopes, you will have saved $1,275—more than enough to complete your Baby Emergency Fund!

You can find the printables for this challenge in the Resource Vault at https://moneytalkwitht.com/resource-vault

**Sell Something:** Do you have items around your house that are just collecting dust? Sell them! Use the funds to quickly build this buffer. You can use online tools like Facebook Marketplace or other selling apps, or you can go old-school: a good old-fashioned yard sale or garage sale still does wonders for generating quick cash.

**Temporary Side Hustle:** Take on a short-term side hustle to generate the cash quickly. I personally drove for ride-sharing and delivery services for about three or four years while I was on my debt-free journey. It's a fantastic way to earn extra money on your own schedule. The faster you hit $1,000, the faster you move on to tackling debt.

Once you have that $1,000 safely tucked away, you have earned the right to move on to the next phase of your financial journey: attacking debt with intensity. You have built a secure foundation.

## The Voice of Doubt: The Slow Grind of Saving

The idea of having a fully funded emergency fund feels amazing. The reality of saving for it can feel slow, frustrating, and sometimes impossible. Let's tackle the common thoughts that can sabotage your efforts to build this crucial safety net.

**Obstacle:** "Saving three to six months of expenses feels impossible. It will take me years to get there. What's the point of even starting?"

**Your Mindset Shift:** Do not focus on the mountain; focus on the first step. Your goal is not to have a fully funded emergency fund tomorrow. Your goal is to save your first $1,000. That's it. We call this a "Baby Emergency Fund." This initial amount is a powerful "crisis buffer" that can stop a small problem (like a flat tire) from becoming a major debt-inducing disaster. Celebrate that first $1,000 milestone. Then, focus on the next $1,000. You will climb this mountain one step at a time, and each step moves you further away from the edge of financial anxiety.

**Obstacle:** "What actually counts as an 'emergency'? I'm tempted to use this money for a vacation/new phone/etc."

**Your Mindset Shift:** An emergency is something that is **urgent, unexpected,** and **necessary**. A job loss? Emergency. A sudden medical bill? Emergency. Your transmission failing? Emergency. A Black Friday sale? Not an emergency. The vacation you've been wanting? That's a goal, not an emergency. The key is to give those nonemergency desires their own separate savings accounts. By creating a "vacation fund" or a "new phone fund," you give yourself permission to save for those things without raiding the one account that is solely dedicated to protecting your future self from disaster.

**Obstacle:** "I finally saved some money, and then a real emergency happened and wiped it out. I'm back at zero. It feels so discouraging."

**Your Mindset Shift:** You are not back at zero! This is not a failure; this is a massive victory. Your emergency fund did its job. It performed its one and only function: it protected you. It allowed you to handle a crisis without going into debt, without derailing your life, and without the crushing stress you would have felt otherwise. You didn't lose money; you *used* your insurance policy. Now, you simply start the process of rebuilding it, knowing with 100% certainty that the system works. You've proven to yourself that you can handle anything life throws at you.

# CHAPTER ELEVEN

# IN CASE OF EMERGENCY, PROTECT THESE FOUR WALLS

*"You cannot build an empire if your 'four walls' are crumbling; stability is the prerequisite for growth."*

—Tiffany Grant

When a financial crisis hits—a sudden job loss, a medical emergency, an unexpected life event—the world can feel like it's spinning out of control. The bills keep coming, the numbers don't add up, and panic sets in. In these moments, it's easy to become paralyzed by the sheer volume of financial obligations. You try to pay a little here, a little there, all while the metaphorical water level continues to rise.

## The Voice of Doubt: Finding Calm in the Crisis

Losing your income is a shock to the system. Your first instincts will likely be panic, fear, and a sense of paralysis. It can feel like the world is ending. Before we talk about what to *do*, we must manage your mindset. Your ability to think clearly is your greatest asset right now.

**Obstacle:** "I'm panicking. I can't think straight. All I can see is every worst-case scenario playing out."

**Your Mindset Shift:** Breathe. Your panic is a normal physiological response to a threat, but it is not your friend. Right now, you are not going to solve everything. You are going to focus on one single task: surviving today. The "four walls" framework we are about to discuss is designed to give your panicked brain a simple, clear set of priorities. It eliminates the need to worry about the 100 things you *could* do and focuses you on the four things you *must* do. Your job is not to see the entire path forward; it is to find the very next step.

**Obstacle:** "I feel so much shame. I must call my credit card company and tell them I can't pay. I feel like a failure."

**Your Mindset Shift:** You must separate your circumstances from your identity. A job loss is an event; it is not a reflection of your worth. The person you will speak to on the phone at the credit card company talks to people in your exact situation all day, every day. You are not a unique failure; you are a human being experiencing a common life event. When you call, you are not a beggar; you are a responsible customer proactively communicating a temporary hardship. State the facts calmly and ask what hardship programs are available. This is a business transaction, not a moral confession.

**Obstacle:** "I should just hide and not answer the phone until I have a new job. It's too stressful to deal with."

**Your Mindset Shift:** Avoidance is tempting, but it is the worst possible strategy. It allows the problem to grow in the dark, and it strips you of your power. Proactive communication, no matter how difficult, keeps you in control. Ignoring a problem gives the other party all the power to make decisions *for* you (like sending you to collections or starting foreclosure proceedings). Making the call yourself allows you to be part of the solution. It is the single most powerful action you can take to protect your financial future during a crisis.

The sense of panic and paralysis you feel during a financial crisis is not a personal failing; it is a predictable biological response. A vast body of research, such as the review by K. Starcke and M. Brand in *Neuroscience & Biobehavioral Reviews*, shows that acute stress significantly alters how our brains function. The prefrontal cortex, the part of your brain responsible for rational thought, long-term planning, and impulse control, is effectively hijacked by the more primitive, emotional parts of your brain. This leads to what's known as **cognitive impairment**, making it incredibly difficult to weigh options, make complex decisions, and see a path forward.

At the same time, as research on the psychological impact of job loss has shown, the event itself threatens one's sense of identity, stability, and control, often leading to significant psychological distress (Brand, 2015). You are not just dealing with a math problem; you are dealing with a profound emotional and psychological event.

This is precisely why a simple, rigid, and prioritized framework like the four walls is so critical. In a moment when your brain's capacity for complex decision-making is severely diminished, you need a pre-made plan that eliminates the noise. The four walls framework acts as a cognitive shortcut, offloading the mental burden of trying to juggle a dozen competing priorities. It tells your panicked brain exactly what matters right now, allowing you to channel your limited mental energy into executing a few clear, essential tasks rather than being paralyzed by an overwhelming number of choices. You are not just following a budget; you are implementing a crisis-management protocol designed to function when you are not at your best.

In a crisis, you cannot do everything. But you can do the most important things.

When your financial house is on fire, your only job is to protect the four walls. Everything else is noise. These are the absolute, nonnegotiable priorities that you must secure to keep your life stable while you navigate the storm. In order of importance, the four walls are the following:

**Housing:** A roof over your head

**Food:** What you need to eat

**Transportation:** Your ability to get to work or seek work

**Utilities and Basic Clothing:** The essentials that make your housing livable and your life functional

This isn't just my advice; it's a principle grounded in one of the most famous psychological theories ever developed: Maslow's Hierarchy of Needs. The psychologist Abraham Maslow argued that humans have a fundamental set of needs ranging from basic physiological requirements to higher-level self-fulfillment. Research by Lee and Hanna (2015) shows that when people set savings goals, they draw on needs across this entire spectrum—from security to self-actualization. As I've said on my podcast, if you can't meet your basic necessities, how can you possibly think further than that? You get stuck.

The four walls are the financial equivalent of that foundation. You must secure your shelter, your food, and your physical safety before you can even begin to think about rebuilding. Trying to pay a credit card bill before you've secured your rent for the month is like trying to decorate a house that's actively on fire. It's a waste of precious resources and energy.

This framework is also consistent with how economists and policy experts define the bare minimum for a safe and decent life. Studies that calculate "basic needs budgets" consistently identify housing, food, and transportation as the core, nonnegotiable pillars of financial stability (Allegretto, 2005). When you focus on the four walls, you are aligning your actions with expert consensus on what truly matters.

Think of this as your personal emergency management plan. In national disaster management, federal policy doesn't try to fund everything at once. It follows a framework that prioritizes certain capabilities and funding streams over others (Donahue and Joyce, 2001). You must act as your own first responder. In a financial crisis, your job is not to please every creditor; your job is to ensure your family's core safety and survival.

Let's break down how to protect each wall when the storm hits.

## WALL 1: HOUSING

This is your top priority. You must keep a roof over your head.

**Action:** Pay your rent or mortgage payment before any other nonessential bill. If you anticipate you cannot make the full payment, communicate with your landlord or lender before the due date.

## WALL 2: FOOD

You and your family must eat. This is not a luxury.

**Action:** Create a bare-bones grocery budget focused on essentials. This is not the time for gourmet meals; it's the time for sustenance. Explore local food banks and SNAP benefits without shame. They exist for this very reason.

# WALL 3: TRANSPORTATION

If you need a car to get to your job, then keeping that car functional is a core need.

**Action:** Ensure you have enough fuel to get to work and that your car payment and insurance are current. If you don't have a car, budget for the public transportation you need to earn an income.

# WALL 4: UTILITIES, BASIC CLOTHING, AND REST

This includes the essentials that keep your home livable and allow you to function. I'm also adding a crucial, often-overlooked need here: Rest.

**Action:** Keep the lights, heat, and water on. Prioritize these over things like internet or cable. Ensure you have clean, functional clothing. But just as importantly, you must give yourself permission to rest. As I realized after moving to Jamaica, the American hustle culture creates a "rest deficit." If they can keep you so tired and burnt out, you'll never have the capacity to think, plan, or escape your situation. Protecting your energy is a core survival tactic.

Everything else—credit cards, personal loans, student loans, medical bills, gym memberships, streaming services—is outside the four walls. During a full-blown crisis, these things must wait.

Adopting this framework is incredibly empowering. In a situation that feels chaotic and out of your control, the four walls give you a clear, actionable plan. It gives you permission to let go of the noise and focus on what truly matters. It is your battle plan to survive the storm, and the first step toward rebuilding on a solid foundation.

# PART 2 ACTION GUIDE

You have moved from the "why" to the "how." You've reframed budgeting as permission, identified your emotional engine, tracked your data, and built your four walls. Now, it is time to solidify these systems. This action guide is your blueprint for the "Systems" phase of your journey. Do not rush this—the house you build here is what will carry you through the storms of life.

## EXERCISE 1: THE "WHY" ENGINE WORKSHEET

In Chapter 6, we identified that a budget without a "why" is just a math problem. Use this space to define the emotional driver for your system.

1. The Surface Goal: What is the first thing you want to achieve? (e.g., "Pay off my $5,000 credit card balance.")
2. The Five Whys: Ask yourself, "Why?" five times to get to the core.
   - *Why do I want to pay off the balance?* Because I'm tired of the monthly payments.
   - *Why?* Because that money could be going toward my savings.
   - *Why is that important?* Because I want to feel secure.
   - *Why?* Because I never want to feel the panic I felt when my car broke down last year.
   - The Core Why: "I am building this system so that I never have to feel the paralysis of financial fear again. I am choosing peace over plastic."

# EXERCISE 2: THE 30-DAY AWARENESS TRACKER

In Chapter 7, we established the rule: Track, don't judge. For the next 30 days, your only job is to gather data.

- Method: Choose your tool (YNAB, Monarch, a notebook, or the "Money Talk with Tiff" spreadsheet).
- The Daily Check-In: Set a recurring alarm on your phone for 8:00 p.m. Spend five minutes recording every transaction from the day.
- The Nonjudgmental Mantra: If you find a purchase that makes you feel guilty, say this out loud: "This is just data. This data is the light that will show me the way forward."

# EXERCISE 3: THE AUTOPILOT RESET (DO MORE, DO LESS, STOP)

Once you have your 30 days of data, use this framework from Chapter 8 to perform your reset.

| Category | Item(s) | The "Why" Alignment |
|---|---|---|
| DO MORE (Nourishes my Why) | *Example: Professional Development* | *Helps me increase my income (Part 3).* |
| DO LESS (Empty Calories) | *Example: Daily Takeout* | *Convenient, but doesn't make me feel "Free."* |
| STOP (The Leaks) | *Example: Unused Gym Membership* | *Zero value; purely a "Money Ghost."* |

# EXERCISE 4: THE MONEY FLOW BLUEPRINT

In Chapter 9, we discussed creating a system that moves with purpose. Map out your flow here.

1. Income Source(s): Where does the money enter the system?
2. The "Pay Yourself First" Stop: Where does the first 10% (or your starting amount) go? (e.g., Ally Savings Bucket)
3. The Bills Reservoir: Which account handles your fixed four walls expenses?
4. The Permission to Spend Account: Where does your "guilt-free" money live? (e.g., a separate checking account with a debit card)

# EXERCISE 5: THE FOUR WALLS TRIAGE LIST

In Chapter 11, we talked about survival mode. If a crisis hit tomorrow, what are the four things you would protect at all costs? List the specific amounts needed for one month of survival.

1. Food: $__________ (Groceries only, no dining out).
2. Utilities: $__________ (Electricity, water, basic phone/internet).
3. Shelter: $__________ (Rent/mortgage and essential insurance).
4. Transportation: $__________ (Gas, basic car payment, or transit pass).

Your Survival Total: $__________

*This is the minimum monthly amount your emergency fund (Chapter 10) needs to cover.*

# THE PART 2 COMMITMENT

I, [Your Name], have designed my architecture of flow. I understand that my system doesn't have to be perfect to be powerful. I commit to tracking my data without shame and telling my money where to go, rather than wondering where it went.

Signature: ______________________________

Ready to put these shifts into motion? Scan the code below to access the **Cycle-Breaker's Resource Vault**, where I've provided downloadable worksheets, budget templates, and video deep-dives for every move in this section.

**Link:** moneytalkwitht.com/moves

# PART 3

# THE ENGINE OF GROWTH

*"But divide your investments among many places, for you do not know what risks might lie ahead."*

—Ecclesiastes 11:2 NLT

You have rebuilt your foundation. You have designed your architecture. You have a money flow system that is steady, intentional, and protected by your Four Walls. But a house, no matter how well-built, needs power to truly come alive. In the world of wealth building, that power is income.

In Part 3, we are moving from the defensive to the offensive. We are shifting our focus from how we manage our resources to how we multiply them. This is where we build the Engine of Growth.

For too long, the conversation around personal finance has been dominated by the scarcity trap. We've been told that the only way to get ahead is to cut more, save more, and live smaller. But there is a limit to how much you can cut; there is no limit to how much you can earn.

This section is about breaking through the ceiling of your current earnings. We will start by addressing the Inner Game of Wealth, using affirmations and visualizations to prepare your mind for a level of success you may have previously thought was "for other people." We'll dismantle the scarcity trap once and for all, replacing it with an abundance mindset that sees opportunities where others see obstacles.

But we aren't just going to "think" our way to wealth. We are going to take strategic, entrepreneurial action.

We will explore the universe of income streams, moving beyond the 9-to-5 to build a diversified portfolio of active and passive revenue. I'll share the "spectrum of income" that allowed me to pay off over $50,000 in debt—from the "hustle" of driving for rideshare apps to the "magnetism" of building a personal brand.

We will master the art of the ask. You'll learn how to negotiate for the salary you deserve and the rates your expertise commands. Because in business and in life, you don't get what you deserve; you get what you have the courage to negotiate.

Finally, we will talk about building your brand. You'll learn how to move from "chasing" opportunities to "attracting" them by owning your digital real estate and providing undeniable value to your community. This is how you move from being a worker to being a financial wellness curator of your own life.

Building this engine requires a new level of internal locus of control. It requires you to stop waiting for a raise, a promotion, or a lucky break, and start creating your own. It requires the audacity to believe that your story—your "why"—is your most valuable asset.

Your system is ready. Your foundation is solid. Now, it's time to turn on the power. Let's start building your engine.

# CHAPTER TWELVE

# THE INNER GAME OF WEALTH

*"Wealth is a game won in the mind long before it's reflected in the numbers."*

—Tiffany Grant

By this point in your journey, you have built the structural foundation of your financial house. You have the tracking, the budget, and the safety net in place. You have moved from a passenger to a pilot, and you are beginning to see the tangible results of your discipline. In a perfect world, the math would always work, the logic would always hold, and the path to wealth would be a straight, predictable line. But as a Cycle-breaker, you know that the world is rarely perfect, and the road to legacy is often paved with unpredictable challenges.

This chapter is about the invisible architecture of your success. While the previous chapters focused on the "mechanics of money," we must now return to the "stewardship of the soul." True wealth is not just about the digits in your bank account; it is about the resilience of your spirit when those digits are tested. Before we move into the high-level strategies of investing and growth, we must ensure that your internal anchor is strong enough to hold you steady when the external numbers don't make sense. We are going to explore the intersection of strategy and faith and how to maintain your peace when you are standing in the gap between your current reality and your future legacy.

## WHEN THE NUMBERS DON'T ADD UP

There will be moments in your financial journey—and in your life journey—when you have done everything right, and yet, the numbers still don't add up. You've tracked every dollar, you've cut every expense, and you've even built your Baby Emergency Fund. But a major setback hits, a season of scarcity arrives, or you find yourself in a situation where logic and math simply cannot provide the answer.

I know this feeling intimately. There were times, especially in those early years as a young single mother, when I was working two jobs, going to school, and budgeting down to the penny, and I still felt like I was drowning. The stress was physical, the worry was constant, and the path forward was completely obscured.

In those moments, when the practical tools fail to provide comfort or a solution, you need a resource that is deeper and more resilient than your bank account balance. You need faith as a lifeline.

## THE STRENGTH THAT SUSTAINS

Faith, in this context, is not just a religious belief; it is the absolute certainty in the unseen. It is the conviction that even when you cannot see the next step, there is a path, and you have the strength to walk it. It is the internal strength that keeps you going when external circumstances are screaming for you to quit.

For me, this meant leaning on my spiritual foundation. When I was facing eviction, or struggling to pay tuition, or dealing with the emotional weight of my personal circumstances, I turned inward. I found that my faith provided three things that money could not:

**Perspective:** It reminded me that my current financial situation was a temporary circumstance, not a permanent identity. My worth was not tied to my net worth.

**Peace:** It allowed me to surrender the worry I couldn't solve. Worrying about money is exhausting and counterproductive. Faith is the practice of letting go of what you cannot control so you can focus your energy on what you can.

**Resilience:** It gave me the quiet confidence that I would find a way through the storm, even if I didn't know how yet. This resilience is what allowed me to keep rowing my boat, even when the waves were high.

## BUILDING YOUR INNER RESOURCE

Just like you budget your money, you must intentionally cultivate your inner strength. You cannot wait until a crisis hits to start building your faith muscle.

**Practice Gratitude:** Even on the hardest days, find three things you are genuinely grateful for. Gratitude shifts your focus from scarcity to abundance and reminds you of the resources you already possess.

**Affirmation and Visualization:** Speak life into your future. Your mind cannot distinguish between a vividly imagined experience and a real one—use this to your advantage to train your mind for success.

# THE POWER OF AFFIRMATION

An affirmation is a powerful statement that declares a goal as already true. The most powerful affirmations are the ones you create for yourself.

Start with "I am" or "I will." These phrases are powerful declarations that put you in the driver's seat.

State it in the positive. Instead of "I will not be in debt," say "I am becoming debt-free."

Keep it in the present tense. Affirmations work best when they declare your goal as a current reality.

Make it emotional. Connect your affirmation to your deep "why." It should make you feel empowered.

## Sample Affirmations

I am a magnet for financial opportunities.

I am worthy of building wealth and living a prosperous life.

I will make wise financial decisions that align with my goals.

I am in control of my money, and I am building a secure future.

Once you have your affirmations, don't just say them—surround yourself with them. Write them on sticky notes and put them in places you see every single day. I used to have them on my bathroom mirror, on the whiteboard in my home office, and in my car. This constant exposure reinforces the message until it becomes an unshakable belief.

# THE POWER OF VISUALIZATION

Sometimes, the anxiety around money is so overwhelming that it's hard to even think clearly. I've had clients on the verge of tears in our sessions for this very reason. In these moments, visualization is a powerful tool to shift from a state of panic to a state of possibility.

If you are feeling overwhelmed, I want you to close your eyes and walk through this exercise with me:

Imagine that everything is perfect. All of your financial concerns are gone. Now, what does your life look like? Where do you live? What are you doing for work? What does your day-to-day routine feel like? Who are you spending your time with?

By vividly imagining this future, you are giving your brain a new target to aim for. You are replacing the picture of stress and scarcity with a picture of peace and abundance. This is the mindset you need to start making effective decisions.

## The Voice of Doubt: Overcoming the Cringe Factor

If you're new to this kind of inner work, practices like affirmations and visualization can feel a bit awkward, or even "cringey," at first. Your logical brain might be screaming that this is silly, woo-woo nonsense. That's a completely normal reaction. Let's address that skepticism head-on.

**Obstacle:** "This feels ridiculous. How is repeating a sentence to myself in the mirror going to change my bank account?"

(*Continued*)

(*Continued*)

**Your Mindset Shift:** You are not trying to magically manifest money out of thin air. You are strategically retraining your brain. For years, your mind has been running on a default script of scarcity and worry. An affirmation is a tool to consciously overwrite that negative programming. Think of it like this: if you wanted to get physically stronger, you would go to the gym and do reps with a dumbbell. Affirmations are reps for your mind. Each time you repeat one, you are strengthening the neural pathways associated with possibility, confidence, and abundance, making it easier to spot opportunities and take positive action in the real world.

**Obstacle:** "I feel like an imposter when I say things like 'I am a magnet for financial opportunities.' I'm broke. I'm lying to myself."

**Your Mindset Shift:** You are not lying; you are speaking to your future self. You are declaring the person you are in the process of becoming. When you started your first day of college, you weren't yet a graduate, but you began to act and think like a student. When you start a new job, you aren't yet an expert, but you adopt the identity of your role. This is the same principle. You are stepping into the identity of a person who is capable of building wealth *before* all the evidence is there. You are acting "as if," which is a powerful catalyst for making it so.

**Obstacle:** "I tried the visualization exercise, but my mind just kept wandering, or all I could picture were my debts."

**Your Mindset Shift:** That's okay. This is a muscle, and it takes practice. Your brain is used to focusing on problems. The goal isn't to have a perfect, cinematic vision every time. The goal is simply to practice redirecting your focus, even for just 60 seconds. If you get distracted, gently guide your thoughts back to the feeling of peace you are trying to cultivate. If all you can do is imagine one small moment of relief—like opening a bill and knowing you can pay it—start there. This isn't about perfection; it's about practice.

The skepticism you might feel is understandable, but the practices of visualization and affirmation are deeply rooted in the fields of neuroscience and psychology. They are not magic; they are targeted mental exercises designed to physically rewire your brain for success.

**Visualization**, or mental imagery, is a powerful tool because your brain often has difficulty distinguishing between a vividly imagined experience and a real one. As research in cognitive neuroscience has shown, when you visualize an action, you activate many of the same neural pathways that are used when you physically perform that action. This mental rehearsal strengthens these pathways, building both your confidence and your competence. A study published in *Npj Mental Health Research* found that receiving positive feedback activates a corticostriatal brain circuit that enhances **self-efficacy**—the belief in your ability to succeed (Shany et al., 2022). When you consistently visualize yourself achieving a financial goal, you are, in effect, creating a memory of a future success, making it feel more achievable and priming your brain to notice the opportunities that will lead you there.

**Affirmations**, or positive self-talk, work in a similar way. Research has shown that self-affirmation activates the brain's reward centers, specifically the ventromedial prefrontal cortex, which is involved in positive valuation and self-related processing (Cascio et al., 2016). This process can buffer against stress and make you more open to behavioral change (Falk et al., 2025). When you consistently repeat an affirmation, you are interrupting negative thought loops and intentionally directing your brain's focus. This isn't about ignoring reality; it's about building up your internal resources and self-efficacy so that you are better equipped to *change* your reality. You are reinforcing the identity of the person you intend to become, which makes it easier to take actions that are aligned with that identity.

By combining these practices, you are engaging in a comprehensive mental training program. You are using visualization to create a clear blueprint for your goals and affirmations to build the unwavering self-belief needed to achieve them.

**Community:** Connect with people who share your values and lift you up. Isolation is the enemy of progress. Whether it's a prayer group, a mastermind, or a supportive friend, surround yourself with people who believe in your vision even when your own belief wavers.

When you fuse this internal strength—this faith—with the practical knowledge of budgeting, you become unstoppable. You have secured your foundation, not just with $1,000 in the bank, but with an unwavering belief in your ability to persevere.

# CHAPTER THIRTEEN

# OVERCOMING THE SCARCITY TRAP

*"Scarcity tells you there isn't enough; stewardship reminds you that you have exactly what you need to start."*

—Tiffany Grant

In the previous chapter, we explored the "inner game" and the role of faith as a lifeline when the numbers don't add up. We established that your spiritual anchor is what allows you to maintain your peace in the gap between your current reality and your future legacy. But as we continue our journey toward stewardship, we must also address the physical and cognitive reality of how financial stress impacts your brain. It is not enough to simply "think positive"; we must understand the biological and behavioral traps that are designed to keep us stuck in a cycle of survival.

This chapter is about the science of the struggle. For many Cyclebreakers, the inability to move forward isn't a result of a lack of willpower or a lack of desire; it is a result of a specific cognitive phenomenon that occurs when we are under constant financial pressure. Before we can fully deploy the high-level strategies of growth and legacy, we must identify the "tunnel vision" that scarcity creates and learn how to widen our perspective. By understanding the mechanics of this trap, you can stop blaming your character and start hacking your environment to reclaim your cognitive bandwidth.

## THE SCARCITY TRAP

If you grew up in a household where money was tight, or if you've experienced financial trauma—like unexpected job loss, medical debt, or the constant anxiety of living paycheck to paycheck—you likely developed a scarcity mindset.

The scarcity mindset is a survival mechanism. It tells you there is never enough. It makes you hoard every penny, fear every bill, and view every potential opportunity through a lens of risk and loss. It's the voice that says, "If I spend this money, it will be gone forever," or "I can't afford to take that risk."

This isn't just a feeling; it's a measurable cognitive state. In their groundbreaking book, *Scarcity: Why Having Too Little Means So Much*, behavioral scientist Sendhil Mullainathan and psychologist Eldar Shafir demonstrated that the condition of scarcity—whether it's a scarcity of money, time, or anything else—captures our minds. It creates tunneling or what I call "tunnel vision" that forces us to focus on the immediate, urgent problem at the expense of everything else (Mullainathan and Shafir, 2013).

This intense focus can be helpful for short-term survival, but it has devastating long-term consequences. It impairs our executive function, reduces our fluid intelligence, and makes us more likely to make impulsive, short-sighted decisions (like taking out a high-interest payday loan).

In essence, the state of scarcity itself makes it harder to escape scarcity. It's a vicious cycle, a psychological trap that keeps people stuck. Understanding that this is a cognitive impairment, not a character flaw, is the first step toward breaking free.

I know this from personal experience. During the 2008–2009 financial crisis, I watched close family members go through the pain of bankruptcies and foreclosures. Seeing their struggle instilled a deep-seated fear of debt in me. I came to believe that credit was an inherently bad thing, a trap to be avoided at all costs. This fear was so strong that I refused to even get a credit card until I was well into my twenties.

For years, I operated from a place of scarcity, believing that avoiding credit entirely was the only way to be safe. What I didn't realize was that I was letting fear close doors for me. It wasn't until I began to re-educate myself and shift my perspective that I understood credit wasn't the enemy; it was a tool. When used responsibly, it could help me achieve my goals. That shift was instrumental in my ability to purchase my first home at 26. Had I held onto that scarcity mindset, I would have never taken the steps necessary to build the credit I needed to make that dream a reality.

This scarcity mindset is an exhausting, self-fulfilling prophecy. When you operate from a place of fear, you unintentionally push away the very opportunities and resources you need to thrive. You become so focused on protecting the little you have that you miss the chance to gain more.

## FROM HOARDING TO HARVESTING

The shift from scarcity to abundance is not about having a lot of money; it's about having a lot of faith and perspective. It's the realization that the world is full of resources and opportunities, and your job is to position yourself to receive them.

For me, this shift happened when I realized that being debt-free was not the end goal—it was the launchpad. I stopped focusing on the debt I needed to eliminate and started focusing on the wealth I needed to create. I stopped viewing every dollar as a potential loss and started viewing every dollar as a seed to be planted.

An abundance mindset changes your behavior in three fundamental ways:

1. It changes your language: You stop saying, "I can't afford that," and start asking, "How can I afford that?" or "Is that aligned with my values right now?"
2. It changes your risk tolerance: You move from being paralyzed by the fear of failure to understanding that failure is simply data—a lesson that gets you closer to success.
3. It changes your generosity: When you believe there is always more to come, you are more willing to share. I believe that money is an energy exchange. By giving—whether it's your time, your knowledge, or your money—you are opening your hands to the world. You can't receive with a closed fist. Generosity is not just a moral good; it is a powerful, physical declaration that you trust more will come. It breaks the cycle of fear and hoarding and creates a flow of abundance in your life.

## Exercise: Identifying Your Limiting Beliefs

The first step to embracing abundance is to identify the scarcity beliefs that are holding you back. These are often deeply ingrained messages you received about money in childhood.

Take a moment to complete these sentences:

People who have a lot of money are ______________________________.

Money is ____________________________________________.

I can't have more money because ______________________________.

If I had more money, I would have to ____________________________.

Once you've identified these beliefs, you can begin to challenge them with the affirmations and visualization techniques we discussed in the last chapter.

## The Voice of Doubt: Everyday Scarcity Traps

Identifying your limiting beliefs is the first step. The next is learning to recognize and challenge the subtle, everyday thoughts that keep you trapped in a scarcity mindset. These thoughts often disguise themselves as practicality or caution, but their root is fear.

**Obstacle:** "I can't invest my money; it's too risky. I might lose it all. It's safer in a savings account."

**Your Mindset Shift:** You are confusing "safe" with "familiar." A savings account feels safe, but due to inflation, the money in it is guaranteed to lose purchasing power over time. That is also a risk. An abundance mindset doesn't ignore risk; it learns to manage it. The shift is from "I can't afford to lose this money" to "I can't afford *not* to have this money working for me." Start small. You don't have to become a day trader. Investing just $50 a month in a low-cost index fund is an act of abundance. It's a declaration that you believe in a future where your money can grow.

(*Continued*)

(*Continued*)

**Obstacle:** "I shouldn't spend money on that course/conference/book. I can just learn it for free on YouTube."

**Your Mindset Shift:** While free resources are valuable, this thought can be a scarcity trap that keeps you from making strategic investments in yourself. An abundance mindset recognizes that your time and focus are your most valuable assets. Sometimes, paying for a structured course or a networking opportunity is the most direct path to a higher income. The question isn't just, "Can I get this for free?" but rather, "What is the potential return on this investment?" Paying for knowledge is an act of faith in your own ability to turn that knowledge into a tangible result.

**Obstacle:** "I have to do everything myself because I can't afford to hire help (a virtual assistant, a babysitter, a house cleaner)."

**Your Mindset Shift:** The scarcity mindset tells you to hoard your money. The abundance mindset tells you to leverage it. If you are spending hours on low-value tasks that someone else could do for $20 an hour, and you could use those same hours to generate $100 in your business, you are not saving money; you are losing $80. Start by delegating just one small task. Use the time you gain to focus on your highest value activities. This is how you break out of the "time for money" trap and begin to scale your success.

# CHAPTER FOURTEEN

# SETTING GOALS YOU ACTUALLY ACHIEVE

*"A goal without a deadline is just a wish; a goal with a plan is a legacy in the making."*

—Tiffany Grant

Understanding the mechanics of the scarcity trap was a vital step in your internal revolution. By recognizing that your past financial "tunnels" were a biological response rather than a character flaw, you have begun to reclaim the cognitive bandwidth necessary to think beyond immediate survival. You are no longer just trying to make it through the day; you are beginning to look toward the horizon. However, having reclaimed your mental energy, the next challenge is deciding exactly where to focus it.

A ship with a powerful engine and a clear-eyed captain is still at the mercy of the currents if there is no destination programmed into the GPS.

To move from the "internal revolution" to the **Engine of Growth**, we must translate your reclaimed bandwidth into a series of strategic milestones. This chapter is about the transition from intention to implementation. We are going to take the "why" you discovered in Part 1 and the "flow" you designed in Part 2 and anchor them to specific, time-bound targets that move you closer to your ultimate vision of stewardship.

# FROM VAGUE WISHES TO CONCRETE WINS

Have you ever set a New Year's resolution only to find it forgotten by February? "I want to save more money." "I want to get out of debt." "I want to be rich." These are not goals; they are wishes. They are daydreams without a deadline, and a dream without a plan is just a wish.

To truly transform your financial life, you need to turn those vague desires into concrete destinations. You need a target. Have you ever seen an archer shoot an arrow without aiming at a bullseye? Of course not. Goal setting is the process of defining your bullseye. It's how you give your financial efforts direction, purpose, and power.

To move your goals from vague dreams to achievable realities, we need a system. Fortunately, decades of research in psychology and management have given us a powerful and effective blueprint. The most enduring of these is the **SMART goal framework**. While the acronym has been adapted over the years, its core principles provide the structure needed to turn abstract desires into concrete plans:

- Specific: Vague goals lead to vague results. Instead of "save more money," a specific goal is "save $5,000 for a down payment on a house."
- Measurable: You must be able to track your progress. "Save $5,000" is measurable; "save more" is not.

- **A**chievable: Your goal should stretch you but not be so outlandish that it's discouraging.
- **R**elevant: The goal must be deeply connected to your "why." It must matter to *you*.
- **T**ime-bound: A goal needs a deadline. "I will save $5,000 in the next 12 months."

Using this framework is more than just an organizing exercise; it's a motivational one. As research has repeatedly shown, setting specific, challenging goals is one of the most reliable ways to increase performance and motivation (Locke and Latham, 2002).

However, even a SMART goal can feel overwhelming if it's too large. This is where a second key principle from behavioral science comes in: the power of **subgoals**.

Research from behavioral scientists like Szu-chi Huang has shown that breaking a large, distant goal into smaller, proximal subgoals is especially powerful early in your journey (Huang et al., 2017). Your brain is wired to respond to progress and rewards. When a goal is too far away, it's easy to lose momentum. When you're starting out, these smaller finish lines—like saving your first $500—provide early wins that build momentum. As you get closer to your ultimate goal, your motivation naturally shifts to focus on the final outcome itself.

By combining these two strategies—using the SMART framework to define your destination and then breaking it down into a series of smaller subgoals—you create a clear road map and a powerful, self-sustaining engine of motivation.

My journey from being a teenage mom to earning my MBA and becoming a business owner wasn't an accident. It was the result of setting one clear, ambitious goal after another. In this chapter, we'll turn your financial wishes into actionable plans using the same powerful framework I use with my clients and in my own life: SMART goals.

## Step 1: Start with Your "Why"

Before you can set a goal, you must know why you want it. As we explored in Chapter 4, your "why" is the emotional engine that will drive you forward when motivation fades. If you haven't done so already, I highly recommend the "Ask Why Five Times" exercise.

"I want to be debt-free." Why?

"So that I can be a good example for my kids." Why?

"Because I want to show them what's possible when you have your money in order." Why?

"Because that wasn't something that was taught to me."

That last answer—that deep, personal reason—is your fuel. When your goals are tied to your core values, they become nonnegotiable.

## Step 2: Make Your Goals SMART

Once you know your "why," it's time to build the "how." The SMART framework is the most effective system I know for creating goals you can actually achieve.

- **S—Specific:** Your goal must be clear and unambiguous.
  - Vague: "I want to pay off my credit card."
  - Specific: "I will pay off my $5,000 Visa card balance."
- **M—Measurable:** You must be able to track your progress with numbers. This is how you know if you're winning.
  - Vague: "I want to save for a down payment."
  - Measurable: "I will save $10,000 for a down payment."
- **A—Achievable:** Your goal should stretch you, but it must be realistic. Setting a goal to become a millionaire in a year on a $50,000 salary is a recipe for discouragement. Start with smaller, attainable steps.

- Unrealistic: "I will pay off $50,000 in student loans in one year on my current income."
- Achievable: "I will pay off my $5,000 credit card in one year."

- **R—Relevant**: Does this goal matter to you? Does it align with your "why"? A goal that doesn't excite you is a goal you won't pursue.
  - Irrelevant: "I should invest in crypto because everyone is talking about it."
  - Relevant: "I will open an investment account to build long-term wealth for my family's future."
- **T—Time-Bound:** A goal needs a deadline. This creates urgency and holds you accountable. When I set my goal to be debt-free by 30, that deadline made me go hard. As the clock ticked, my focus intensified.
  - Vague: "I'll pay off my car someday."
  - Time-Bound: "I will pay off my car by December 31, 2026."

## The Voice of Doubt: Why Goals Fizzle Out

We've all been there. Fired up on January 1 with a list of resolutions, only to find our motivation has vanished by February. Setting a goal is easy; achieving it is hard. The failure often isn't in the goal itself, but in the mental traps we fall into along the way. Let's get ahead of them.

**Obstacle:** "My goal feels so big and far away, I don't even know where to start. It's overwhelming."

**Your Mindset Shift:** You don't climb a mountain in one giant leap; you do it one step at a time. A big goal like "buy a house" is not a goal; it's a dream. Your job is to break that dream down into a series of small, actionable steps. Your first goal isn't "buy a house"; it's "save the first $1,000 for a down payment." Your next goal is "improve my credit score by 20 points." By focusing only on the very next step, you build momentum and turn an overwhelming dream into a manageable project.

(*Continued*)

*(Continued)*

**Obstacle:** "I set a goal, but I'm not making progress fast enough. I feel like a failure, so I might as well just quit."

**Your Mindset Shift:** You are confusing progress with perfection. The path to any meaningful goal is never a straight line; it's a messy, winding road with setbacks and detours. The goal isn't to have a perfect journey; it's to maintain forward momentum, no matter how slow. Did you only save $50 this month instead of your planned $100? That is not a failure. That is a $50 victory. You are $50 closer than you were last month. Celebrate the small wins relentlessly, because they are the fuel that will get you through the long journey.

**Obstacle:** "I feel like I 'should' be saving for retirement, but I'm just not motivated. It doesn't feel urgent or exciting."

**Your Mindset Shift:** You have a goal without a "why." A goal that isn't connected to a deep, emotional driver is just a chore on your to-do list. "Saving for retirement" is abstract. What does that life actually look like for you? Is it the freedom to live by the sea in Jamaica, like I did? Is it the ability to travel and see your grandchildren? Is it the peace of mind of never having to worry about money again? Take the time to vividly picture the life that goal will give you. When the goal is attached to a powerful feeling, the motivation will follow. If you can't connect to it emotionally, it's probably not your real goal.

## Putting It All Together: Your SMART Goal Statement

When you combine these elements, you create a powerful statement of intent. I always start my goals with "I will." There is power in declaring what you are going to do.

Let's transform a vague wish into a powerful SMART goal:

- Vague Wish: "I want to pay off my credit card."
- SMART Goal: "I will pay off my $5,000 in credit card debt in 12 months by paying $500 a month towards it. I will achieve this

by cutting my entertainment budget and not using the card during this time."

That's not a wish; that's a plan.

## Step 3: Organize and Implement

Most of us have more than one goal. You might want to build your emergency fund, pay off a car, and start investing. Trying to do everything at once is a recipe for overwhelm.

**List and Categorize:** Write down all your financial goals. I recommend starting with at least three. Now, sort them into two columns: Short Term (less than a year) and Long Term (more than a year).

**Prioritize:** Within each column, order your goals. You can order them by timeline or by what's most important to you right now. Do you need the security of an emergency fund first? Or is the high-interest credit card causing you the most stress? Put that goal at the top.

**Break It Down:** Look at your big, long-term goals. How can you break them down into smaller, short-term goals? If your long-term goal is to be completely debt-free in five years, a short-term goal might be to pay off one specific credit card this year. This makes a huge, intimidating goal feel manageable.

**Integrate with Your Budget:** This is where the magic happens. Look at your top-priority goal. Go back to your budget from Chapter 6. Where is the money going to come from? Every dollar left over after your essentials are covered should be aimed directly at that number one goal.

## Step 4: Stay the Course When Motivation Fades

Setting the goal is the easy part. Sticking with it when life gets in the way is the real challenge. Here are the strategies that have kept me and my clients on track.

**Make It Visual:** You need daily reminders of what you're working toward. Create a vision board. Print a picture of your dream house and stick it on your refrigerator. Write your goal on a sticky note and put it on your bathroom mirror. Make it impossible to forget what you're fighting for.

**Make It Public:** Accountability is a powerful motivator. When I started my blog, *Money Talk with Tiff*, a big reason was to publicly declare my goal of being debt-free by 30. Tell your spouse, a trusted friend, or your social media followers. When you know others are watching, you're more likely to follow through.

**Embrace the Power of Affirmation:** As we discussed in the last chapter, your self-talk matters. If you tell yourself, "I'll never get out of debt," you won't. Use your affirmations to declare your success in advance.

**Don't Be Afraid to Tweak:** Life happens. An emergency might pop up and derail your timeline. That's okay. It's not a failure; it's a detour. Go back to your SMART goal and adjust the timeline. Maybe you won't be debt-free by June, but you can be by November. The goal isn't to be perfect; it's to keep moving forward. Even when I didn't hit my "debt-free by 30" goal, I looked back and saw just how much I had accomplished. I simply adjusted the timeline and kept going.

By using this framework, you're not just hoping for a better financial future—you're actively building it, one specific, measurable, achievable, relevant, and time-bound step at a time.

# CHAPTER FIFTEEN

# THE UMBRELLA METHOD

*"Don't just work for your money; build an umbrella of income that works while you rest."*

—Tiffany Grant

We have spent the beginning of this section addressing the "inner game" of your growth. You have dismantled the scarcity trap, realigned your faith, and set the SMART goals that will act as the GPS for your future. You have reclaimed your cognitive bandwidth and prepared your mind to handle a level of abundance that the "bulletproof persona" could never have sustained. But as we know, a clear vision and a strong mindset are the fuel; now, we need the vehicle.

This chapter is where we move from the "why" of growth to the "how." For many Cycle-breakers, the realization eventually sets in that you cannot save your way out of a significant income gap. You have optimized your spending, but the math of your legacy requires a bigger shovel. We are going to explore how to strategically expand your "pie" without losing your peace. By implementing the Umbrella Method, you will learn to build a diversified engine of income that leverages your existing human capital, allowing you to move from the exhaustion of the "hustle" to the efficiency of a CEO.

## THE INCOME PROBLEM: EXPANDING THE PIE

In the world of budgeting, there is a point of diminishing returns. You can cut expenses, cancel subscriptions, and optimize every category, but if your income is less than your essential needs, you don't have a spending problem—you have an income problem.

I know this feeling intimately. There was a time in my life when I was using government benefits and timing my school refund checks just to make sure rent was paid. The wake-up call came when a bank told me flat-out that I "didn't make enough" for a simple $200 line of credit. I realized then that if I was ever going to get ahead, I had to expand the pie, not just slice it differently.

That realization lit a fire in me. My goal was to be debt-free by thirty, and I was willing to do whatever it took. While working a full-time job and going to school, I added a new stream: I started driving for Uber and Lyft. For three years, that was my life. The result? In the first year alone, I paid off more than $50,000 in debt.

But as I drove those miles, I realized something critical: hustle is a season, but strategy is a lifestyle. I couldn't drive forever. I needed to move from being an employee—or a gig worker—to being the CEO of my own income.

# FROM EMPLOYEE TO CEO: THE MINDSET OF AN ENTREPRENEUR

For generations, we were taught a single path to financial stability: get a good, secure job and stay there. But as we've all seen, the "secure job" is a myth. Relying on a single source of income is one of the riskiest financial strategies you can employ. Building multiple income streams is no longer a luxury; it is a necessity for the prudent.

Think of your financial life as a bridge supported by multiple pillars. If one pillar cracks, the bridge remains standing. If your life is supported by only one pillar—your primary job—and that pillar cracks, the entire structure collapses.

My journey to full-time entrepreneurship wasn't a single leap; it was a series of calculated steps. The real breakthrough came when I stopped trying to build separate, disconnected businesses—a soap business, a blog, a logistics company—and started building one cohesive structure. I consolidated everything under one brand: *Money Talk with Tiff.*

# THE UMBRELLA METHOD: ONE BRAND, MANY RIBS

The Umbrella Method is the strategy of consolidating your expertise under one canopy. Instead of running in five different directions, you create different income streams that all support one another.

- The Handle and Canopy: This is your core brand—your "why," your unique expertise, and your reputation.

- The Ribs: These are your different income streams. Because they sit under the same canopy, they share the same audience and the same mission.

Under the *Money Talk with Tiff* umbrella, I built three specific types of "ribs":

1. Active/Service Income (The Cash Flow Starter): This is trading time for money. For me, this was one-on-one financial counseling and corporate workshops. It's the fastest way to generate cash today.
2. Scalable/Product Income (The Lever): This is where you "do the work once and sell it many times." This includes my digital courses, like *Budget Nirvana*, and the book you are holding right now.
3. Passive/Residual Income (The Wealth Builder): This is money that comes in regardless of whether you are "at the office," such as brand partnerships and affiliate marketing for tools I genuinely use, like Ally Bank or YNAB.

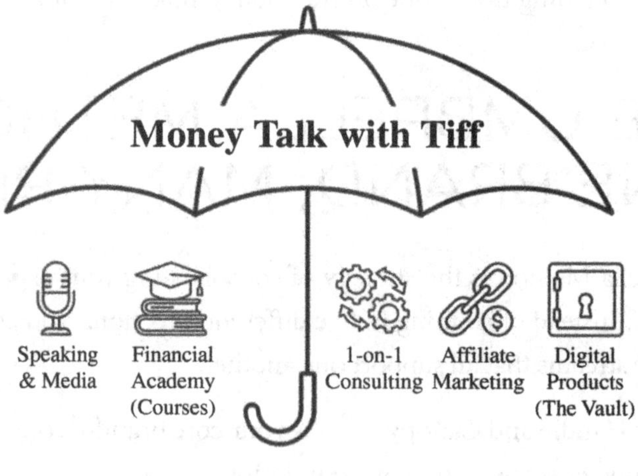

# THE SIDE HUSTLE SELECTION MATRIX

Not every opportunity is a good one. To avoid the exhaustion of "context switching," I use a simple matrix to vet new ideas. Rate a potential stream on a scale of 1–5 across these criteria:

- Time Commitment: Does this require 20 hours a week or 20 minutes?
- Startup Cost: Do you need expensive equipment or just a laptop?
- Skill Alignment: Does this leverage what you already know?
- Scalability: Can this grow without requiring more of your personal time?
- Brand Synergy: Does this fit under your existing umbrella?

The Rule of 15: If a project doesn't score at least a 15 out of 25, it is a distraction. Let it go so you can focus on the streams that actually move the needle.

# CASE STUDY: MARCUS AND THE UMBRELLA METHOD REVOLUTION

When I first met Marcus, he was a talented graphic designer with a stable 9-to-5, but he lived in constant fear of a layoff. He felt his entire life hung by a single thread.

We realized Marcus was viewing his career as a single pole in the ground. We needed to build him an umbrella.

- Rib 1 (Active): Marcus started taking on two high-end freelance branding projects a month. By using the "Art of the Ask" (which we will cover in Chapter 17), he earned an extra $1,500 a month with minimal extra hours.
- Rib 2 (Scalable): He took the templates he created for clients and turned them into a "Brand Identity Toolkit" for a digital marketplace. It now generates $500 a month in "sleep money."
- Rib 3 (Authority): He began sharing his process on LinkedIn, which led to paid speaking invitations.

The breakthrough for Marcus didn't happen when he hit a certain dollar amount; it happened when he realized that his employer was now just one of several "clients" under his umbrella. He had moved from a defensive posture to an offensive one.

## THE TAX STEWARD MINDSET

As you move to multiple streams, your relationship with the government changes. You are no longer just an employee; you are a tax steward.

The 30% Rule: For every dollar that comes in under your umbrella, immediately move 30% into a separate "tax buffer" account. This isn't your money; it's the government's money that you are temporarily holding. Shifting to this mindset early prevents the "success trap," where your business is growing but your tax debt is growing even faster.

# THE LEAP OF FAITH

Leaving a 9-to-5 is a calculated risk. You do it when the following are true:

1. You know your numbers inside and out.
2. You have a proven, consistent stream of income from your business.
3. You have a three to six months cash buffer to weather the initial storms.
4. Your "why" is so strong that the fear of staying put is greater than the fear of leaping.

Building multiple income streams isn't just about making more money. It's about creating resilience, freedom, and control. It is the ultimate expression of your internal locus of control.

## The Voice of Doubt: "I Don't Have the Time or the Skills"

The idea of building another income stream can feel exhausting before you even begin. Your plate is already full. The voices of doubt will tell you it's a luxury you can't afford in terms of time, energy, or talent. Let's dismantle those beliefs right now.

**Obstacle:** "I'm already working a full-time job and taking care of my family. I literally have no extra time. How can I possibly start something else?"

**Your Mindset Shift:** You are looking for hours when you should be looking for minutes. You don't need to find 20 hours a week to start.

(*Continued*)

(*Continued*)

You need to find 20 minutes a day. Can you wake up 20 minutes earlier? Can you trade 20 minutes of scrolling on social media for 20 minutes of research? The goal is not to build a second full-time job overnight. The goal is to create a tiny snowball of momentum. Small, consistent efforts over time build empires. Start with a time commitment that is so small it feels almost ridiculous and then be fiercely consistent with it.

**Obstacle:** "I don't have any special skills that someone would pay for. I'm not an expert in anything."

**Your Mindset Shift:** You are dramatically underestimating the value of the knowledge you already possess. You don't have to be the world's foremost expert to provide value. You just need to know a little bit more than someone else. Are you the person everyone asks for help with their resume? That's a service. Are you great at planning kids' birthday parties? That's a service. Do you know how to navigate the local government office efficiently? That's a service. Start by making a list of things you are good at, things you enjoy, and problems you have solved for yourself or others. Your first income stream is almost certainly hiding in that list.

**Obstacle:** "What if I try and it fails? I'll have wasted all that time and money for nothing."

**Your Mindset Shift:** There is no such thing as failure in this process; there is only data collection. If you launch a small side project and it doesn't make money, you haven't failed. You have learned what the market doesn't want. You have gained valuable data that will inform your next attempt. The only true failure is allowing the fear of a potential outcome to stop you from taking action in the first place. An abundance mindset knows that every "failure" is just a tuition payment for the education of success.

# THE SPECTRUM OF INCOME: FROM FULLY ACTIVE TO MOSTLY PASSIVE

Income isn't just a binary choice between a 9-to-5 (active) and sipping margaritas on a beach while money magically appears (passive). It's a spectrum.

**Active Income:** This is a direct trade of your time for money. If you stop working, the money stops coming in. Your salary from a job is the classic example. Freelance work, consulting, and even my early side hustle of driving for Uber and Lyft fall into this category. You are actively performing a service.

**Passive Income:** This is where you earn money with minimal active effort after an initial investment of time or money. I want to be very clear about this: nothing is truly passive from day one. There is always upfront work. The goal is to build a system that eventually generates income without your constant, direct involvement.

The magic happens when you use your active income (from your job or an active side hustle) to build assets that generate passive income.

# A UNIVERSE OF IDEAS: FINDING YOUR NEXT INCOME STREAM

The biggest hurdle to starting is often a lack of ideas. To help you, here is a universe of possibilities, broken down by category. This is not an exhaustive list but a starting point to get your creative juices flowing. As you read, don't just look for what you *can* do; look for what *excites* you.

# Leverage Your Existing Skills and Knowledge

You are already an expert in something. These ideas involve packaging what you already know and selling it to others who want to learn.

- **Freelance Your Day Job:** Are you a writer, graphic designer, bookkeeper, or social media manager? Offer your skills on a project basis to small businesses on platforms like **Upwork** or **Fiverr**.
- **Become a Tutor or Coach:** Are you great at math, a second language, or playing an instrument? Offer tutoring services online or in your community. Did you successfully navigate a difficult career change? Coach others on how to do the same.
- **Create a "Done-for-You" Service:** Are you the person everyone asks for help with their resume, their college application essays, or planning a vacation itinerary? Turn that skill into a paid service.
- **Sell Digital Templates:** Are you a wizard with spreadsheets, Canva, or Notion? Create and sell budget templates, social media graphic packs, or project management dashboards on platforms like **Etsy** or **Gumroad**.

# The Gig Economy and Task-based Work

These are the modern-day side hustles. They offer maximum flexibility and are perfect for earning quick cash in your spare time. This is exactly how I started with Uber and Lyft.

- **Rideshare and Delivery:** The classics for a reason. Drive for **Uber** or **Lyft** or deliver food with **DoorDash** or **Uber Eats**. You work exactly when you want to.

- **Task-based Services:** Use platforms like **TaskRabbit** to get paid for assembling furniture, running errands, doing handyman work, or providing moving help.
- **User Testing and Surveys:** Get paid for your opinion. Websites like **UserTesting.com** pay you to test websites and apps, while platforms like **Respondent.io** offer paid research studies.

## Build a Digital Asset (The Path to Passive Income)

These ideas require more upfront work but have the potential to generate income while you sleep. This is the ultimate goal for many.

- **Start a Niche Blog or YouTube Channel:** Pick a topic you are passionate about—gardening, vintage video games, baking, personal finance for nurses—and create content. Over time, you can monetize it with ads, affiliate links (like I do with my blog), and sponsorships.
- **Write and Self-publish an eBook:** Do you have a specific expertise or a story to tell? Write a short eBook and publish it on **Amazon KDP (Kindle Direct Publishing)**. It costs nothing to publish, and it can sell for years.
- **Create an Online Course:** Package your knowledge into a video or text-based course on platforms like **Teachable** or **Kajabi**. Your one-time effort can serve thousands of students.

## The Local and Physical World

Don't underestimate the power of providing services in your own neighborhood.

- **Pet Services:** Offer dog walking, pet sitting, or grooming services. People will always spend money on their furry family members.

- **Home and Yard Services:** Provide house cleaning, lawn mowing, landscaping, or home organization services.
- **Notary Public:** Becoming a mobile notary can be a lucrative and flexible side business, especially if you specialize in serving real estate agents or law offices.

The key is to pick one idea that feels exciting and achievable *for you* and then take the smallest possible first step to get started.

But the first question I always get is, "Tiffany, I get it, but what am I good at?" Let's find out.

# HOW TO FIND YOUR INCOME STREAM: AN INVENTORY OF YOU

Often, others see our talents before we do. This exercise is designed to help you see what they see. Grab a notebook and make three lists:

**The Joy List:** Write down everything you genuinely enjoy doing.

**The Help List:** What do people always ask you for help with?

**The Pattern List:** What themes or activities keep showing up in your life?

I had a client who, through this exercise, saw a clear pattern: cleaning. She loved keeping a spotless house and found it genuinely therapeutic. I told her, "There are people like me out there who do not enjoy cleaning." That spark was all she needed. She started a successful cleaning business. Your next income stream is hiding in those lists.

# A CRITICAL WARNING: NOT EVERY PASSION IS A PAYCHECK

I need to give you a warning that I learned the hard way. Not every passion needs to be monetized. At one point, I got into soap-making. I loved the craft, but when I turned it into a business, the demand turned my relaxing hobby into a stressful obligation. If turning a passion into a business makes you miserable, let it remain a passion.

# THE ULTIMATE GOAL: ALIGNMENT, NOT MISERY

Building income streams is supposed to make your life easier, not harder. Yes, there's a ramp-up period. But if a side hustle starts to make you miserable or you realize it doesn't align with your values, let it go. I've had countless businesses since I was five years old. I try things, keep what sticks, and discard what doesn't. You cannot be afraid to pivot.

I once built a business that made half a million dollars in revenue in a single year. By every external metric, it was a massive success. But I was completely miserable running it. I realized I could work on *Money Talk with Tiff*, have more fun, and be happier. So, I made the difficult decision to let the half-million-dollar business go.

Sometimes, the most powerful money move is knowing when to walk away. The goal isn't just to make more money; it's to build a life you actually want to live.

# CHAPTER SIXTEEN

# THE REVENUE TRAP

*"High profit at the expense of high peace is just a different kind of poverty."*

—Tiffany Grant

In the previous chapter, we explored the mechanics of the Umbrella Method and the strategic importance of expanding your income. We established that for a Cycle-breaker, increasing your "shovel" is a vital part of building a lasting legacy. You have begun to see yourself not just as a worker, but as a CEO of your own revenue streams. It is an empowering shift, and the momentum of seeing your gross numbers grow can be intoxicating. However, a dangerous shadow often follows rapid growth—a trap that many entrepreneurs fall into just as they think they've finally won the game.

This chapter is the guardrail for your growth. It is the cautionary tale that every steward must hear before they scale. We are going to talk about the difference between building a business that serves your life and building a business that consumes it. As you move toward higher levels of revenue, you must maintain a fierce commitment to the "ROI of Peace" we discussed in the earlier stages of this journey. Before you add the next truck, the next client, or the next stream to your umbrella, you must ensure that you aren't accidentally building a high-revenue prison.

## THE MIRAGE OF THE HALF-MILLION

In the world of entrepreneurship, there is a number that carries an almost mystical weight: the half-million. We are told that once you hit $500,000 in revenue, you've "made it." You've scaled. You've proven the concept. You are officially a success.

In late 2021, I was living that success. On paper, the money moves were working perfectly. Our logistics business was at its peak. We had 10 trucks and vans on the road, their sides emblazoned with our logos—a physical manifestation of the empire I was building. Every day, the bank notifications chimed with deposits from brokers. We were traveling, taking vacations, and to the outside world, I was the embodiment of the "boss girl" aesthetic.

But I remember a specific afternoon, sitting at my desk, staring at the accounting software. The screen showed a revenue line that would make most founders celebrate. But as I looked closer at the overhead, the fuel costs, the maintenance, and the payroll, a cold realization washed over me: the net profit didn't justify the soul-crushing exhaustion I was feeling.

I was making the most money I had ever made in my life, and I had never been more miserable.

I turned to my husband at the time and said the words every "hustler" is trained to fear: "We should close this. It doesn't make sense anymore."

He looked at me like I was crazy. "Close it? We just need to run more trucks," he argued. But "running more" meant I would have to work more. And I was already working 24 hours a day. I was the dispatcher. I was the on-call crisis manager. I was the one keeping the wheels turning while my own internal engine was seizing up.

This is the Revenue Trap. It is the moment when your business stops being a vehicle for your freedom and starts being a more expensive form of bondage. It is the proof that revenue is a vanity metric, profit is a sanity metric, but peace is the ultimate metric.

## THE COVID-19 PIVOT: A STRATEGIC TRAP

To understand how I ended up in a $500,000 prison, you need to understand the "why" behind the business. In early 2020, my primary business, *Money Talk with Tiff*, was thriving. I had a calendar full of speaking engagements across multiple states and countries. Speaking was my bread and butter, my passion, and my primary income stream.

Then, COVID-19 hit.

Overnight, every single event was canceled. The world shut down, and my main revenue stream evaporated. As a Cycle-breaker and a mother, my High-functioning Survival Mode kicked in. I couldn't just sit and wait for the world to reopen. We needed a pivot.

My husband had always wanted to start a logistics company. At the time, it seemed like a brilliant strategic move. While the rest of the world was at a standstill, trucks were the only things moving. We were essential. We were recession-proof. I did the research, established the entity, and brought the business to fruition.

But here is the lesson I want you to underline: just because a move is "strategic" doesn't mean it's aligned.

I was building a business based on a scarcity trap response—the fear of losing income—rather than building a business based on my internal locus of control and my true purpose. I had traded a business I loved for a business that "kept the wheels turning," and in doing so, I handed over the keys to my peace of mind.

# THE 24-HOUR PRISON

A day in the life of that logistics company was a masterclass in what I now call the "Bandwidth Tax." As we discussed in Part 2, financial stress robs you of your cognitive capacity. But operational stress does the same.

I was never "off." My phone was an extension of my hand, and it was a dangerous attachment. If a driver had a tire blowout at 3:00 a.m. in a different time zone, I was the one who got the call. I had to coordinate with brokers, find roadside assistance, and ensure the load wasn't late. I was home all day, but I wasn't *present*. My kids saw their mother constantly tethered to a screen, reacting to crises that never seemed to end.

I felt a bone-deep drain that no amount of "pleasure vacations" could fix. We would go on trips, but I was still dispatching from the beach. I was still arguing with brokers from the hotel room.

Looking back, my history as a teen mom played a massive role in why I stayed in that grind so long. As we explored in Chapter 1, when you start your journey by trying to "prove everyone wrong," you develop a pathological fear of failure. I didn't want to fail in business. I didn't want to fail in my marriage. I didn't want to fail in my finances. I felt that if I quit, I was admitting that the people who doubted the 17-year-old version of me were right.

I was using my resilience—one of the pillars of PsyCap—against myself. I was "bouncing back" into a situation that was actively destroying me.

## THE HIDDEN TAX: TOXIC PARTNERSHIPS

In business, we talk about taxes like the self-employment tax or the corporate tax. But there is a hidden tax that can bankrupt you faster than the IRS: the Toxic Partnership Tax.

During this $500,000 year, I was dealing with a partner who wasn't just unsupportive—he was a drain on the business's actual productivity. While I was handling the 3:00 a.m. calls and the accounting, he was often absent or, worse, creating conflict at home that made it impossible for me to focus.

He would use my professional identity as a weapon. Whenever we faced the financial issues that come with high-overhead businesses—like the mounting credit card debt we were using to keep the trucks running—he would throw my credentials in my face.

"Aren't you a financial counselor?" he would sneer. "We shouldn't be having these issues."

It was a psychological game designed to keep me in High-functioning Survival Mode. He knew he couldn't run the business without me, so he used my fear of professional shame to keep me tethered to the work.

This is the intersection of financial abuse and entrepreneurship. When your business success is used as a tool of isolation, and your professional expertise is used as a point of ridicule, the "revenue" you are generating is being paid for with your soul.

# THE AFC® PARADOX: HELPING OTHERS WHILE DROWNING

The most painful part of this era was the persona conflict.

Since 2017, I had been the "Money Girl." I was an Accredited Financial Counselor® (AFC). I was helping hundreds of clients get out of debt, fix their credit, and build their architecture of flow. I was meeting one-on-one with clients, giving them the tools to live their best financial lives, and then hanging up the phone to face my own depreciating net worth.

Behind the scenes, my personal finances were in shambles. As a result of the logistics business's overhead and the personal chaos at home, we were racking up credit card debt. I was watching the very things I taught against happen in my own life.

It felt like I was living a lie. I felt like an imposter. But the truth was more complex: I was a high-performing professional who was trapped in a low-performing environment.

I realized that when you drift away from your purpose—when you stop being a steward of your gifts and start being an owner of a trap—life gets harder, not easier. The money becomes harder to make, and even harder to keep.

# THE BREAKING POINT AND THE PROTECTION ORDER

The end didn't come because the revenue stopped. It came because the safety did.

In December 2021, I went to see a divorce attorney. I thought I was just there to talk about ending a marriage. But as I explained the situation—the verbal abuse, the stalking, the drug use I had recently discovered, and the physical incidents—the lawyer stopped me.

"Tiffany," he said, his voice grave. "You don't just need a divorce. You need a protection order. You are in danger."

It is a strange thing to realize that other people can see the fire in your house before you can. I was so used to "managing" the chaos that I didn't realize the house was about to collapse.

The day I went to the courthouse to apply for the *ex parte* order was the most emotional day of my life. I had to retell the story to the court, to the judge, and to myself. But as I signed those papers, I felt a shift in my locus of control. For the first time in a year, I wasn't reacting to a driver or a husband. I was making a move for my own survival.

When the order was served, my ex-husband was out on a run in another state. I called everyone who worked for us and told them I was leaving the company.

Their response was the ultimate validation. They asked me, "Who are we going to work for now?" and every single one of them quit. They told me they were only there because of me. They refused to work for him.

In that moment, I realized that I was the asset. The trucks were just metal. The revenue was just numbers. My human capital and my reputation were the only things that truly mattered.

## THE STEWARDSHIP SHIFT: CHOOSING PEACE OVER PROFIT

Moving to Jamaica in May 2024 was the final step in escaping the Revenue Trap.

I chose Jamaica for many reasons—health, lifestyle, and a return to my roots—but the biggest reason was the need for a Peace Wall. I needed to live in an environment where I didn't have to look over my shoulder every time I saw a sprinter van or a box truck. I needed to trade the PTSD of that $500,000 year for the Veranda Moment I have now.

Today, I look at that 2021 revenue completely differently. I don't work nearly as much as I did then, but I have more in my pocket because my overhead is low and my peace is high.

I have moved from an owner mindset to a stewardship mindset.

When you think you "own" a business, you feel you must cling to it, even if it's killing you. But when you are a steward, you realize you are just a manager of God's resources for a season. If a business is no longer fulfilling its purpose—if it is no longer serving the "Good of Me" or the "Good of God"—I am now much quicker to cut the cord.

I gave up the logistics business. I am currently thinking about dissolving my construction business. I am no longer afraid of "failing" in the eyes of the world because I know that the only true failure is staying in a situation that robs you of your ability to be a present mother and a peaceful soul.

## TIFF'S TAKEAWAY: THE ROI OF PEACE

If you are currently obsessed with hitting your first $100k or $500k, I want you to stop and perform a Peace Audit.

Ask yourself: Is this an Engine of Growth, or is it a Revenue Trap?

True wealth is not just the money coming in; it is the freedom to step away from the screen. It is the ability to sleep through the night without a 3:00 a.m. crisis. It is the realization that you would rather have $100,000 and a quiet mind than $500,000 and a shattered spirit.

In the next chapter, we will talk about how to build a business that actually supports this kind of peace. But for now, I want you to remember this formula:

$$ROI = (Net\ Profit + Personal\ Peace) \div Time\ Invested$$

Don't guess your peace score. Download my **ROI of Peace Worksheet** (see Figure 16.1) the Resource Vault to audit your current business or job.

If the "Personal Peace" variable in your life is negative, your ROI is zero. No matter what the bank account says.

**Figure 16.1 The ROI of peace matrix—identifying the revenue trap vs. the steward.**

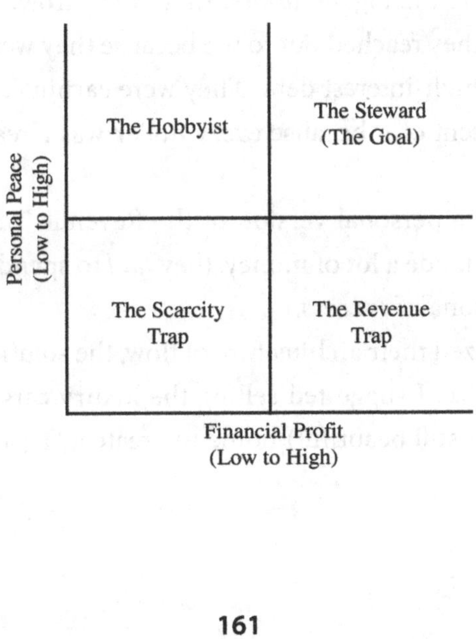

In 2021, the Bulletproof Persona I built at seventeen was no longer protecting me; it was suffocating me. I was so afraid that a "failed" business would prove my early critics right that I used my Hyper-independence to carry the weight of 10 trucks and a toxic marriage alone. I thought that if the mask slipped, I would lose everything. I didn't realize that the mask was the very thing keeping me from the peace I was working so hard to buy.

## CLIENT SPOTLIGHT: THE GOLDEN HANDCUFFS OF THE JONESES

I once worked with a couple who, on the outside, looked like the ultimate success story. They both earned multiple six-figure salaries. They lived in a sprawling mansion, drove high-end luxury cars, and wore the latest designer labels. They were "the Joneses" that everyone else was trying to keep up with.

But behind the mahogany doors, they were drowning. Despite their massive income, they reached out to me because they were carrying multiple six figures in high-interest debt. They were earning a fortune, but they couldn't enjoy a cent of it because every dollar was already spoken for by their creditors.

They were in a personal version of the Revenue Trap. They believed that because they made a lot of money, they *had* to spend a lot of money to maintain the persona of success.

When I analyzed their architecture of flow, the solution was clear: they needed to downsize. I suggested selling the luxury cars and moving to a more modest (but still beautiful) home to create a "Peace Buffer" in their budget.

The resistance was immediate. Their egos were tied to their assets. They felt that taking a step back in lifestyle was an admission of failure. I had to help them see that they were currently in a prison of their own making.

## The Lesson

Sometimes you must take a strategic step back to move 10 steps forward. We eventually negotiated a compromise: they sold one car and moved to a house that was $2,000 less per month in carrying costs. That $2,000 became the engine for their debt-payoff plan. By sacrificing the image of wealth for a season, they were able to build the reality of wealth. They learned that net peace is more valuable than a high-profile zip code.

# ACTION GUIDE: THE REVENUE TRAP AUDIT

*"Don't build a business that you eventually need a vacation from. Build a life you don't want to escape."*

—Tiffany Grant

## Exercise 1: The Peace-to-profit Ratio

In this chapter, we introduced the formula for true ROI. Use your most recent month of data to calculate yours.

1. Net Profit: (Total Revenue – All Expenses/Taxes) = $__________
2. Personal Peace Score: On a scale of −10 (Constant Crisis) to +10 (Total Flow), how did you feel running the business this month? Score: __________

3. **Time Invested:** How many hours did you actually work (including "hidden" hours like 3 a.m. calls or answering emails at dinner)? Hours: __________

The Formula:

$$ROI = (Net\,Profit + (Peace\,Score \times 1000)) \div Time\,Invested$$

(Note: If your peace score is negative, notice how quickly your ROI drops, regardless of the profit.)

## Exercise 2: Identifying the "Hidden Taxes"

List the three biggest drains on your energy right now. Are they operational (systems), financial (overhead), or relational (partners/clients)?

- Drain 1: ____________________ (Type: __________)
- Drain 2: ____________________ (Type: __________)
- Drain 3: ____________________ (Type: __________)

## Exercise 3: The "Owner vs. Steward" Decision Matrix

For every major project or business line under your umbrella, ask:

- Does this serve the "Good of Me" (My health and family)? [Yes/No]
- Does this serve the "Good of God/Purpose"? [Yes/No]
- If you passed away tomorrow, would this legacy be worth the life energy you are spending on it today? [Yes/No]

# CHAPTER SEVENTEEN

# THE STRATEGIC ADVISORY TEAM

*"You are the CEO of your life, but even a CEO needs a council of wise advisors."*

—Tiffany Grant

In the previous chapter, we looked at the high cost of the Revenue Trap—the moment where your growth begins to outpace your peace. We saw how the Bulletproof Persona, while useful for early survival, eventually becomes a bottleneck that prevents true scaling and stewardship. If you are going to avoid the prison of a half-million-dollar business that robs you of your sleep, you must be willing to dismantle the myth of the solo-grind. You must move from being the person who answers every call and solves every problem to being the visionary who leads a specialized team.

This chapter is about building the infrastructure of your support. As a Cycle-breaker, your Hyper-independence has been your shield, but to enter the next phase of your legacy, you must trade that shield for a "Council of Stewards." We are going to identify the specific professional roles—from the AFC® to the CFP®—that will act as your strategic "pit crew." By surrounding yourself with experts who care for the technical details of your wealth, you buy back the time and mental energy required to focus on your highest purpose. Before you take another step toward expansion, we are going to ensure you have the right voices at your table.

# PERSONAL FINANCE IS A TEAM SPORT

In the early days of your financial journey, you are the athlete. You are the one doing the heavy lifting, tracking every cent on the linoleum floor, and making the hard choices to silence the noise. But as you move from the internal revolution to the Engine of Growth, the game changes. You can no longer afford to be a solo player. To build a legacy that lasts, you must realize that personal finance is not a solo mission—it is a team sport.

One of the most dangerous myths in entrepreneurship is the "self-made" narrative. We are taught to believe that the most successful founders are the ones who can do it all. But through my years of working with high-net-worth individuals and interviewing hundreds of financial experts, I have found the opposite to be true: The most successful people are those who are the best at building a pit crew.

True financial empowerment comes from identifying who has the specialized knowledge you lack and bringing them into your circle. When you are running a business or managing a growing household, you aren't just looking for help; you are building a Council of Stewards.

These are the professionals who will help you manage God's resources with precision, protection, and peace. If I had built this council during my logistics years, I wouldn't have been dispatching trucks at 3:00 a.m. while my own net worth depreciated. I would have had a strategic board to spot the red flags before they became a prison.

## DECODING THE ALPHABET SOUP: WHO DO YOU NEED?

When you start looking for professional help, you will be met with a "word search" of credentials. It can be overwhelming, but understanding these roles is the first step in moving from being a bank teller in your life to being the CEO.

### The Accredited Financial Counselor (AFC): The Behavioral Specialist

The AFC is your foundational partner. If you find yourself on a "hamster wheel"—working hard but not seeing your goals materialize—this is where you start. Think of an AFC as the personal trainer for your money.

While many in the finance industry focus solely on the math, the counseling approach focuses on the behavior. We help you with the short-to-medium-term moves: budgeting, debt payoff, and building that initial architecture of flow. We are trained to look at the emotional money ghosts that keep you from hitting your targets. You call an AFC when you know *what* to do, but you can't seem to make yourself *do* it.

## The Certified Financial Planner (CFP): The Long-term Architect

Once your foundation is steady and you are ready to look 30 years into the future, you graduate to a CFP. While the AFC focuses on the "now," the CFP focuses on the "forever." They look at your holistic financial view—retirement, estate planning, and long-term wealth building.

When vetting a planner, you must look for the "F-word": fiduciary. A fiduciary is legally obligated to act in your best interest, not their own. This is a nonnegotiable standard. Before hiring a planner, you should ask three critical questions:

- "How do you get paid?" (Ensure they aren't just earning commissions on the products they sell you.)
- "Who do you work for?" (Ensure they work for *you*, not a specific brokerage or insurance company.)
- "What is your investment strategy?" (It should be tailored to your values and risk tolerance, not a generic script.)

## The Chartered Financial Analyst (CFA): The Technical Expert

The CFA is often considered the "practical PhD" of finance. These professionals specialize in high-level security valuation and portfolio management. While you may not interact with a CFA daily, they are the technical experts behind the scenes of major investment funds.

Understanding the role of a CFA helps you realize that true wealth building is a science of discipline and institutional-grade rigor. It reminds us to ignore the "get rich quick" trends of social media and focus on the technical fundamentals of the long game.

# THE TAX GUARDRAILS: CPAS, EAS, AND RED FLAGS

Your tax preparer is perhaps the most frequent collaborator on your team. But as a business owner, there is a massive difference between a "data entry clerk" and a tax strategist.

There are only three types of professionals who can fully represent you before the IRS: CPAs (certified public accountants), enrolled agents (EAs), and attorneys. If you are a Cycle-breaker building a business, you need someone who understands the tax code and can guide you through legitimate deductions—like the business portion of your cell phone or your home office—without triggering an audit.

Red Flags to Watch for in Tax Prep:

- The "Ghost" Preparer: If they do your taxes but refuse to sign the return or provide a PTIN (Preparer Tax Identification Number), they are leaving you with 100% of the liability.
- The Percentage-based Fee: If a preparer charges you a percentage of your refund, this is a major red flag. It incentivizes them to use "aggressive" or illegal math to inflate your refund.
- The Original Document Trap: Never give away your original documents. A true professional only needs digital uploads or copies.

## The Voice of Doubt: "Can I Really Afford a Team?"

When you are a Cycle-breaker, you are used to being the one who makes a dollar out of 15 cents. You've built your life on the back of your own grit and DIY spirit. So, when someone tells you to go hire a CPA, a financial counselor, or a fiduciary planner, the voice of doubt doesn't just whisper—it screams.

(*Continued*)

*(Continued)*

Let's address the three most common money ghosts that appear when it's time to build your Council of Stewards.

**Obstacle:** "I'm not making enough money to need a team yet. I'll hire a CPA when I hit six figures. Right now, I can just use a basic software and hope for the best. Paying a professional feels like a luxury I haven't earned."

**Your Mindset Shift:** You don't hire a team because you are wealthy; you hire a team so that you can become wealthy. This is the difference between expense thinking and investment thinking.

If you wait until you are "successful" to get professional help, you will likely spend those early years making expensive mistakes—missing deductions, triggering avoidable audits, or setting up business structures that will cost thousands to fix later. A good tax strategist or financial counselor often pays for themselves in the "found money" they identify through better systems and tax efficiency. You aren't "spending" money on a team; you are buying insurance against your own blind spots.

**Obstacle:** "Nobody will care about my money as much as I do. I've worked too hard for this. If I hand over the books or the planning to someone else, they might miss something, or worse, take advantage of me. I'm the only one I can trust."

**Your Mindset Shift:** This is the Hyper-independence trap wearing a new mask. While it's true that you are the ultimate steward of your life, "caring" is not the same as "competence."

You can care deeply about your car, but that doesn't mean you should perform your own transmission repair. Building a council isn't about "handing over" your power; it's about empowering your oversight. When you have a fiduciary CFP or an enrolled agent, you aren't abdicating responsibility—you are gaining a second set of expert eyes. Integrity-based professionals operate under strict ethical codes and legal requirements (like the Fiduciary Standard) specifically designed to protect you. Trust, but verify. A team doesn't replace your eyes; it gives you a telescope.

**Obstacle:** "I'm embarrassed for a professional to see how messy my numbers are. My books are a disaster. I have personal and business expenses commingled, I'm behind on my filings, and I'm honestly ashamed of my debt. I need to 'clean it up' before I show it to an expert."

**The Mindset Shift:** This is like trying to get in shape before you go to the gym. Professionals—especially AFCs and specialized bookkeepers—have seen it all. They aren't there to judge your past; they are there to architect your future.

In my own Revenue Trap year, the shame of my mounting credit card debt kept me from seeking help sooner. I thought that as a financial wellness curator, I shouldn't have those problems. But the moment I let a professional into the room, the shame evaporated and was replaced by a plan. Shame dies in the light of strategy. Your "mess" is just data to a professional. Don't let your ego keep you in a prison that an expert could help you unlock in a single afternoon.

## MOVING FROM OWNER TO CHIEF STEWARD

The reason most entrepreneurs hit a Revenue Trap is that they refuse to delegate the financial oversight of their lives. They stay in the owner mindset, clutching every receipt and stressing over every line item because they believe their Hyper-independence is their superpower.

When you transition to a stewardship mindset, you realize that your job is to lead the team, not play every position. You are the manager of the vision; your Council of Stewards handles the execution.

## The ROI of a Team

You might hesitate at the cost of a CPA or a financial counselor. But remember our formula:

$$ROI = (Net\,Profit + Personal\,Peace) \div Time\,Invested$$

By paying for expertise, you are buying back your time and protecting your peace. You are ensuring that when a "tire blows out" in your financial life, you have a pit crew ready to fix it so you can stay focused on the race.

# TIFF'S TAKEAWAY: YOUR FIRST MEETING

I want you to audit your current "team." Do you have a squad, or are you a solo act? Your first move this week isn't to hire five people; it's to identify the gap.

If your books are a mess and you're guessing at your numbers, your first hire is a bookkeeper or an EA. If your mindset and trauma are holding you back from sticking to a plan, seek an AFC. If you are building wealth but have no idea how to protect it for your children, find a fiduciary CFP.

Stop trying to be the expert in everything. Be the leader of your legacy. Build your council and let them help you turn your money moves into a lifetime of mindset shifts.

# ACTION GUIDE: THE COUNCIL OF STEWARDS VETTING CHECKLIST

Building your team is a strategic money move, but hiring the wrong person can be a Revenue Trap of its own. Use this checklist to vet potential members of your Council of Stewards. Whether you are looking for an AFC, CFP, or CPA, these questions will help you separate the experts from the money ghosts.

## Phase 1: The Initial Screening (The Nonnegotiables)

Before you even book a discovery call, verify these three pillars of professional integrity:

- ☐ Credential Verification: Does the professional hold the specific designation they claim (AFC, CFP, CPA, EA)? Verify their standing on the official board website (e.g., AFCPE.org or CFP.net).
- ☐ The Fiduciary Standard: For financial planners and advisors, will they sign a written statement confirming they will act as a fiduciary in all aspects of the relationship?
- ☐ Regulatory History: Check the SEC's Investment Adviser Public Disclosure (IAPD) or FINRA's BrokerCheck for any history of disciplinary actions or consumer complaints.

# Phase 2: The Interview (Questions to Ask)

During your first meeting, don't be afraid to be the CEO of the conversation. Use these questions to gauge their alignment with your goals:

1. How are you compensated?
   - *What to listen for:* A clear, transparent explanation of fees (flat fee, hourly, or percentage of assets). Be wary of anyone who says they are "free" or only paid via commissions from products they sell you.
2. Who is your typical client?
   - *What to listen for:* You want someone who understands your specific stage of life or business. If you are a Cycle-breaker building a business, an advisor who only works with ultra-high-net-worth retirees may not understand your unique challenges.
3. What is your philosophy on [debt/investing/taxes]?
   - *What to listen for:* Alignment with your core values. If you believe in paying yourself first and avoiding high-interest debt, but they are pushing aggressive leverage, they aren't the right fit for your council.
4. How often will we communicate, and what does that look like?
   - *What to listen for:* A defined process. Will you have quarterly reviews? Do they offer an online portal? You are looking for a partner, not a "once-a-year" ghost.

# Phase 3: The Red Flag Audit

If you encounter any of the following during the vetting process, it is a signal to walk away:

☐ The "Secret Sauce" Pitch: They claim to have a "proprietary" strategy or "insider" knowledge that others don't have.

- ☐ Pressure Tactics: They urge you to sign a contract or move money immediately to avoid "missing out."
- ☐ Lack of Transparency: They are vague about their fees or how they handle conflicts of interest.
- ☐ The Original Document Demand: They insist on keeping your original tax documents or records rather than accepting copies or digital uploads.
- ☐ The "Ghost" Preparer Sign-off: A tax preparer who asks you to sign a blank return or refuses to sign the return themselves as the paid preparer.

## Phase 4: The Stewardship Decision

After the meeting, ask yourself these questions:

- Did they explain complex concepts in a way I actually understood, or did they use "alphabet soup" to make themselves look smart?
- Do I feel a sense of peace or pressure after talking to them?

# CHAPTER EIGHTEEN

# THE ART OF THE ASK

*"Closed mouths don't get fed, and unasked questions don't get answered."*

—Tiffany Grant

In the previous chapter, we focused on building your Council of Stewards—the team of experts who provide the specialized knowledge and oversight necessary to protect your wealth. By bringing in a strategic associate, a CPA, or a financial counselor, you have effectively moved from a solo-grind to a leadership position. You have recognized that you don't have to have all the answers to be a successful steward. However, even with the best team in the world behind you, there is one skill that you, as the CEO of your life, must master personally. You are the primary advocate for your vision, and your ability to communicate your value is what determines the speed at which your Engine of Growth can run.

This chapter is about the power of the ask. Negotiation is often viewed as a confrontational or intimidating process reserved for corporate boardrooms, but for the Cycle-breaker, it is a daily tool for resource optimization. Whether you are advocating for a higher salary, lower interest rates, or better terms on a business contract, your willingness to negotiate is a direct reflection of your internal locus of control. We are going to dismantle the fear of the word "no" and replace it with a strategic framework that allows you to claim the value you've worked so hard to create. Before we move into the final stages of your legacy, we must ensure that you have the confidence and the tactics to ensure you never leave money on the table.

## "I'M ALLERGIC TO FULL PRICE"

I have a running joke that I'm allergic to paying full price for anything, but it's mostly true. Negotiation isn't just for high-stakes business deals or buying a car; it's a vital life skill that can save you thousands of dollars and earn you even more. Whether you're negotiating a salary, a business contract, your monthly bills, or even items on your credit report, the ability to ask for what you want is a muscle you must develop.

Many people shy away from negotiating because they're afraid of hearing "no" or appearing confrontational. But the truth is, most of the time, you don't know what kind of deal you can get until you ask. The worst they can say is no, but the best-case scenario could change your financial life.

This chapter is your guide to becoming a better negotiator. We'll break the process down into three phases: the preparation, the inner game of confidence, and the conversation itself.

# PHASE 1: THE PREP WORK (BEFORE YOU EVEN SPEAK)

Effective negotiation begins long before you sit down at the table. Success is born from research and strategy.

**Educate Yourself:** Research is nonnegotiable.

- Negotiating a salary? Use sites like Glassdoor and Salary.com to research what your role and similar titles are paying in your geographic area. Knowledge is your leverage.
- Buying a car? Use Kelley Blue Book or check Facebook Marketplace to see what the vehicle you want is actually selling for. A car salesman once told me they take advantage of people who don't come in knowledgeable. Don't be that person.
- Lowering a bill? Research what new customers are paying for the same service. This gives you a powerful benchmark to ask for.

**Know Your Audience (and Their Motivation):** Who are you talking to? If you're calling a cable company, the frontline customer service rep isn't incentivized to give you a deal. Their job is to handle basic queries. You need to ask for the "retention" or "cancellation" department. Those are the people whose job it is to keep you as a customer. Always try to understand the other person's priorities to frame your request as a win for them too.

**Define Your Target:** What is your ideal outcome? What is the absolute minimum you're willing to accept? You must know your numbers before you start. If you're selling your car, have an ideal price and a walk-away price. If you don't define your target, you'll have no idea if you've hit it.

**Have a Plan B (and C):** Think outside the box. If you're negotiating a raise and the company can't meet your number for budget reasons, what else would you accept? A title change? A certification that the company pays for? More vacation days? Sometimes a nonmonetary "yes" is easier for them to give and just as valuable for you.

# PHASE 2: THE CONFIDENCE GAME

Once your research is done, you need to prepare your mind. If you don't believe you deserve it, you'll never convince them.

**Practice Power Poses:** This might feel silly, but it works. Before a call or meeting, stand with your hands on your hips and your chest up, or raise your arms in a "V" shape. Some people find that standing in an expansive pose before an important meeting helps them feel more confident—whether it's the posture itself or just the ritual, if it works for you, use it!

**Breathe:** When we're nervous, our breathing becomes shallow, our voice gets shaky, and we lose clarity. Before you start, practice box breathing: inhale for four seconds, hold for four, exhale for four, and hold for four. It calms your nervous system and centers your mind.

**Master Active Listening:** The best negotiators are the best listeners. Active listening means you give the other person your full attention. You're not just waiting for your turn to talk; you're genuinely hearing what they're saying, picking up on cues, and understanding their position.

## The Voice of Doubt: Silencing the Fear of "No"

All the preparation in the world won't help if, in the moment, your own mind sabotages you. The fear of negotiation is rarely about the process itself; it's about the stories we tell ourselves about what it means to ask for more.

**Obstacle:** "If I ask for more money, they'll think I'm greedy or ungrateful. They might even get angry or rescind the job offer."

**Your Mindset Shift:** You are reframing this as a confrontation when it is simply a standard business conversation. Companies *expect* to negotiate. They have a budget range, and their initial offer is rarely the top of that range. By asking for what you're worth based on your research, you are not being greedy; you are demonstrating that you are a savvy professional who understands your value in the marketplace. It's a sign of confidence, not arrogance.

**Obstacle:** "I don't want to seem difficult or rock the boat. I should just be happy with what they offered."

**Your Mindset Shift:** This is a classic scarcity mindset, believing that you should accept whatever scraps are offered. An abundance mindset knows that your value is not determined by someone else's first offer. The most expensive financial mistake you can make is accepting a starting salary that is below your market value because every future raise and job offer will be based on that artificially low number. By negotiating now, you are not just earning more today; you are increasing your lifetime earning potential by hundreds of thousands of dollars.

**Obstacle:** "I'm not a 'negotiator.' I'm just not good at that kind of thing. I'll probably mess it up."

**Your Mindset Shift:** You negotiate every single day. You negotiate with your kids about bedtime, with your partner about what to have for dinner, and with yourself about whether to go to the gym. You have the skill; you just need to apply it in a new context. This isn't about being a slick, fast-talking character from a movie. It's about being prepared, knowing your numbers, and calmly and respectfully stating your case. It is a learnable skill, not an innate personality trait.

# PHASE 3: AT THE NEGOTIATION TABLE

You've done the prep, you're feeling confident—now it's time to have the conversation.

**Aim for a Win-Win:** Negotiation is a dance, not a battle. The goal is not to crush the other person; it's to find a solution where both parties feel good about the outcome. You never know when you'll cross paths with someone again. I've seen people who were rude in an entry-level role have their resume come across my desk years later. Always treat people with respect.

**Let Them Offer First (If Possible):** There's a saying in negotiation: the first person to state a number often loses. When you're negotiating a salary, for example, try to get them to give you their range first. This prevents you from accidentally lowballing yourself.

**Get Comfortable with Silence:** This is a superpower. After you make your offer, stop talking. We often feel the need to fill the silence because it's awkward, and we end up negotiating against ourselves ("I'm asking for $80,000 … but I could do $75,000"). Make your statement, then be quiet. Let the silence do the work. It forces the other person to respond.

**Anchor High:** If you do have to make the first offer, start with an anchor. This is a number that is higher than your ideal outcome. If you want to sell your car for $15,000, you might list it for $17,500. This gives you room to be "talked down" while still ending up at or above your target.

The anchoring effect is a well-known cognitive bias that we normally experience.

First identified by psychologists Amos Tversky and Daniel Kahneman, anchoring refers to our brain's tendency to rely too heavily on the first piece of information offered (the "anchor") when making decisions. Whether estimating quantities or entering a negotiation, that initial anchor powerfully shapes what follows (Tversky and Kahneman, 1974).

By making the first offer and setting a high (but reasonable) anchor, you immediately frame the negotiation around your desired outcome. Even if your initial number is rejected, it has a powerful psychological effect, making your *actual* target number seem much more reasonable in comparison. If you let them anchor first with a lowball offer, the entire conversation will be an uphill battle to get back to a fair number. By anchoring high yourself, you take control of the negotiation's starting point and significantly increase your chances of landing at or above your goal.

**Offer Options:** If your Plan A is rejected, bring out your Plan B. "I understand you can't meet the salary I requested, but would you be open to a title change to senior manager and an extra week of paid vacation?" This shows flexibility and keeps the conversation moving toward a "yes."

Negotiation is a skill that gets better with practice. Start small. Try negotiating your next cell phone bill or asking for a discount on a floor model. The more you do it, the more confident you'll become, and the more you'll realize that you have the power to get what you deserve.

## THE HIDDEN PAYCHECK: MAXIMIZING FINANCIAL WELLNESS AT WORK

When most people think about their income, they only look at one number: the net pay that hits their bank account every two weeks. But as a financial wellness curator and former HR professional, I want you to look at your total compensation statement.

Your employer-provided benefits are not just "perks"; they are a critical part of your Umbrella of income. If you aren't maximizing these benefits, you are essentially giving yourself a pay cut. Let's look at the four most common areas where you can find "hidden money" to fuel your financial revolution.

## The Retirement Match: The Only True "Free Money"

If your employer offers a 401(k), 403(b), or Thrift Savings Plan match and you aren't contributing enough to get the full amount, you are leaving your own money on the table.

- The Move: View the match as a 100% return on your investment. If you put in 6% and they match 6%, you have doubled your money before it even hits the market.
- Tiff's Tip: If you are in crisis triage (Part 2), you might need to pause this temporarily. But the moment you have your $1,000 buffer, your very next move should be to capture every penny of that match. It is the most efficient way to pay yourself first.

## The HSA: The "Triple Tax Advantage" Powerhouse

If you have a high-deductible health plan (HDHP), you likely have access to a Health Savings Account (HSA). Most people use this as a short-term debit card for copays, but for a Cycle-breaker, the HSA is a secret wealth-building weapon.

- The Advantage: Money goes in tax-free, grows tax-free, and comes out tax-free for medical expenses.

- The Long Game: If you can afford to pay for your current medical expenses out-of-pocket, you can leave the money in your HSA to be invested. After age 65, it functions like a traditional IRA for non-medical expenses but remains tax-free for medical ones. It is the ultimate health wall (Chapter 11) insurance policy.

## The EAP: Your Mental Health Architecture

Most companies offer an employee assistance program (EAP), yet fewer than 5% of employees ever use it. An EAP typically provides three to six free counseling sessions per year for you and your household members.

- The Move: In Part 1, we talked about the importance of silencing your money ghosts. Therapy is expensive, but your EAP makes it accessible.
- Tiff's Tip: Use your EAP sessions to work through the "frugality trauma" or "scarcity mindset" we discussed. It's a way to build your PsyCap on your employer's dime.

## Professional Development and Tuition Reimbursement

In Chapter 2, we established that your human capital is your greatest asset. Many employers have a budget to pay for your certifications, conferences, or even a degree—provided it relates to your role.

- The Move: Don't wait for your boss to offer it. Find a certification (like a Google Career Certificate or a Lean Six Sigma belt) that increases your market value and present it as a way to "add more value to the team."

- The Result: You are using your 9-to-5 to fund the skills that will eventually allow you to build your own Umbrella.

## The "Hidden" Insurance: Disability and Life

We often overlook the "boring" benefits like short-term disability and long-term disability. But for a solo parent or a Cycle-breaker, these are the ultimate safety nets.

- The Move: Ensure you are enrolled in at least the base level of disability insurance. Your ability to earn an income is your most valuable asset; you must insure it just like you insure your car.
- Tiff's Tip: Be careful with employer-provided life insurance. It's a great start, but it's "rented" insurance. If you lose your job, you lose the coverage or it gets more expensive. Always aim to have a private term-life policy that stays with you regardless of your employer.

# CHAPTER NINETEEN

# BUILDING YOUR BRAND AND ATTRACTING OPPORTUNITIES

*"Your brand is the shadow your character casts in the marketplace."*

—Tiffany Grant

In the previous chapter, we mastered the "Art of the Ask." You have learned that negotiation is a vital muscle for any Cycle-breaker, allowing you to advocate for your resources and ensure that you are fairly compensated for your Human Capital. You are now equipped to walk into any room and claim the value you've worked so hard to create. However, as you move toward the final stages of the **Engine of Growth**, you must

**Figure 19.1 The Umbrella Method—scaling multiple income streams under one master brand.**

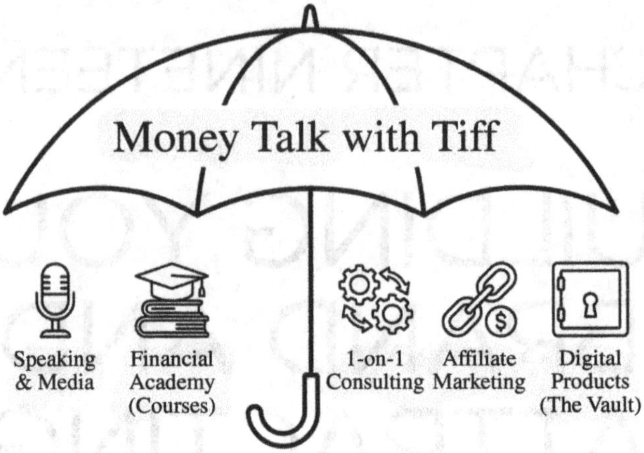


realize that there is a limit to how many rooms you can physically enter. To achieve true scalability and move toward the **Autopilot Life**, you must build an asset that speaks for you even when you aren't in the room (see Figure 19.1).

This chapter is about the transition from the active work of negotiation to the magnetic power of branding. While negotiation is about how you *ask* for value, branding is about how you *attract* it. By aligning your personal history, your stated values, and your professional expertise into a cohesive identity, you create a reputation that precedes you.

We are going to explore how to move from the exhaustion of the "hustle" to the efficiency of "attraction marketing." Before we move into the mechanics of geo-arbitrage and lifestyle design, we must ensure that you have built a brand that is not only profitable but authentically you.

# FROM CHASING TO ATTRACTING

In the beginning of your entrepreneurial journey, you spend most of your time chasing: chasing clients, chasing opportunities, chasing exposure. But a powerful shift happens when you stop chasing and start attracting. This shift occurs when you move from simply offering a service to building a brand.

This shift from "chasing" to "attracting" is grounded in the psychological principle of Brand Authenticity. In a world saturated with polished, corporate messaging, consumers are increasingly drawn to what researchers call "true-to-self" authenticity.

Studies published in journals like Psychology & Marketing have found that brand authenticity has a direct and powerful impact on brand trust (Portal et al., 2019). When an audience perceives a personal brand as authentic—meaning the creator's actions are aligned with their stated values and personal history—it triggers brand trust, the foundation of "attraction marketing." Instead of you having to convince people to listen, your authenticity creates a natural pull, making your audience more likely to seek out your services and remain loyal to your community. By being "authentically you," as we'll discuss, you aren't just being honest; you are strategically building the most powerful asset a business can have: an unshakeable bond of trust with your audience.

A brand is more than a logo or a website; it's a promise. It's the reputation you build, the value you consistently provide, and the community you cultivate. When your brand is strong, opportunities don't just knock—they line up at your door. Brands want to partner with you, media outlets want to feature you, and ideal clients seek you out.

The *Money Talk with Tiff* platform wasn't built overnight. It was the result of a consistent, multi-year effort to share my knowledge and build a community, one piece of content at a time. Here's how you can do the same.

# STEP 1: FIND YOUR PLATFORM AND PLANT YOUR FLAG

You can't be everywhere at once. You need a "home base"—a central hub where you can consistently share your expertise and direct your audience. For me, that was my blog, moneytalkwitht.com.

## The Risk of Digital Sharecropping

Why do I insist on a website when you could just build a following on TikTok or Instagram for free? It comes down to a concept known as "Digital Sharecropping."

Coined by journalist and author Nicholas Carr, digital sharecropping describes the risk of building your entire brand on "rented land"—platforms owned by someone else. When you build exclusively on social media, you are providing free content that increases the platform's value, while you remain vulnerable to their whims. If the algorithm changes, or if the platform decides to charge for reach (or disappears entirely), your "crops"—your audience and your income—can be wiped out overnight.

Owning your digital real estate is an act of Internal Locus of Control. By moving your audience from social media to a website and email list you own, you ensure that you—not a billionaire CEO—control the gates to your business.

# Choosing Your Address: 2026 Domain Best Practices

Your domain name (your URL) is your digital street address. In 2026, the competition for attention is fiercer than ever, so your address needs to be easy to find and impossible to forget. Here is how to pick a winner:

- The "Radio Test": If you said your domain name over the radio, would people know exactly how to spell it? Avoid hyphens, numbers (is it "5" or "five"?), and "creative" spellings that require explanation.
- Short and Snappy: Aim for under 14 characters. The shorter it is, the less room there is for a typo.
- The .com Standard: While extensions like .co, .blog, or .biz are common, .com is still the gold standard for trust and memorability. If your name isn't available in.com, consider adding a verb (e.g., GetTiffanyGrant.com) rather than settling for an obscure extension.
- Check the Handles: Before you hit "buy," make sure the matching handles are available on the social platforms you plan to use. Consistency across your URL and your @username is key to a professional brand.

# Choosing Your Construction Site: The Platform Comparison

Once you have your address, you need to decide what kind of "building" you're going to put on it. Here is how the big three stack up for creators in 2026:

| Platform | The Vibe | Pros | Cons |
|---|---|---|---|
| WordPress.org | The Mansion | You own the land and the house. Unlimited customization and the best SEO tools in the world. | Steep learning curve. You are responsible for your own maintenance and security. |
| Squarespace | The Luxury Apartment | Beautiful, polished, and "all-in-one." You don't have to worry about the tech; you just move in and decorate. | You pay a higher monthly "rent." You can't knock down walls (limited customization) if you outgrow it. |
| Substack | The Shared Workspace | Perfect for writers. Built-in discovery and a simple "write and send" workflow. | They take a 10% cut of your subscription revenue, and your design options are very limited. |

**My Advice:** If you are serious about building a long-term, scalable brand, WordPress is the ultimate move. It's what I use for *Money Talk with Tiff* because I want total control over my SEO and my monetization. However, if technology makes you break out in hives, start with Squarespace or Substack. The most important thing is that you plant your flag somewhere that you own. You can always hire someone later.

# STEP 2: GIVE AWAY YOUR BEST STUFF FOR FREE

This might sound counterintuitive, but it's the secret to building trust and authority. Before anyone will pay you for your knowledge, you have to prove you have knowledge worth paying for.

For years, I shared everything I was learning on my blog and podcast for free. I talked about budgeting, getting out of debt, setting goals, and the mindset shifts that were changing my own life. This consistent output of high-value content did three things:

It Built Trust: It showed my audience that I was genuinely invested in their success, not just in making a sale.

It Established Authority: It positioned me as an Expert in the field of personal finance.

It Created a Content Library: This library of free content became a powerful marketing engine, attracting new people through search engines and social media shares.

Don't be afraid that giving away free content will stop people from buying from you. The opposite is true. The people who consume and benefit from your free content are the most likely to become your paying customers when they're ready to take the next step.

# STEP 3: BUILD YOUR COMMUNITY (YOUR EMAIL LIST)

Your email list is your single most valuable business asset. It's a direct line of communication to your most engaged followers that isn't dependent on a social media algorithm.

Offer a "Lead Magnet": To encourage people to sign up, offer them something of value in exchange for their email address. This could be a free guide, a checklist, a webinar, or a savings challenge printable—like the 50-envelope challenge I offer on my site.

If the 50-envelope challenge doesn't quite fit your brand, don't worry. The "universe of ideas" for lead magnets is vast. The key is to solve one specific problem for your audience, quickly and effectively. Here are a few categories of lead magnets to spark your creativity:

1. **The "Quick Win" Checklist or Cheat Sheet**

   People love resources they can consume in under five minutes.

   - **Example:** "The 10-Point Pre-Flight Checklist for Your First Rental Property" or "The Ultimate Salary Negotiation Script: Exactly What to Say to Get a 10% Raise."
   - **Why it works:** It's low-friction and provides immediate value.

2. **The "Interactive" Quiz**

   Quizzes are incredibly engaging because they provide personalized results. This has given me the most results over the years.

   - **Example:** "What's Your Money Personality?" or "Is Your Side Hustle Idea Actually Profitable? Take the Two-Minute Test."
   - **Why it works:** It taps into the reader's desire for self-discovery and gives you deep insights into your audience's needs.

3. **The "Done-For-You" Template or Worksheet**

   If you've created a system that works, share the bones of it.

   - **Example:** A "Monthly Budget Spreadsheet" (like the one we discussed in Chapter 9), a "Debt Snowball Calculator," or a "Social Media Content Calendar for Freelancers."
   - **Why it works:** You are saving the reader time and effort by doing the heavy lifting for them.

4. **The "Educational" Mini-Course or Email Series**

   This is perfect for complex topics that need to be broken down into bite-sized pieces.

   - **Example:** "Five Days to a Better Credit Score" or "The Beginner's Guide to Investing: A Seven-Day Email Journey."
   - **Why it works:** It builds a habit of the reader opening your emails and establishes you as a teacher and authority over several days.

5. **The "Resource Vault" or "Tool Kit"**

   Curate a list of the tools and resources you personally use and recommend.

- **Example:** "My Top 10 Apps for Managing a Remote Business" or "The Financial Wellness Curator's Reading List: Five Books That Changed My Life."
- **Why it works:** It leverages your curated taste and expertise, positioning you as a trusted advisor.

**Pro-Tip:** Don't overthink your first lead magnet. It doesn't have to be a 50-page ebook. In fact, shorter is often better. Pick the one that you could create in a single afternoon and get it out there. You can always iterate and improve it later based on the feedback you get from your growing community.

Nurture the Relationship: Don't just email your list when you want to sell something. Send them a regular newsletter with personal updates, valuable tips, and links to your latest content. My "The Deep Dive with Tiff" newsletter is where I share more personal insights, connecting with my audience on a deeper level.

# STEP 4: BE AUTHENTICALLY YOU

In a crowded online world, the one thing you have that no one else does is your story. People connect with people, not with faceless corporations.

I've always been open about my journey: being a teen mom, my struggles with debt, my health challenges, and my move to Jamaica. I share pictures of myself working from my veranda. This authenticity isn't a marketing tactic; it's just who I am. But it has been the key to building a loyal community that trusts me and relates to my journey.

Don't be afraid to share your personality, your struggles, and your wins. Your story is your superpower. It's what will make you stand out and attract the people who are meant to be in your orbit.

## The Voice of Doubt: Overcoming the Fear of Being Seen

Building a personal brand requires a level of visibility that can feel incredibly vulnerable. It's one thing to drive for a rideshare app; it's another to put your face and your story on the internet. Let's silence the voices that tell you to stay small.

**Obstacle:** *"Who am I to be an 'expert'? There are so many people out there who know more than I do. I feel like an imposter."*

**Your Mindset Shift:** You are not an imposter; you are a guide. You don't need to know everything; you just need to be two steps ahead of the person you are helping. Your value isn't in having all the answers, but in sharing your unique perspective and your lived experience. Remember, people don't just want information; they want a transformation they can relate to. Your "teen mom" story or your "move to Jamaica" isn't a distraction from your expertise—it's the very thing that makes your expertise accessible and trustworthy.

**Obstacle:** *"I don't want to be 'that person' who is always posting about themselves. It feels self-centered and annoying."*

**Your Mindset Shift:** Shift your focus from promotion to service. If you have knowledge that can help someone get out of debt, sleep better at night, or provide for their family, then staying silent is actually a disservice. Your brand is not a monument to yourself; it is a lighthouse for others. When you share value, you aren't "posting about yourself"—you are providing a solution. If you are authentically helping people, the right audience will find you helpful, not annoying.

**Obstacle:** *"What if people judge me or leave mean comments? I'm not sure I can handle the criticism."*

**Your Mindset Shift:** Criticism is often a sign of reach, not a reflection of your worth. As your brand grows, you will inevitably attract people who aren't your "tribe." That's okay. In fact, it's a good thing. A brand that appeals to everyone appeals to no one. Your goal is to be a magnet—and magnets both attract and repel. Focus on the people whose lives you are changing, and let the noise of the others fade into the background. Your community is built on the people who stay, not the ones who leave.

When you consistently show up, provide immense value, build a community, and do it all with authenticity, you create a powerful brand. That brand becomes a magnet, pulling in the clients, partnerships, and opportunities that will take your business to the next level.

# PART 3 ACTION GUIDE

You have shifted your mindset and built your architecture. Now, it is time to fuel the engine. In this section, we explored how to increase your value in the marketplace, build multiple streams of income under one brand, and master the art of negotiation. This Action Guide is designed to help you move from "earning a living" to "designing an income."

## EXERCISE 1: YOUR HUMAN CAPITAL AUDIT

In Chapter 12, we discussed the human capital theory—the idea that your skills and knowledge are your most valuable assets.

1. The Inventory: List three skills you currently possess that people pay for (e.g., project management, graphic design, empathetic listening).
2. The Gap Analysis: Look at the "next level" in your career or business. What is one certification, degree, or skill (like the AFC or an MBA) that would act as a "multiplier" for your income?
3. The Investment Plan: What is the first step toward acquiring that skill? (e.g., "Register for a Coursera certification by Friday.")

# EXERCISE 2: THE SIDE HUSTLE SELECTION MATRIX

Before you add a new rib to your "Umbrella," you must ensure it isn't a distraction. Use the matrix from Chapter 15 to vet your next idea.

Idea: ______________________________

| Criteria | Score (1–5) | Notes |
|---|---|---|
| Time Commitment | | *Is it a second job or scalable?* |
| Startup Cost | | *Can I start with what I have?* |
| Skill Alignment | | *Does this use my existing expertise?* |
| Scalability | | *Can it grow without more of my hours?* |
| Brand Synergy | | *Does it fit under my Umbrella?* |
| TOTAL SCORE | /25 | |

The Verdict: If the score is below 15, put this idea in the "Someday" folder. If it's 15 or higher, move to Exercise 3.

# EXERCISE 3: MAPPING YOUR UMBRELLA

In Chapter 15, we integrated your personal story with the Umbrella Method. Draw your own Umbrella here.

- The Canopy (Your Brand Name/Mission): ______________________
- Rib 1 (Active/Service): ______________________________

- Rib 2 (Scalable/Product): ______________________
- Rib 3 (Passive/Residual): ______________________

# EXERCISE 4: THE "ART OF THE ASK" SCRIPT BUILDER

In Chapter 17, we discussed the psychology of negotiation. Use this template to prepare for your next "ask," whether it's a raise, a brand partnership, or a higher project rate.

1. The Value Anchor: "Over the last [Time Period], I have [Specific Achievement, e.g., increased revenue by 15% / saved the team 20 hours a week]."
2. The Market Reality: "Based on my research and my [Credentials/Experience], the current market value for this level of impact is [Target Amount]."
3. The Ask: "I would like to adjust my [Salary/Rate] to [Target Amount] to reflect this value."
4. The "Silence" Move: Write "STAY SILENT" in big letters here. After you make the ask, do not speak until they do.

# EXERCISE 5: THE BRAND IDENTITY WORKSHEET

Your brand is the "handle" of your Umbrella. Define it in three sentences:

1. Who do you serve? ______________________
2. What problem do you solve? ______________________
3. How do you want them to feel? ______________________

## Client Spotlight: Marcus and the Umbrella Revolution Revisited

Remember Marcus from Chapter 15? When I first met Marcus, he was the definition of "working hard but staying still." He was a talented graphic designer with a stable 9-to-5 job, but he felt a constant, low-level hum of anxiety. Despite his talent, he was terrified of a layoff. He felt that his entire financial life was hanging by a single thread—his employer's satisfaction.

Marcus was stuck in a defensive posture. He was budgeting perfectly (Part 2), but he wasn't growing. He was managing his "four walls," but he wasn't building a fortress.

### *Identifying the "Single-stream" Risk*

Marcus's biggest hurdle was a mindset shift. He believed that starting a business was "risky." I challenged him to look at it differently: Is it riskier to have one employer who controls 100% of your income, or to have five clients who each control 20%?

We realized that Marcus was viewing his career as a single pole in the ground. If that pole snapped, everything collapsed. We needed to build him an Umbrella.

### *Building the Ribs of the Umbrella*

We didn't ask Marcus to quit his job. Instead, we used the Side Hustle Selection Matrix (Part 3 Action Guide) to identify how he could leverage his existing human capital without burning out.

1. Rib 1: The Service (Active Income): Marcus started taking on two high-end freelance branding projects per month. Because he used the Art of the Ask scripts to set his rates based on value rather than hours, he was able to earn an extra $1,500 a month with only 10 hours of additional work.

(*Continued*)

(*Continued*)

2. Rib 2: The Product (Scalable Income): Marcus took the templates he created for his freelance clients and turned them into a brand identity toolkit for small businesses. He put this on a digital marketplace. It took 40 hours to build once, but it now generates \$300–\$500 a month in "sleep money."
3. Rib 3: The Authority (Brand Income): Marcus started sharing his design process on LinkedIn, positioning himself not just as a designer, but as a strategic brand architect. This led to a corporate wellness workshop invitation—a fourth rib he hadn't even considered.

### *The Result: The Shift in Power*

The most powerful moment for Marcus didn't come when he hit a certain dollar amount. It came during a performance review at his 9-to-5.

In the past, Marcus would have walked into that room with his hat in his hand, hoping for a 3% raise. This time, he walked in knowing that his Umbrella was already covering 60% of his living expenses. He used the value anchor technique to present his contributions to the company. When his boss hesitated on the salary adjustment, Marcus didn't feel panic; he felt peace. He knew he had options.

Eventually, the company agreed to his terms. They didn't do it because they were nice; they did it because Marcus showed up as a CEO, not a teller.

**Tiff's Takeaway:** Marcus's story shows us that multiple streams of income aren't just about the money—they are about the power dynamic. When you build an Umbrella, you stop being a "renter" in your career and start being the landlord. You move from a position of need to a position of value.

Ready to put these shifts into motion? Scan the following code to access the **Cycle-breaker's Resource Vault**, where I've provided downloadable worksheets, budget templates, and video deep dives for every move in this section.

**Link:** moneytalkwitht.com/moves

# PART 4

# THE AUTOPILOT LIFE

*"My people will live in safety, quietly at home. They will be at rest."*

—Isaiah 32:18 NLT

We have spent the last three sections of this book doing the heavy lifting. You have excavated your mindset, architected your flow, and built an engine of growth that is capable of carrying you toward your wildest dreams. But if you stop here, you are still the primary operator of that machinery. You are still the one turning the gears every single day.

In Part 4, we are going to flip the final switch. We are moving from active management to the autopilot life.

For me, flipping this switch required a literal change in my team structure. As I prepared for my move to Jamaica, I brought on a strategic associate to manage the operational "gates" of my business. This move allowed me to shift from being the bottleneck to being the visionary, proving that you don't have to be the one turning every gear to maintain a high-impact legacy.

Most people spend their entire lives in a state of high-alert vigilance over their finances. They are constantly checking balances, manually moving money to pay bills, and agonizing over every transaction. This constant state of "doing" creates a massive leak in your mental bandwidth. It leads to decision fatigue, a psychological exhaustion that robs you of the creativity and energy you need to be a visionary in your business and a present force in your family.

In this section, we are going to reclaim that bandwidth through the power of automation.

We will explore how to set up a system that handles the "must-dos" of your financial life without you having to lift a finger. We'll talk about the ultimate system—a tri-party workflow that combines technology, professional support, and behavioral accountability. You'll learn how to automate your savings, your debt repayments, and even your seasonal utility spikes so that your money flow becomes as natural and invisible as the air you breathe.

But automation is not the end goal; it is the enabler.

The real purpose of putting your life on autopilot is to give you the freedom to engage in lifestyle design. For me, that meant taking the leap and moving my life to Negril, Jamaica. It meant realizing that I didn't have to wait for retirement to live a life of simplicity, health, and beauty.

We will dive into the concept of geo-arbitrage and the expat goal. You'll see how I used the systems in this book to buy back my health and design a life that supports my healing rather than draining my spirit. We'll talk about the "Health Wall"—the realization that your environment is the most powerful biological reset you have.

Living on autopilot doesn't mean you stop caring; it means you start choosing. It means you stop spending your energy on the mundane so you can spend it on the meaningful.

You have built the foundation. You have powered the engine. Now, it's time to take your hands off the wheel and trust the system you've created. It's time to stop working for your money and start letting your money—and your systems—work for you.

Welcome to the autopilot life. Let's design your destination.

# CHAPTER TWENTY

# AUTOMATION IN LIFE AND BUSINESS

*"Systems are the 'autopilot' that allow you to reclaim your cognitive bandwidth for the things that matter."*

—Tiffany Grant

In the previous chapter, we explored the power of building an authentic brand. You have learned how to move from the exhaustion of "chasing" to the magnetic pull of "attracting," creating a reputation that precedes you and opens doors you didn't even have to knock on. By aligning your values with your professional identity, you have built a powerful Engine of Growth. However, as your brand begins to attract more opportunities, you will quickly discover a new bottleneck: yourself. If every new opportunity requires your direct, manual intervention, your success will eventually become your greatest source of stress.

This chapter represents the transition into **Part 4: The Autopilot Life**. We are moving from the strategy of growth to the science of sustainability. To truly live as a steward and not just a high-level worker, you must learn to remove yourself as the primary gear in your own machinery. We are going to explore how to protect your most finite and valuable resource—your mental energy—by shifting from active management to automated flow. By installing the right systems in both your life and your business, you buy back the cognitive bandwidth required to stay in your "Zone of Genius" while your legacy continues to build itself.

## THE ENTREPRENEUR'S MOST VALUABLE ASSET

What is the most valuable asset an entrepreneur has? It's not money, it's not a great idea, and it's not a strong brand. It's mental energy.

Your focus, creativity, and decision-making power are finite resources. Every ounce of energy you spend worrying about whether a bill was paid, manually transferring money to savings, or stressing about your personal finances is energy that you cannot spend on growing your business, serving your clients, or creating your next big opportunity.

The ultimate goal of mastering your money is not just to have more of it; it's to think about it less. This is achieved through the most powerful tool in the entrepreneur's arsenal: automation.

The reason mental energy is so critical—and so easily depleted—is a psychological phenomenon known as decision fatigue. Popularized by social psychologist Roy F. Baumeister, this concept explains that our ability to make high-quality decisions may erode after a long session of making choices, no matter how small they are (Baumeister and Tierney, 2011). Note: While widely discussed, the underlying research has faced replication challenges, with some large studies finding weaker effects than originally reported.

Every time you must decide to move money to savings, or remember to pay the electric bill, you are using up a portion of your "executive function." For an entrepreneur, this is a dangerous leak in your most important resource. By the time you sit down to work on your business strategy or a client proposal, your brain is already tired from managing the minutiae of your personal finances. Automation isn't just a convenience; it's a strategic preservation of your cognitive bandwidth.

Furthermore, the "separate buckets" system we are building leverages a principle called mental accounting. Nobel Prize-winning economist Richard Thaler discovered that humans tend to categorize money into different "accounts" based on its source or intended use (Thaler, 1999). When all your money is in one big pile, your brain struggles to distinguish between "rent money" and "taco Tuesday money." By physically separating these into different bank accounts and automating the flow between them, you are working with your brain's natural tendencies. You are creating "choice architecture" that makes financial success the path of least resistance (Thaler and Sunstein, 2009).

## YOUR PERSONAL LIFE ON AUTOPILOT

Just as you build systems to automate your business (like email sequences or social media schedulers), you must build systems to automate your personal financial life. This is the final step that transitions you from actively managing your money to simply overseeing it.

This is the true "Budget Nirvana"—a state where your financial goals are being met automatically in the background, freeing you to focus on what truly matters.

Here's how to build your personal automation system:

## Automate Your Paycheck

**Pay Yourself First, Automatically:** Set up your direct deposit to split your paycheck. A portion should go directly into your savings or investment accounts before you even see it. This makes "paying yourself first" a nonnegotiable, automated habit.

**Create Separate "Buckets":** Have your paycheck deposited into multiple accounts. For example, you could have a primary checking account for bills, a separate checking account for discretionary spending (your "fun money"), and a high-yield savings account for your emergency fund.

## Automate Your Bills

Every predictable bill—your mortgage/rent, car payment, insurance, cell phone, and utilities—should be on autopay. Set it and forget it. This eliminates the risk of late fees and the mental energy spent tracking due dates.

**Use a "Bills" Account:** By having a dedicated checking account just for bills, you can ensure the money is always there, separate from your daily spending money.

## Automate Your Savings and Investments

**Emergency Fund:** Set up a recurring automatic transfer from your checking account to your high-yield savings account every single payday until your fund is complete.

**Investing:** Whether it's a 401(k), an IRA, or a brokerage account, set up automatic monthly or biweekly contributions. This is how you build wealth consistently over time, without having to make a decision every month.

## Automate Your Debt Repayment

Set up automatic payments for at least the minimum amount on all debts to avoid missed payments.

For the debt you are aggressively paying down (your top priority from Chapter 10), set up an additional, automatic payment for the extra amount you budgeted.

When you have fully automated your financial life, you only need to check in once a month to ensure the system is running smoothly. The machine is working for you, 24/7, freeing up your mind to focus on the high-level, creative work that only you can do.

# THE PREDICTABILITY HACK: EQUAL PAYMENT PLANS

One of the most common reasons automation systems break is the unpredictability of seasonal expenses. You've set up your beautiful money flow system, your transfers are scheduled, and your "bills account" is perfectly balanced—and then August hits. Suddenly, your electricity bill doubles because of the air conditioning, or your heating bill spikes in January, leaving your carefully planned system in the red.

To build a truly resilient system, you need to move from reactive billing to predictable flow.

This is where you leverage a tool that most utility companies offer but few people use: equal payment plans (sometimes called "levelized billing" or "budget billing").

## How It Works

Instead of paying for exactly what you use each month—which results in high "peaks" in the summer/winter and "valleys" in the spring/fall—the utility company looks at your total usage over the last 12 months and divides it into 12 equal payments.

For example, if your total annual electricity cost is $2,400, instead of paying $100 in April and $400 in August, you pay exactly $200 every single month.

## Why This Is a CEO Move

As the CEO of your household, your goal is to eliminate surprises. When your bills are the same amount every month, your automation becomes "set it and forget it."

1. No More "Buffer" Stress: You don't have to keep extra "just in case" money in your bills account for seasonal spikes.
2. Perfect Automation: You can set your automatic transfer from your income account to your bills account for the exact amount of your levelized bill, knowing it will cover the cost 100% of the time.
3. Mental Bandwidth: You stop dreading the arrival of the utility email. You already know the number.

## The Action Step

This week, I want you to log in to your accounts for electricity, water, and natural gas. Look for "budget billing" or "equal payment" options. Most companies allow you to enroll with a single click. If you don't see it online, give them a quick call and ask, "Do you offer an equal payment plan based on my average usage?"

By smoothing out these peaks and valleys, you aren't just making your budget easier to manage; you are reinforcing the autopilot mindset. You are taking a variable that used to control you and turning it into a predictable line item that you control.

## The Voice of Doubt: Overcoming the Fear of Autopilot

Even when the logic of automation is clear, handing over the "controls" to a system can trigger a new set of anxieties. If you've spent years in survival mode, watching every penny to ensure you don't drown, "setting and forgetting" can feel like a dangerous lack of vigilance. Let's address those fears.

**Obstacle:** "If I automate everything, I'll lose touch with my money. I'm afraid I won't know what's happening, and I'll end up overspending or missing something important."

**Your Mindset Shift:** Automation is not abandonment; it is delegation. Think of your automation system as your first "hire." You are moving from being the bank teller of your life—manually moving every dollar—to being the CEO. A CEO doesn't process the payroll, but they do review the financial reports. By automating the repetitive tasks, you actually gain better clarity because your "available balance" becomes a true reflection of what you have left to spend, not a confusing mix of "money that's already spoken for."

**Obstacle:** "What if a bill hits and the money isn't there? I'm terrified of overdraft fees and the system failing."

**Your Mindset Shift:** This fear is exactly why the bills account and the buffer are so important. Automation actually reduces the risk of human error—like forgetting a due date or miscalculating a balance

(*Continued*)

(*Continued*)

in your head. It forces you to be honest about your fixed costs. If you are worried about the timing, start by automating just one small, consistent bill. Once you see the system work, you'll gain the confidence to add the rest. You aren't giving up control; you are creating a more reliable form of it.

**Obstacle:** "I feel like I 'should' be more hands-on. If I don't feel the 'pain' of paying the bill, will I lose my discipline?"

**Your Mindset Shift:** We aren't looking for pain; we are looking for progress. Discipline is a finite resource, and as an entrepreneur, you need to save yours for the big decisions that grow your business. Relying on "feeling the pain" to stay disciplined is an exhausting way to live. Let the system handle the discipline of the must-dos so you can use your creativity for the could-dos.

This is the final money move. It's the system that allows you to scale your life and your business, turning your financial foundation into a launchpad for your biggest ambitions.

# CHAPTER TWENTY-ONE

# THE EXPAT GOAL

*"Peace is a place you can move to, both geographically and mentally."*

—Tiffany Grant

In the previous chapter, we explored the power of automation as the ultimate preservation of your mental energy. You have learned how to remove yourself as the bottleneck in your own financial machinery, allowing your "architecture of flow" to run without your constant, manual intervention. By installing these systems, you have successfully bought back your cognitive bandwidth and moved into the autopilot life. But once you are no longer tethered to the bank teller tasks of your existence, a profound question emerges: Now that you can work from anywhere, where does your soul actually want to be?

This chapter is the culmination of the **autopilot life**. For many Cycle-breakers, the final move isn't just about achieving a number in a bank account; it is about the audacity to redesign your entire environment to support your health, your peace, and your purpose. We are going to move beyond the theory of geo-arbitrage and look at the practical, high-stakes reality of moving your life across borders. Whether your

"Jamaica" is a tropical island, a quiet mountain town, or simply a home where you are finally present for your children, the goal is the same: to ensure that your external environment finally reflects the internal revolution you've worked so hard to achieve.

# THE ULTIMATE "WHY"

Sometimes, a goal isn't just about a number in a bank account; it's about a fundamental shift in your entire life. It's about designing a reality that aligns with your deepest values. For me, that goal was moving to Jamaica.

This wasn't a decision I made lightly. It was born from a series of profound realizations about my health, my environment, and the kind of life I wanted for myself and my children. For months, I had been battling a mysterious illness. My blood pressure was out of control, I was experiencing severe swelling, and I was in and out of hospitals. Doctors couldn't find the cause, but a trip to Jamaica in February 2024 provided a clue. Without my medication, my symptoms vanished. It became clear that my environment in the United States—from the food to the stress—was literally making me sick.

That was my "why." It wasn't just about a change of scenery; it was about a change for my health, my peace of mind, and my family's well-being. I wanted a simpler, more active lifestyle, surrounded by fresh food and a strong sense of community. I wanted to trade the constant stress of the American hustle for the feeling of being truly wealthy in health and spirit.

My business, *Money Talk with Tiff*, which I started in 2017 and took full-time in 2019, had already given me location independence. The question was no longer if I could move, but how and when.

This pursuit of a life designed on my own terms is a practical application of self-determination theory (SDT), a macro theory of human motivation developed by psychologists Edward Deci and Richard Ryan. SDT posits that for a human to thrive and experience true well-being, three innate psychological needs must be met: autonomy, competence, and relatedness.

My move to Jamaica was, at its core, a move for autonomy—the need to feel in control of one's own life and choices. In the United States, I felt like I was on a treadmill I couldn't stop. By choosing a simpler lifestyle and leveraging geo-arbitrage, I reclaimed my autonomy. Research shows that when we act out of our own interests and values (autonomous motivation) rather than external pressures, we experience higher levels of creativity, persistence, and physical health (Deci and Ryan, 2017).

Furthermore, the concept of lifestyle design, popularized by authors like Tim Ferriss, challenges the traditional "deferred life plan"—the idea that you work 40 years at a job you may not love to finally enjoy life at sixty-five. Ferriss's work in *The Four-Hour Workweek* introduced the idea of "mini-retirements" and using currency differences to live like a millionaire on a middle-class income. By combining these economic strategies with the psychological need for autonomy, we aren't just "escaping" a job; we are intentionally constructing a life where work supports our well-being rather than draining it.

# CASE STUDY: MAKING THE MOVE TO JAMAICA

That huge, life-altering dream became a reality in May 2024. Here's how I applied the SMART goal framework to make it happen:

- S—Specific: The goal was clear: "Relocate myself and my two youngest children to Negril, Jamaica, and establish our new life there, supported by my location-independent business, *Money Talk with Tiff*."

- M—Measurable: I set concrete milestones to track my progress:
  - Secure all necessary legal paperwork for residency.
  - Find and secure a suitable home in our target parish.
  - Arrange for the children's schooling.
  - Ensure the business infrastructure (internet, banking) was functional in the new location.
  - Successfully move our essential belongings.
- A—Achievable: The key to making this massive goal achievable was breaking it down. I had already built a business that could be run from anywhere, which was the most critical piece. The next steps were logistical. I dedicated time each day to research—visa requirements, housing options, and the cost of living. I also had to prepare mentally and emotionally for leaving behind the only country I had ever known.
- R—Relevant: This goal was the ultimate expression of my "why." Every step, from selling possessions to packing suitcases, was directly tied to my desire for better health, a stronger community connection, and a more fulfilling life for my family. This deep relevance was the fuel that kept me going when challenges arose.
- T—Time-bound: I set a firm deadline: May 2024. This created the necessary urgency to get everything done. Having a target date turned a vague dream of "one day" into a concrete, time-sensitive project.

## Client Spotlight: The Domestic Geo-arbitrage

While I was in the middle of my own move to Jamaica, I began working with a single mother in a high-cost-of-living state. She had a "good" life—a nice house, a stable job, and a reliable car—but she was miserable. The "convenience tax" and the high overhead of her environment meant she was working constantly just to sustain a life she didn't even like.

She wanted a change, but she felt that as a single mom, a big move was irresponsible.

Our paths crossed at the perfect time. I was able to show her my own "CFO-level" move to Negril and explain that her desire for a new environment wasn't a whim—it was a strategic life design move. We applied the principles of geo-arbitrage to her situation. We looked for a state that offered a better lifestyle fit, lower taxes, and a lower cost of living, while still allowing her to earn her current salary through a remote role.

I guided her through the same vetting process I used for Jamaica:

- The Extended Stay: She visited her target state multiple times to "test-drive" the culture.
- The Job Hunt: We ensured her income was secure before the moving trucks arrived.
- The Community Audit: We looked for schools and support systems that would replace what she was leaving behind.

### *The Outcome*

She made the move. Today, she lives in a state she loves, working a job that values her, and enjoying a lifestyle she previously thought was reserved for "rich people." She did it all as a single mom, proving that your environment is a choice, not a life sentence.

### *The Lesson*

Your cortisol ROI is directly tied to your zip code. Don't be afraid to make big changes if your current environment is taxing your soul. As I always say: The person with the lowest expenses has the most options.

# THE JOURNEY IS THE DESTINATION

Moving to another country wasn't a simple, linear process. It was a journey filled with learning, adapting, and embracing a new way of life. I learned to live with less, finding joy in simplicity, like washing clothes by hand and picking fruit from my own yard. I discovered that true wealth isn't about the accumulation of "stuff," but about health, community, and peace.

When you are in survival mode, the Four Walls are about keeping the lights on. But when you move into the realm of lifestyle design, the Four Walls shift. They become the pillars that support your peace, your health, and your long-term success. Before I moved to Negril, I had to ensure these Four Walls were solid. If even one is shaky, your "paradise" can quickly become a source of stress.

## Wall 1: Health (The Catalyst)

For me, this was the primary wall. In the United States, my health was failing because my environment was toxic. High blood pressure and chronic stress were my daily companions. When evaluating a new location, you must look beyond the scenery and look at the healthcare infrastructure and the lifestyle it encourages.

- **The Veranda Effect:** Does the environment force you to slow down? In Jamaica, my "office" is my veranda. The salt air and the slower pace aren't just perks; they are my medicine.
- **Access to Care:** Research the local clinics and specialists. Don't assume "island life" means "no care." I found that while the systems are different, the personalized care and the focus on holistic wellness in Jamaica far exceeded my high-stress experiences in the US medical system.

## The Biological Reset: Why Your Environment Is Your Health

When I moved to Negril, I wasn't just looking for a better view; I was looking for a better baseline for my health. While it felt like a personal intuition, there is a vast body of research that explains why changing your environment can fundamentally change your biology. As evolutionary anthropologists have shown, human biology evolved for natural settings—frequent movement, exposure to nature, and short bursts of stress—while modern industrial environments create a fundamental mismatch that overstimulates stress systems and erodes health (Shaw and Longman, 2025).

## The Healthy Immigrant Effect (and the Reverse)

In public health, researchers often discuss the "healthy immigrant effect." Studies, such as those by J.T. McDonald and S. Kennedy, have shown that immigrants often arrive in their new countries with health profiles that are significantly better than the native-born population. However, over time that health advantage tends to disappear (McDonald and Kennedy, 2004).

For many of us in the diaspora, moving back or moving to a simpler, more intentional environment is a way to reclaim that original health advantage. By stepping out of the high-cortisol, "hustle at all costs" culture of the United States, you are essentially performing a biological reset. You are moving from an environment that promotes chronic stress to one that promotes longevity.

## Environmental Psychology: The Power of Blue and Green Spaces

This isn't just about escaping stress; it's about what you are moving toward. Environmental psychology—the study of how our surroundings affect our well-being—shows that consistent exposure to blue spaces (the ocean) and green spaces (nature) has a measurable impact on our mental and physical health (Gifford, 2014).

Research on nature exposure has found reductions in stress biomarkers and improvements in cognitive function (Hunter et al., 2019). When you can walk to a fresh fruit stand instead of driving to a supermarket, or when your morning "commute" involves looking at the Caribbean Sea, you are lowering your body's "allostatic load"—the wear and tear from chronic stress (McEwen, 2000).

In my health wall calculation, I don't just look at the cost of insurance; I look at the cost of not living in an environment that supports my healing. Geo-arbitrage isn't just about saving money; it's about buying back your health by choosing an environment that does the heavy lifting for you.

## Wall 2: Safety (The Reality)

This is the wall that most people worry about, often based on sensationalized news reports. Safety is a nuanced conversation that requires moving past headlines and into local reality.

- **Local Knowledge vs. Media Perception:** Safety in a new country is about integration and awareness. It's about knowing your neighbors, understanding local customs, and moving with respect.
- **The "Vibe" Check:** When I moved to Negril, I didn't just look at crime statistics; I looked at the community. Do people look out for one another? Is there a sense of collective responsibility? I felt safer on my veranda in Jamaica than I did in many high-traffic areas in the United States because I took the time to build relationships and understand the local rhythm.

## Wall 3: Community (The Connection)

You cannot thrive in isolation. This wall is about moving from being a "tourist" to being a "resident." It's about contribution.

- **Advocacy and Integration:** To truly feel at home, you must give back to the land that is hosting you. My work with the Negril Chamber of Commerce and organizing stakeholder meetings wasn't just about business; it was about planting roots.
- **Grassroots Impact:** When Hurricane Melissa hit, our community didn't wait for outside help; we organized our own relief. That sense of belonging—knowing that you are part of a unified set of voices advocating for a better future—is what turns a house in a foreign country into a home.

## Beyond the Brochure: How to Vet Your New Home

When you're looking at a new location from your laptop in the United States, everything looks like a postcard. But to live there successfully, you must look beyond the tourism marketing and understand the local infrastructure. You aren't looking for perfection; you are looking for a community where you can contribute and grow. Here is how I vet a community from the inside out:

- **Look for the "Unified Voices":** Every community has challenges. The question is: are people working together to solve them? I looked for organizations like the **Negril Chamber of Commerce**. While no organization is perfect—and I've been vocal about the need for better management and transparency—the existence of a Chamber means there is a structured way for stakeholders to talk to the government.
- **Identify the "Stakeholders":** Before you move, research who the local leaders are. Are they accessible? When I organized stakeholder meetings to prepare for a visit from a government minister, I saw firsthand that change in a place like Negril happens through grassroots unity. If you see a community that is fragmented and not talking to one another, that's a red flag for your long-term peace.

- **Test the "Crisis Response":** You don't know a community until you see it in a crisis. When Hurricane Melissa hit and the power went out, I didn't see panic; I saw neighbors checking on neighbors. I saw a grassroots food relief effort form overnight. A community that can organize its own groceries and hot meals when the official systems fail is a community with a strong, resilient heart.
- **The "Respect First" Rule**: The biggest mistake expats make is trying to "fix" their new home to look like their old one. Vetting a community means asking yourself: *Can I respect the local rhythm, even when it's frustrating?* Integration is a two-way street. You bring your skills and your advocacy, but you must also bring a deep respect for the history and the culture of the people who were there long before you arrived.

By vetting the community through the lens of advocacy and contribution, you move from being a guest to being a stakeholder. You aren't just living in a place; you are helping to build its future.

## Wall 4: Cost (The Strategy)

This is where the geo-arbitrage math comes to life. This wall is about ensuring your lifestyle is sustainable and that your money goes further without sacrificing quality.

- **The Rent Swap:** In North Carolina, my rental property generates a profit of about $815 per month. By doing the math, my housing in "paradise" is effectively paid for by my investments back home.
- **Value-based Spending:** Cost isn't just about being "cheap"; it's about value. In Jamaica, I spend less on "stuff" and more on fresh, local food and experiences. The Do More, Do Less, Stop framework from Chapter 8 becomes incredibly easy to apply when the environment itself discourages mindless consumerism.

## The Voice of Doubt: Overcoming the "Someday" Syndrome

For many, the idea of moving to a tropical island or living a nomadic lifestyle sounds like a dream reserved for the ultra-wealthy or the retired. When I first started talking about Jamaica, the voices of doubt—both internal and external—were loud. Let's address the most common mental blocks that keep people from designing their own version of "paradise."

**Obstacle:** "I could never do that. I have a family, a mortgage, and too many responsibilities to just pick up and leave."

**Your Mindset Shift:** Lifestyle design isn't about "picking up and leaving" your responsibilities; it's about realigning them. You don't have to move to Jamaica to design your life. Maybe your expat goal is simply moving to a lower-cost city in the United States so you can work part-time and spend more time with your kids. The shift is from seeing your current life as a fixed cage to seeing it as a series of choices. You aren't stuck; you are just currently choosing your current circumstances. Once you realize that, you gain the power to choose something else.

**Obstacle:** "It's too risky. What if the economy shifts, or I get sick, or I can't find community in a new place?"

**Your Mindset Shift:** There is a risk in staying exactly where you are too. There was a risk in me staying in the United States with uncontrolled high blood pressure and a high-stress lifestyle. We often over-calculate the risk of change and under-calculate the risk of stagnation. An abundance mindset approaches risk with a plan. You don't just jump; you build a parachute (like the emergency fund we built in Chapter 10 and the multiple income streams from Chapter 16). Community and security are things you build, not things you find.

(*Continued*)

(*Continued*)

**Obstacle:** "I'd miss my family and friends too much. I don't want to be isolated."

**Your Mindset Shift:** We live in the most connected era in human history. Moving away doesn't mean moving out of their lives. In fact, when I moved to Jamaica, my interactions with my loved ones became more intentional. When people visit, it's high-quality, dedicated time. Plus, by designing a life you love, you become a more vibrant, happy version of yourself for the people you care about. You aren't leaving them; you are leading the way by showing them what's possible.

# LIFESTYLE DESIGN LAB: THE GEO-ARBITRAGE WORKSHEET

It's time to move from the "what if" to the "how much." Use this worksheet to compare your current Four Walls with a potential new location. Don't worry about being perfect; use estimates from sites like Numbeo or Expatistan to get a baseline for your target destination.

### The Survival Comparison (Monthly Costs)

| Category | Current Location ($) | Target Location ($) | Difference (+/–) |
|---|---|---|---|
| **Shelter** (Rent/Mortgage) | | | |
| **Utilities** (Electric, Water, Internet) | | | |
| **Food** (Groceries and Dining Out) | | | |
| **Transportation** (Car, Insurance, Transit) | | | |
| **TOTAL SURVIVAL COST** | $ | $ | $ |

**The Thriving Comparison (Monthly Costs)**

| Category | Current Location ($) | Target Location ($) | Difference (+/–) |
|---|---|---|---|
| **Healthcare** (Insurance/Out-of-pocket) | | | |
| **Wellness** (Gym, Spa, Fresh Markets) | | | |
| **Community** (Club dues, Socializing) | | | |
| **Help** (Housekeeping, Childcare) | | | |
| TOTAL THRIVING COST | $ | $ | $ |

**The Geo-Arbitrage Calculation**

1. **Current Total Monthly Spend:** $__________
2. **Target Total Monthly Spend:** $__________
3. **Monthly Savings/Surplus:** $__________ (Line 1 minus Line 2)
4. **Annual Surplus:** $__________ (Line 3 multiplied by 12)

**Reflection Questions:**

- **The "Why" Check:** If you moved to this new location and saved the "Annual Surplus" amount, how much faster would you reach your ultimate financial goal?
- **The Quality-of-life Check:** Look at the "Thriving" section. Which of these categories would improve the most in your target location?
- **The "Safety Net" Check:** Based on the "Target Total Monthly Spend," how many months of expenses would your current emergency fund cover in this new location? (You might find that a three-month fund in the United States is a nine-month fund in your target destination!)

**Pro-Tip:** Remember my rent-swap strategy. Is there an asset you own (like a rental property or a side hustle) that could completely cover the "Survival" costs in your new location? When your basic needs are covered by passive or semi-passive income, you have achieved true lifestyle autonomy.

This move, which started as a SMART goal, became the ultimate mindset shift. It proved that with a clear vision, a strong "why," and a practical plan, it is possible to design the life you truly want to live.

# THE EXPAT MATH: FINANCIAL MECHANICS OF FREEDOM

While the decision to move may be driven by the heart, the ability to stay is governed by the math. For many, the idea of living abroad feels like a dream that requires a massive windfall or a lottery win to achieve. But for the Cycle-breaker who has mastered the **architecture of flow**, relocation isn't a gamble—it is a calculated maneuver. It is the moment where you stop looking at your bank account as a consumer and start looking at your life as an enterprise that requires a high return on investment.

To make this shift, you must be willing to look past the "vacation" surface and dive into the underlying mechanics of how money actually moves across borders. You must move from a mindset of spending to a mindset of reallocation. By applying a professional financial lens to your personal geography, you can unlock a level of freedom that most people believe is impossible. This is where we move from the "why" of the veranda to the "how" of the balance sheet.

# The CFO of Your Own Life

When I told people I was moving to Jamaica in May 2024, many assumed I was retiring or taking a permanent vacation. To the outside world, a move to the Caribbean is a luxury—a reward for years of hard work. But as a Fractional CFO and an AFC, I wasn't looking for a getaway. I was performing a strategic asset reallocation.

In business, a CFO's job is to ensure that every dollar of capital is deployed where it generates the highest return. As I looked at my life in North Carolina, I realized that my capital (my time, my money, and my mental energy) was being deployed in a high-cost, high-stress market that was yielding a diminishing return on my peace.

I decided to apply the same principles I use for my corporate clients to my personal life. I didn't just move for the sun; I moved for the geo-arbitrage.

# Understanding Geo-arbitrage: The Ultimate Money Move

Geo-arbitrage is the strategic practice of earning money in a strong economy (like the US dollar) while spending it in a lower-cost environment. It is the ultimate money move because it allows you to instantly increase your net peace without necessarily increasing your gross revenue.

Think of it this way: If you earn $10,000 a month in a city where your basic Four Walls (Housing, Utilities, Food, Transport) cost $8,000, your freedom margin is only $2,000. You are forced to stay in High-functioning Survival Mode just to keep the lights on.

However, if you take that same $10,000 income to an environment where those same Four Walls cost $3,000, your freedom margin jumps to $7,000. You haven't worked a single extra hour, yet you are suddenly 3.5 times "wealthier" in terms of disposable capital and time.

# The Math: North Carolina vs. Negril

To make this real, let's look at the actual mechanics of the shift. While every expat's journey is different, the expat math generally breaks down into three categories: fixed costs, variable costs, and the hidden tax of convenience.

## The Housing and Utility Pivot

In the United States, housing is typically the largest drain on the architecture of flow. Between mortgages, property taxes, homeowner association fees, and the ever-rising cost of climate control (HVAC), many Americans are "house poor."

When I moved to Negril, my housing costs transformed. By opting for a local lifestyle rather than a tourist-centric one, I was able to secure a home that allowed me to work from my veranda—surrounded by nature rather than a concrete office.

- The US Reality: High fixed costs that require a high revenue floor to sustain.
- The Jamaica Reality: Lower fixed costs that lower your break-even point, allowing you to be more selective with your clients and projects.

## The Food and Local Economy

In the United States, we pay a premium for convenience culture. We spend thousands on processed foods, delivery apps, and out-of-season produce. In Jamaica, the math shifts toward the local economy.

By shopping at the local markets in Westmoreland and eating what is in season, I am not just saving money; I am investing in my human capital (health). The "cost per nutrient" is significantly lower when you are buying directly from the farmer. This is a strategic move that supports my current health goals, such as managing my iron levels and preparing for a healthy pregnancy, at a fraction of the cost of a "high-end" health food store in the United States.

### The Business Overhead

As a business owner, geo-arbitrage also applies to your operations. By establishing localized "Negril Community Rates" for my workshops and hiring local talent—like my project manager for Negril Masonry and Construction—I am able to stimulate the local economy while maintaining a lean business model. My "Three-bucket System" (Operations, Safety/Tax, Personal) becomes much easier to manage when the "Operations" bucket isn't being emptied by high US-based overhead.

## THE CORTISOL ROI: MEASURING THE INTANGIBLES

In Chapter 16, we introduced the formula for the ROI of Peace. But there is a biological component to this math that every founder needs to understand: the cortisol ROI.

Cortisol is the "stress hormone." When you are in the Revenue Trap—constantly looking over your shoulder, worrying about the next tire blowout, or living in an environment that triggers your PTSD—your cortisol levels stay chronically high. High cortisol doesn't just damage your health; it damages your efficacy (the "E" in PsyCap). It makes you reactive instead of proactive. It makes you make expensive decisions out of fear.

By moving to a peaceful environment, I am effectively lowering my biological tax.

The Formula for Cortisol ROI:

$$ROI\ (Cortisol) = \frac{Increase\ in}{Decision\ Quality} \div \frac{Reduction\ in}{Stress\ Triggers}$$

When I sit on my veranda at 6:30 a.m. for my daily Bible study, my brain is in a state of flow. I am making CFO-level decisions for my brand and my clients from a place of abundance, not scarcity. I am no longer paying the Hyper-independence tax of trying to outrun my environment.

# THE HEALTH WALL: YOUR MOST VALUABLE ASSET

We often talk about the Four Walls of finance, but we forget the fifth wall: your health.

As I navigate my pregnancy as a solo parent in 2026, the expat math has become even more critical. In the United States, the cost of health-care and childcare can be a Revenue Trap of its own. In Jamaica, I have been able to build a support system—including an extended visit from my mother and a localized team—that allows me to prioritize my "Slow Fourth Trimester."

If I were still in the US grind culture, I would be pressured to return to work within weeks to sustain my high overhead. Here, the math allows me to "pay myself first" in the form of time and recovery. This is not a luxury; it is a strategic reserve. By protecting my health now, I am ensuring that I have the longevity to manage my legacy for decades to come.

# TIFF'S TAKEAWAY: GEO-ARBITRAGE WHERE YOU ARE

You don't have to move to Jamaica to apply the expat math. You can practice geo-arbitrage within your own borders or even within your own business.

1. Domestic Geo-arbitrage: Can you move from a high-tax, high-cost city to a lower-cost area that offers the same quality of life?
2. Digital Geo-arbitrage: Are you earning in a high-value currency (like selling digital products to a global market) while keeping your expenses local?
3. The Convenience Audit: How much are you paying for "convenience" because you are too stressed to cook or manage your own systems?

The goal of the autopilot life isn't to stop working; it's to stop working for the wrong reasons. Use the math to buy back your time. Lower your overhead to raise your peace. Remember: The person with the lowest expenses has the most options.

### The Voice of Doubt: "Is It Selfish to Leave?"

As you read about my move to Jamaica, you might hear a whisper of doubt. This is a common money ghost for Cycle-breakers, especially those from marginalized communities.

(*Continued*)

(*Continued*)

**Obstacle:** "If I move away to find my peace, am I abandoning my community? Am I being selfish by prioritizing my own 'cortisol ROI' while others are still struggling in the system I left behind?"

**The Mindset Shift:** You cannot pour from an empty cup. For years, I was the Strong One in a high-stress environment, and it nearly broke me. By moving to a place of peace, I haven't stopped serving my community; I have increased my capacity to serve.

Because my overhead is lower and my peace is higher, I was able to organize grassroots food relief after Hurricane Melissa. I am able to lead an investment circle for the "Shifting Wealth & Shaping Futures" program. I am able to write this book to give *you* the blueprint.

Choosing peace isn't an act of abandonment; it is an act of stewardship. You are managing the most important resource you have—yourself—so that you can be a more effective leader for everyone else. Your peace is a prerequisite for your purpose.

# THE EXPAT LIFE TECHNICAL TOOLKIT: BUILDING YOUR GLOBAL PARACHUTE

Designing a life in a new country—whether it's the lush hills of Jamaica, the coastal towns of Portugal, or the vibrant streets of Mexico City—is an act of extreme autonomy. But as any financial wellness curator will tell you, freedom without a system is just chaos. To successfully move your life and your business across borders, you need more than a passport; you need a technical infrastructure that protects your Four Walls while you scale your Umbrella.

This toolkit is designed to help you navigate the three most complex pillars of the expat journey: choosing your destination, managing your global banking, and staying on the right side of the IRS.

# Pillar 1: The Geo-arbitrage Index

Geo-arbitrage is the strategic move of earning in a "strong" currency (like the US dollar) while spending in a "weaker" local economy. This allows you to accelerate your wealth-building by lowering your cost of living without lowering your quality of life.

When evaluating a potential "Jamaica" moment, you must look beyond the scenery and analyze the Cycle-breaker metrics: cost of housing, speed of internet (for your digital Umbrella), and the ease of residency. Here are five popular destinations for 2025, compared through the lens of a multi-stream entrepreneur:

| Destination | Monthly Four Walls (Estimated) | The "Why" for Cycle-breakers | Residency Ease |
|---|---|---|---|
| Negril, Jamaica | $1,800–$2,500 | High quality of life, fresh food, strong community, and English-speaking. | Moderate (Work permits/ Residency) |
| Mexico City, Mexico | $1,500–$2,200 | World-class culture, incredible food, and a massive community of entrepreneurs. | Easy (Temporary Resident Visa) |
| Lisbon, Portugal | $2,200–$3,000 | Safety, high-speed infrastructure, and a gateway to the rest of Europe. | Moderate (D7 or Digital Nomad Visa) |
| Medellín, Colombia | $1,200–$1,800 | The ultimate geo-arbitrage play. Modern amenities at a fraction of US costs. | Easy (Digital Nomad Visa) |
| Bali, Indonesia | $1,500–$2,500 | The "spiritual home" of the digital nomad. Excellent for wellness and focus. | Moderate (B211A or Remote Worker Visa) |

**Tiff's Tip:** Don't just look at the total cost. Look at the "Rent-Swap" potential. If you own a home in the United States that can rent for $2,500, and your total life in Medellín costs $1,800, your housing is not just "free"—it is a $700-per-month engine of growth.

# Pillar 2: The Global Banking Infrastructure

The biggest friction point for expats is often the most basic: getting to your money. If you are constantly paying 3% foreign transaction fees or $5 ATM fees, you are "leaking" money that should be going toward your "pay yourself first" goal.

To build a borderless money flow system, you need a "Stewardship Stack" that includes the following:

1. The "No-Fee" Anchor Account: You need a US-based bank that understands international travelers.
   - Charles Schwab High Yield Investor Checking: This is the gold standard for expats. They refund all ATM fees worldwide and have zero foreign transaction fees.
   - Capital One 360: Excellent for no-fee transactions and a user-friendly app for managing your bills account from abroad.
2. The Multi-currency Hub: If you are paying local contractors or receiving payments in different currencies, you need Wise (formerly TransferWise). Wise allows you to hold balances in 50+ currencies and exchange them at the mid-market rate (the "real" exchange rate), saving you thousands over traditional bank wires.
3. The Digital Wallet Strategy: Ensure your primary cards are loaded into Apple Pay or Google Pay. In many countries, "tap-to-pay" is

more common than swiping, and it provides an extra layer of security by not exposing your physical card numbers.

# Pillar 3: The Digital Nomad Tax Guide (The FEIE)

This is the section where most people get overwhelmed, but as a financial wellness curator, I need you to hear this: the IRS has a very long reach. US citizens are taxed on their worldwide income regardless of where they live. However, the US government offers a powerful tool to prevent double taxation and encourage global entrepreneurship: the Foreign Earned Income Exclusion (FEIE).

**What is the FEIE?**

The FEIE allows you to exclude a significant portion of your foreign-earned income from US federal income tax. For the 2024 tax year, the exclusion amount is $126,500 per person. If you and a spouse both qualify, you could potentially exclude over a quarter-million dollars from federal taxes.

**How do you qualify?**

You can't just go on a long vacation and claim the exclusion. You must meet one of two rigorous tests:

1. The Physical Presence Test: You must be physically present in a foreign country (or countries) for at least 330 full days during any period of 12 consecutive months.
    - Warning: Even a quick trip back to the United States for a wedding or a funeral counts against your 35 days of "US time." You must track your travel dates with surgical precision.
2. The Bona Fide Residence Test: You must be a resident of a foreign country for an uninterrupted period that includes an entire tax year. This requires more "proof" of life—like a long-term lease, a local ID, and paying local taxes.

**The self-employment tax trap**

Here is the "fine print" for my fellow entrepreneurs: the FEIE only excludes income tax. It does not exclude Self-Employment Tax (Social Security and Medicare). Even if you exclude all $126,500 of your income from income tax, you will still owe approximately 15.3% in self-employment tax on your net profit. This is why your tax buffer (Chapter 19) remains nonnegotiable. Please talk to a qualified tax professional for your particular circumstances.

## Pillar 4: The Health Wall Abroad

In Chapter 11, we defined the Health Wall as a core component of your survival. When you move abroad, your US health insurance likely becomes useless. You have three primary options:

1. International Private Medical Insurance (IPMI): Comprehensive global coverage (e.g., Cigna Global or Bupa). This is the most expensive option but provides the most "US-like" experience and allows you to seek care anywhere in the world.
2. Digital Nomad Insurance: Specialized, lower-cost insurance for travelers (e.g., SafetyWing or World Nomads). These are excellent for emergencies and accidents but often do not cover routine care or pre-existing conditions.
3. Local Private Insurance: In many countries (like Mexico or Portugal), you can purchase high-quality local private insurance for a fraction of the cost of a US policy. This is often the best move for those seeking long-term residency.

**The Health Wall move**

Before you move, have a full physical and dental check-up in the United States. Research the top-rated hospital in your target destination and save their emergency number in your phone. Your peace of mind is the foundation of your productivity.

# PART 4 ACTION GUIDE

You have built your engine; now it is time to engage the cruise control. The goal of this section was to move you from being the "operator" of your financial life to being the "architect." This Action Guide is designed to help you audit your current systems, eliminate friction, and begin the exciting work of designing a life that is no longer tethered to a desk or a debt.

## EXERCISE 1: THE AUTOMATION AUDIT

In Chapter 19, we discussed moving from "reactive billing" to "predictable flow." Use this audit to see how much of your life is currently on autopilot.

The Set It and Forget It Checklist:

- Income: Is your paycheck automatically split between your "Bills," "Savings," and "Spending" accounts?
- Fixed Bills: Are your utilities, rent/mortgage, and insurance on autopay?
- The Predictability Hack: Have you enrolled in equal payment plans for your seasonal utilities?
- Credit Building: Is your training wheels card set to pay the statement balance in full automatically?
- Wealth Building: Is your "pay yourself first" amount (Chapter 4) automatically transferred to your investment or high-yield savings account on payday?

The Friction Point: Identify the one bill or transfer you still handle manually every month. Why? What is the one move you can take today to automate it?

# EXERCISE 2: THE "CEO VS. TELLER" TIME LOG

For one week, track every time you must log into a financial app or think about a bill.

- The Goal: Reduce your bank teller time (data entry, moving money, paying bills) to less than 60 minutes per month.
- The Shift: Use that reclaimed time for CEO activities: researching new income streams (Part 3), learning a new skill (Part 1), or spending time with your "why."

# EXERCISE 3: THE LIFE DESIGN CANVAS (YOUR "JAMAICA" MOMENT)

Chapter 20 explored the concept of geo-arbitrage and lifestyle design. You don't have to move to the Caribbean to live a life of permission, but you do have to define what that life looks like.

1. The Location: If you could live anywhere in the world for three months without it affecting your income, where would you go?

2. The Daily Rhythm: Describe your perfect Tuesday in that location. What time do you wake up? What do you do for work? Who are you with?
3. The Cost of Freedom: Research the actual cost of living in that location.
   - Current Monthly Expenses: $__________
   - Target Location Monthly Expenses: $__________
4. The Gap: What is the difference between your current reality and this vision? Is it a money gap, a mindset gap, or a system gap?

# EXERCISE 4: THE DIGITAL NOMAD/EXPAT READINESS CHECKLIST

If your "why" involves location independence or moving abroad, use this preliminary checklist to identify your next steps.

- Income Portability: Can your "Umbrella" (Chapter 15) function entirely online?
- Banking Infrastructure: Do you have a bank (like Charles Schwab or Ally) that allows for international travel without excessive fees?
- Tax Strategy: Have you consulted with a professional about the tax implications of working from your target location?
- Health and Safety: Have you researched international health insurance or the Health Wall (Chapter 11) requirements of your new home?

# THE PART 4 COMMITMENT

I, [Your Name], have designed my autopilot life. I commit to removing myself as the bottleneck in my own financial system. I will use automation to protect my time and my peace, and I will have the audacity to design a life that reflects my deepest values, not my deepest fears.

Signature: ______________________________

Ready to put these shifts into motion? Scan the code below to access the **Cycle-breaker's Resource Vault**, where I've provided downloadable worksheets, budget templates, and video deep-dives for every move in this section.

**Link:** moneytalkwitht.com/moves

# PART 5

# THE LEGACY SHIFT

*"Good people leave an inheritance to their grandchildren, but the sinner's wealth passes to the godly."*

—Proverbs 13:22 NLT

We have reached the final and most significant turn in our journey.

You have done the internal work of Part 1, the structural work of Part 2, the growth work of Part 3, and the lifestyle work of Part 4. You are now living a life that is intentional, automated, and aligned with your deepest "why." For many, this is where the story ends. They have reached their "paradise," and they are content to enjoy the fruits of their labor.

But for the Cycle-breaker, there is one more move to make.

In Part 5, we are moving from Personal Success to Generational Significance. We are making the Legacy Shift.

A legacy is not just a pile of money that you leave behind in a will. If you pass down a million dollars but you haven't passed down the mindset required to manage it, you haven't left a legacy—you've left a burden. True legacy is the transmission of values, wisdom, and systems. It is the process of ensuring that the internal locus of control you've fought so hard to build becomes the default setting for the next generation.

For me, this shift is deeply personal. My journey began as a seventeen-year-old mother trying to survive. Today, as I prepare to welcome a new life into our family while living the life I designed in Jamaica, I am acutely aware that my children are watching. They aren't just watching how I spend money; they are watching how I view money. They are absorbing my relationship with risk, my commitment to stewardship, and my belief in abundance.

In this final section, we will explore how to become a financial socializer.

We will talk about how to teach your children the internal locus of control from an early age, moving beyond the piggy bank to teach them about human capital, earned income, and the power of compound interest. We'll discuss the practical money moves for the next generation—from setting up Custodial Roth IRAs to using the "Authorized User" strategy to build their credit history before they even leave the house.

We will also look at the Legacy Letter—a document that distills your story, your values, and your "why" into a North Star for your family. This is where you ensure that your grandfather's wisdom, your "linoleum floor" moments, and your "veranda" victories are preserved as a blueprint for those who will walk the path after you.

The legacy shift requires you to look past your own lifetime. It requires the humility to realize that you are a link in a chain, and the audacity to decide that you will be the strongest link that chain has ever seen.

You have built a life of permission. Now, it's time to build a heritage of power.

Let's finish the work. Let's build your legacy.

# CHAPTER TWENTY-TWO

# THE GENERATIONAL SHIFT

*"The greatest inheritance you can leave your children isn't a trust fund; it's the mindset that knows how to build one."*

—Tiffany Grant

In the previous chapters, we have focused on the architecture of your own freedom. You have moved from the "Internal Revolution" of Part 1 to "The Autopilot Life" of Part 4. You have built the systems, expanded the income, and perhaps even redesigned your environment to support your highest peace. For many, this is where the journey ends—at the point of personal autonomy. But for the Cycle-breaker, personal freedom is only the midpoint. The ultimate goal of stewardship is not just to change your own life, but to change the trajectory of your entire family tree.

This chapter represents the transition into **Part 5: The Legacy Shift**. We are moving from the "me" to the "we." To build a legacy that lasts, you must realize that the wealth you've created is a tool for empowerment, not just a safety net for your own comfort. We are going to explore how to pass down the three-legged stool of wealth—financial, human, and psychological capital—to the next generation. Before we conclude our journey, we must ensure that the cycles you've broken stay broken and that the children who follow you inherit not just your assets, but the unshakeable mindset required to manage them.

# THE FULL CIRCLE MOMENT

My journey with money didn't start in a boardroom or a bank; it started in a moment of sheer terror when I realized I was seventeen, pregnant, and financially unprepared for the life that was coming. My son was the original "why" that fueled every late-night study session and every dollar I scraped together for my first emergency fund.

Now, as I sit on my veranda in Jamaica, preparing for the arrival of my next child in February 2026, I realize that the greatest gift I can give them isn't a trust fund or a paid-off house—though those things are wonderful. The greatest gift is the internal locus of control that I had to fight so hard to find for myself.

Generational wealth is often discussed in terms of assets—stocks, real estate, and businesses. But true generational wealth is a three-legged stool: financial capital (the money), human capital (the skills and education), and PsyCap (the mindset) (see Figure 22.1).

If you leave the money without the mindset, the money will eventually disappear. But if you leave the mindset, the money can always be rebuilt.

**Figure 22.1 The legacy stool—why mindset and education are the necessary supports for money.**

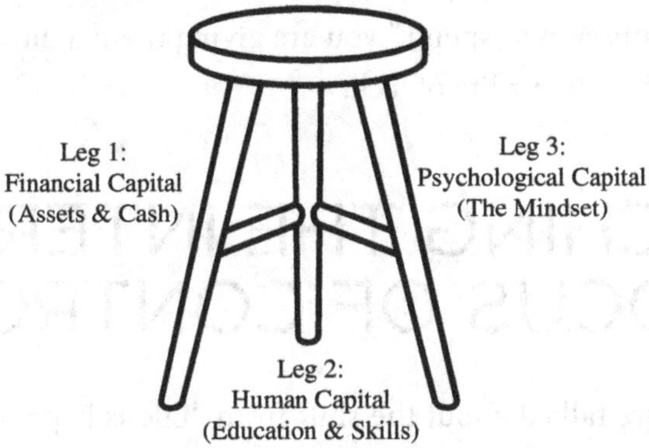


# THE SCIENCE OF THE DINNER TABLE: FINANCIAL SOCIALIZATION

We often think that "teaching kids about money" means sitting them down for a lecture on compound interest. But the reality is much more subtle. Researchers call this process financial socialization—the lifelong process by which children acquire the values, knowledge, and behaviors that shape their financial future (Gudmunson and Danes, 2011).

Studies have shown that children as young as seven have already formed their basic money habits. They aren't learning from what you *say*; they are learning from what you *do*. They see how you react when a bill comes in the mail. They hear the tone of your voice when you talk about the cost of groceries. They notice if money is a source of joy and opportunity or a source of shame and conflict (Whitebread and Bingham, 2013).

As a "Cycle-breaker," your job is to be intentional about the financial atmosphere of your home. You are the "chief financial socializer." By modeling the "pay yourself first" principle and showing them how you use your budget as "permission to spend," you are giving them a blueprint for a life of freedom rather than a life of lack.

# TEACHING THE INTERNAL LOCUS OF CONTROL

In Chapter 1, we talked about the shift from "Life is happening to me" to "I am making life happen." Teaching this to children is the ultimate defense against the intergenerational transmission of poverty.

When a child asks for a toy and the response is, "We can't afford that," we are inadvertently teaching them that money is a scarce, external force that controls our happiness. We are teaching an external locus of control.

Instead, try shifting the language to choice and agency: "That toy isn't in our spending plan for this month because we are choosing to use our money for our trip to the beach instead." This small shift teaches the child that money is a tool used to fulfill values, and that *we* are the ones in the driver's seat.

# THE AGE-APPROPRIATE ROADMAP

You don't have to teach everything at once. Like building a credit score, building financial literacy is a marathon.

- The Early Years (Ages 3–7): The Three Jars. Introduce the concept of "Give, Save, Spend." When they receive money, help them divide it physically. This makes the abstract concept of "allocation" tangible.

- The Middle Years (Ages 8–12): The Power of the Pivot. This is the time to introduce an allowance—not as a "salary" for chores, but as a training tool. Let them make small mistakes. If they spend their entire allowance on candy on Monday, don't "bail them out" on Wednesday. Let them feel the natural consequence of a choice in a safe environment.
- The Teen Years (Ages 13–18): The Launchpad. This is where we move into the money moves we've discussed in this book.
  - The Authorized User Strategy: As we discussed in Chapter 3, adding your teen as an authorized user on a credit card you manage responsibly can give them a massive head start on their credit history before they even leave home.

## The Cycle-breaker's Move: From Credit Fear to Credit Power

In Chapter 3, I shared my deep-seated fear of credit—the "binder of cards" that represented trauma, loss, and the ghost of the 2008 financial crisis. For years, I thought the best way to protect my children from that pain was to keep them away from credit entirely. I thought that if they didn't have the "tools," they couldn't get hurt.

But I was wrong. By keeping them in the dark, I was leaving them to figure out a complex, high-stakes system on their own once they turned eighteen. I was sending them into the world without a shield. Today, I use a strategy that turns my own responsible credit habits into a launchpad for my children: The Authorized User Strategy.

### *What It Is*

Most major credit card issuers allow you to add a "secondary" or "authorized user" to your account. When you add your child, the entire history of that specific credit card account—the age of the account and the record of on-time payments—is reported on their credit file as well as yours.

(*Continued*)

(*Continued*)

### *Why It's a Cycle-breaker*

While I had to fight tooth and nail to build my credit from scratch after a crisis, my children can enter adulthood with a credit score already in the 700s. They won't have to start with high-interest, "predatory" cards or struggle to get approved for their first apartment. They start with the "A+" grade that I had to earn through years of manual labor and mindset shifts.

### *How to Do It Safely (The "Drawer Method")*

The fear most parents have is: *"What if my teenager goes on a shopping spree with my card?"* Here is the secret: They don't actually need the physical card.

1. Add them as an authorized user to your oldest, most reliable credit card (one with zero balance and a perfect payment history).
2. When the card arrives in the mail with their name on it, put it in a drawer. Or better yet, shred it.

The credit bureaus don't care if the child ever touches the card; they only care that the child is associated with a perfectly managed account. You maintain 100% control of the spending, while they reap 100% of the "reputation" benefit.

### *The Parent's Guide to the 700+ Club (The Timeline)*

To make this strategy most effective, I recommend following this timeline to transition from building their score to building their knowledge:

- Phase 1: The "Invisible" Foundation (Ages 0–13): Add your child as an authorized user. Some banks allow this as early as birth, while others require the child to be 13. This builds the "length of history" that is so hard to get later in life.

- Phase 2: The "Training Wheels" Phase (Ages 14–17): Open a youth checking and savings account. Use this to teach them how to monitor a balance. Explain that the "invisible" credit score you are building for them is a tool they must respect.
- Phase 3: The "Launch" Phase (Age 18): Help them apply for their first student credit card in their own name. Because of the history you built, they will likely be approved for a quality card immediately. Teach them to put one small subscription on it and set it to autopay in full.

### *The Golden Rule for Parents*

You can only give what you have. Never add a child as an authorized user to an account that has a history of late payments or high utilization. If you miss a payment on that card, it will hurt their score just as much as yours. You are moving from a legacy of avoidance to a legacy of mastery. You are ensuring that for them, credit is never a monster—it's just another tool in their well-stocked toolkit.

- The Roth IRA for Kids: If your teen has earned income (from a summer job or a side hustle), you can open a Custodial Roth IRA. Showing them a compound interest calculator and how their $500 summer contribution could grow to tens of thousands by retirement is a lesson they will never forget.

## THE ULTIMATE TIME MACHINE: THE CUSTODIAL ROTH IRA

If I could go back and give my 17-year-old-self one piece of financial advice, it wouldn't be about saving more or spending less. It would be about time. In the world of wealth building, time is a more valuable currency than dollars.

This is why one of the most powerful moves you can make for your children is helping them open a Custodial Roth IRA.

## The Magic of the Head Start

Most people don't start thinking about retirement until their thirties or forties. By then, they've missed out on decades of compound interest. But imagine if your child started at fifteen.

A Roth IRA is an account where you contribute money that has already been taxed, and in exchange, that money—and every penny of profit it earns—is 100% tax-free when it's withdrawn in retirement. For a child who is likely in the lowest tax bracket they will ever be in, this is the ultimate strategic move.

## The Requirement: Earned Income

To contribute to a Roth IRA, a child must have "earned income." This doesn't mean they need a 9-to-5. It means they need to be paid for a service.

- The Entrepreneurial Angle: As a business owner, I look for ways to involve my children in *Money Talk with Tiff.* Whether they are helping with basic filing, acting as "models" for social media content, or assisting with event setup, I pay them a fair market wage for their work.
- The Neighborhood Hustle: If your child mows lawns, babysits, or tutors, that counts as earned income too.

## The Parent Match: Building the Habit

Here is where you can supercharge the lesson. Tell your child: "For every dollar you earn and choose to invest in your Roth IRA, I will match it."

This does two things:

1. It Incentivizes the Habit: It teaches them that investing is a priority worth rewarding.
2. It Preserves Their "Fun" Money: They can still spend their hard-earned money on the things they want today, while you help them build their tomorrow.

## The Lesson in Compound Interest

Sit down with your child and a compound interest calculator. Show them that a single $1,000 investment made at age 15, assuming a 7% return, could grow to over $30,000 by the time they are 65—without them ever adding another cent. Now, imagine if they added just $50 a month. That number jumps to over $250,000.

By setting up this account, you aren't just giving them money; you are giving them the perspective of a long-term thinker. You are teaching them to look past Friday's paycheck and toward a lifetime of security. You are ensuring that they never have to "catch up" on their future, because you helped them start the race while everyone else was still at the starting line.

# THE PRACTICAL TOOLKIT FOR LEGACY

Beyond the conversations, there are structural moves you can make to solidify this generational shift:

1. 529 College Savings Plans: Investing in their human capital by ensuring their education doesn't come with the debt trap we discussed in Part 2.

2. UTMA/UGMA Accounts: These are custodial accounts that allow you to hold assets for a minor. It's a great way to start their investment journey early.
3. The Family Money Meeting: Once a month, have a "Pulse Call" for the family. Review the goals, celebrate the wins (like hitting a savings milestone), and discuss the "why" behind your family's financial decisions.

# THE CYCLE-BREAKER'S AGE-BY-AGE GUIDE TO FINANCIAL SOCIALIZATION

Financial literacy is not a one-time conversation you have when your child gets their first job; it is a 20-year apprenticeship. As a financial wellness curator, I view money as a language. If you want your children to be fluent, they need to hear it spoken, practice the vocabulary, and eventually, write their own stories.

The following guide is designed to help you move from being a Provider to being a financial socializer. It breaks down the specific money moves and mindset shifts you should introduce at every stage of your child's development.

## Phase 1: The Foundation (Ages 3–5)

The Goal: To introduce the concept that money is a finite resource used for choices, and to build the muscle of delayed gratification.

At this age, children are in the "observation" phase. They see you swipe a card or tap a phone, and to them, it looks like magic. Your job is to make the invisible visible.

- The Mindset Shift: From "I Want" to "I Choose." Introduce the idea that we cannot have everything, so we must choose what is most important. When you are at the market, give them two options: "We can get the strawberries or the blueberries, but not both today. Which do you choose?"
- The Money Move: The Three Jars. Replace the traditional piggy bank with three clear jars labeled Give, Save, and Spend. Using clear jars is vital because children need to *see* the money growing.
- The Activity: The "Wait" Game. To build the Resilience and Optimism pillars of PsyCap, practice small moments of delayed gratification. If they want a $5 toy, have them save their "spend" money for two weeks. When they finally buy it, celebrate the victory of the wait.

## Phase 2: The Family Economy (Ages 6–11)

The Goal: To establish the link between effort and income, and to introduce the architecture of flow on a micro-scale.

This is the age where "allowance" often becomes a point of contention. In a Cycle-breaker household, we move away from "allowance" (which implies entitlement) and toward "commissions" (which implies agency).

- The Mindset Shift: The Steward's Heart. Teach them that they are managers of their resources. Introduce the "Four Walls" concept (Chapter 11) in a kid-friendly way. Explain that the family has "must-haves" (house, food) and "nice-to-haves" (toys, treats).
- The Money Move: The Commission System. Identify "citizen chores" (things they do because they live in the house, like making their bed) and "commission chores" (extra tasks they can do to earn money, like washing the car or helping with the garden). This teaches the internal locus of control: if I want more money, I have the power to earn it.

- The Activity: The Grocery Detective. Take them to the store with a $20 bill and a list of five items. Their job is to find the best value for each item. If they come in under $20, they get to keep 50% of the "savings" for their Spend jar. This builds efficacy in a real-world setting.

# Phase 3: The Training Wheels (Ages 12–14)

The Goal: To transition from physical cash to digital systems and to introduce the concept of human capital.

As your children enter middle school, the peer pressure to spend increases. This is the time to anchor them in their "why" and show them how the autopilot life (Part 4) works.

- The Mindset Shift: Human capital as an asset. Start talking about their interests as potential income streams. If they love video games, talk about the people who code them, test them, and market them. Help them see themselves as producers, not just consumers.
- The Money Move: The youth checking account. Open a joint youth checking account with a debit card. This is the "training wheels" phase of the money flow system. Transfer their commissions into this account and let them manage their own "Spend" category digitally.
- The Activity: The subscription audit. If they want a subscription (like Roblox or Spotify), have them pay for it out of their own account. Once a month, sit down and ask: "Is this still a Rank 10 for you? Or should we 'Stop' this and move the money to 'Do More' of something else?" (Chapter 8).

# Phase 4: The Launchpad (Ages 15–18)

The Goal: To build their "reputation" (credit) and prepare them for the Art of the Ask.

These are the high-stakes years. Your goal is to ensure that when they turn eighteen, they aren't starting from zero—they are starting with a foundation of power.

- The Mindset Shift: The internal locus of growth. Focus on negotiation and self-advocacy. When they want a summer job or an internship, use the Art of the Ask scripts (Chapter 17) to help them prepare for the interview. Teach them that their time has a market value.
- The Money Move: The authorized user strategy. As discussed in Chapter 21, this is the ultimate legacy move. Add them to your oldest, most well-managed credit card. Use the "drawer method" to keep the card safe while their credit score climbs.
- The Money Move: The Custodial Roth IRA. If they have earned income from a part-time job, open a Custodial Roth IRA. Show them a compound interest calculator. Explain that a $1,000 investment at age sixteen could be worth over $50,000 by the time they retire—without them ever adding another cent. This is the "Legacy Shift" in action.
- The Activity: The first "CEO date." Once a quarter, have them present a "financial report" to you. What did they earn? What did they save? What is their big goal for the next six months? Treat them like the CEO of their own life.

## Phase 5: The Generational Partner (Ages 19+)

The Goal: To transition from a teacher to a strategic advisor.

Once they are adults, your role shifts. You are no longer managing their flow; you are curating their legacy.

- The Mindset Shift: Interdependence over independence. Teach them that wealth is a team sport. Encourage them to build their own strategic advisory team (Appendix) and to continue their education using the "Syllabus for Success."
- The Money Move: The transition to primary. Help them move from being an authorized user to having their own primary credit card. Ensure they understand the "set it and forget it" automation from Chapter 19.
- The Activity: The legacy letter exchange. When they reach a major milestone (graduation, first "real" job, marriage), give them your legacy letter. Invite them to write their own. This is the moment the chain is officially strengthened.

# "AM I DOING ENOUGH?"

If you are starting this journey late, or if you are still working through your own debt, you might feel a pang of guilt. You might think, *"I wish I had known this when my oldest was five."*

Listen to me: The best time to plant a tree was 20 years ago; the second best time is today. Your children don't need a perfect financial role model; they need an honest one. By allowing them to see you work through your own money moves, you are teaching them the most important lesson of all: resilience. You are showing them that even if you start at a crossroads, you can always choose a new direction.

## The Voice of Doubt: Overcoming the Parent's Financial Fear

Even when we want the best for our children, our own money ghosts can make us hesitant to lead. If you are still working through your own financial journey, you might feel like a fraud trying to teach your kids. Let's silence those voices.

**Obstacle:** "I've made so many mistakes with money. Who am I to teach my kids? I don't want to pass on my failures."

**Your Mindset Shift:** Your "mistakes" are actually your most valuable teaching tools. Being a perfect example is impossible; being an honest example is life changing. Tell your kids, "I didn't understand credit when I was younger, and it cost me. That's why I'm teaching you how to use it as a tool now." Your transparency removes the shame and mystery from money, making them more likely to come to you when they have questions.

**Obstacle:** "I don't want to 'spoil' them or make them obsessed with money. Shouldn't kids just be kids?"

**Your Mindset Shift:** Teaching financial literacy isn't about creating "mini-capitalists"; it's about creating capable adults. Money is a tool for living, like fire or a car. You wouldn't let your child play with fire without teaching them how to use it safely, and you wouldn't give them the keys to a car without driving lessons. Giving them financial knowledge is an act of protection, not a loss of innocence.

**Obstacle:** "I don't have enough money yet to set up big accounts or leave an inheritance. Is it even worth starting?"

**Your Mindset Shift:** Legacy is built in cents before it's built in dollars. The habit of saving $5 a month in a custodial account is more powerful than a $10,000 gift later in life because it teaches the system. You are building their PsyCap—their hope, resilience, and optimism. That mindset will earn them more money over their lifetime than any single check you could write.

# THE FAMILY MONEY DATE: YOUR MONTHLY CONNECTION GUIDE

Goal: To normalize the conversation around money, celebrate wins, and align the family's spending with its values.

Tone: Curious, encouraging, and collaborative. (No judgment allowed!)

Frequency: Once a month (aim for 20–30 minutes).

## Part 1: The Celebration (Five Minutes)

*Start with the positive to lower defenses and build PsyCap.*

- The Win: What is one financial win we had as a family this month? (e.g., "We stayed under our grocery budget," or "We saved enough for that new board game.")
- The Gratitude: What is one thing we are grateful for that didn't cost any money?

## Part 2: The Pulse Check (10 Minutes)

*Review the system you built in Part 3 of the book.*

- The Big Goal: How close are we to our next big family goal? (e.g., The "Beach Trip Fund" or the "New Computer Fund.")

- The Giving Update: Who did we help this month? Review your "Give" jar or the family's charitable contributions.
- The Budget Review: (For older kids/teens) Look at one category together. "We planned to spend $X on eating out; we actually spent $Y. Do we need to adjust for next month?"

## Part 3: The Mini-lesson (Five Minutes)

*Introduce one concept from the book in a simple way.*

- This Month's Topic: (Pick one)
    - The "Why": Why are we choosing to save for [Goal] instead of buying [Impulse Item] today?
    - Internal Locus of Control: "If we want to earn extra money for [Item], what are three ways we could make that happen?"
    - The Power of Time: Show a compound interest calculator and how $5 grows over 10 years.

## Part 4: The Ask and the Action (Five Minutes)

- The Kid's Corner: "Is there anything you're saving for right now that you need help planning for?"
- The Action Item: What is one specific money move we are making as a family before our next meeting?

# HOW TO LEAD YOUR FIRST MEETING: A PARENT'S GUIDE

If you didn't grow up with these conversations, the first meeting might feel a little awkward. That's okay! Here is how to ensure it's a success:

1. Keep It "Snack-able": Literally. Bring snacks. Make this a time the kids look forward to. If they associate money talk with treats and positive attention, they will carry that positive association into adulthood.
2. Be the "Chief Vulnerability Officer": You don't have to have it all figured out. It is incredibly powerful to say, "I'm still learning how to be better at [Budgeting/Saving], and I want us to learn together." This removes the "perfection" barrier.
3. Focus on Agency, Not Scarcity: Avoid saying "We can't." Instead, use the language of priority. "We are prioritizing our savings right now so that we can have [Future Benefit]."
4. Make It Visual: Use a "Goal Thermometer" on the fridge or clear jars for "Give, Save, Spend." Children (and many adults!) need to see the progress to feel the momentum.
5. End on a High Note: Always end the meeting by reaffirming the family's "why." Remind everyone that money is just a tool we use to build the life we want together.

# CHAPTER TWENTY-THREE

# THE STEWARDSHIP MANIFESTO

*"Stewardship is the realization that you don't own the resources—you are just the one trusted to make them flourish."*

—Tiffany Grant

You have traveled a long way from the "linoleum floor" of survival. You have dismantled your money ghosts, built a robust architecture of flow, and engineered a life that allows for both growth and peace. You have even looked beyond your own horizon to ensure that the next generation inherits the mindset required to sustain the legacy you've started. By every worldly metric, you have arrived. You are the architect, the CEO, and the Cycle-breaker. But as you stand at this summit, you may find that a new kind of pressure begins to mount—the pressure to maintain, protect, and control everything you have worked so hard to build.

This final chapter is the resolution to that pressure. It is the moment where we move from the tactical to the transcendent. To truly finish the journey from survival to legacy, you must be willing to trade your most prized title for a more powerful one. We are going to explore the radical freedom that comes when you stop carrying the heavy burden of ownership and embrace the strategic grace of stewardship. This is the "manifesto" that will ensure your wealth remains a source of flourishing rather than a source of fear. Before you close this book and step fully into your new life, we must ensure that your heart is as well-positioned as your balance sheet.

# THE FINAL SHIFT: FROM OWNER TO MANAGER

Throughout this book, we have talked about building an architecture of flow, mastering the Engine of Growth, and designing an autopilot life. But as you stand at the summit of your financial journey, there is one final, radical shift you must make if you want your wealth to result in lasting peace.

You must stop viewing yourself as the owner of your life and start viewing yourself as the steward.

In our modern culture, we are obsessed with ownership. We want to own our homes, our businesses, our time, and our destiny. We wear our "owner" titles like badges of honor. But as I've learned through the fires of a $500,000 "revenue trap" and the peace of a Jamaican veranda, ownership is often a heavy, exhausting illusion.

When you believe you own something, you feel you must protect it, control it, and worry over it. But when you realize you are a steward, the weight shifts. A steward is a manager. A steward is someone entrusted with another person's resources to grow them, protect them, and use them for a specific purpose.

In my own spiritual journey, this realization changed everything. I realized that God is the source of the order in my life, and I am simply the "royal representative" tasked with managing His blessings with integrity. This isn't just a religious concept; it is the ultimate strategic advantage for a business owner.

Becoming a steward is the final act of dismantling the Bulletproof Persona. For over a decade, I believed that my safety was found in my ability to be invincible. But as a steward, I have learned that my safety is found in my surrender. I no longer have to be "bulletproof" because I am no longer the source of the protection—I am simply the manager of the resources. Putting down the armor didn't make me weak; it made me free to finally enjoy the life I had built.

# THE THREE PILLARS OF THE STEWARDSHIP MINDSET

Through my years of study and conversations with spiritual financial leaders, I have identified three core principles that define the stewardship mindset.

## Money Is a Powerful Tool, but a Terrible God

There is a common misunderstanding that "money is the root of all evil." But ancient wisdom actually tells us that it is the *love* of money that causes the trouble.

When you love money—when you idolize it—you make it your master. And money is a cruel master. It will demand your sleep, your health, your integrity, and your relationships. If you are chasing a number just for the sake of the number, you are building a golden calf that will eventually crush you.

However, when you view money as a tool, it becomes a beautiful resource for good. A hammer can be used to destroy a house or build a shelter for the homeless; the hammer isn't the problem, the hand holding it is. Stewardship starts with a heart check: Are you using money to expand your purpose, or are you letting money shrink your soul?

## Capacity Precedes Blessing

We often pray for "more." More revenue, more clients, more opportunities. But the law of stewardship suggests that we are rarely blessed with more until we have proven we can manage what we already have.

If you cannot manage a $50,000 salary with integrity and order, why would you be trusted with $500,000? If your current architecture of flow is a mess of commingled funds and late fees, "more money" will only magnify the chaos. Stewardship is the process of expanding your capacity. By being a "good manager" of the little, you signal to the universe (and to God) that you are ready for the much.

## Wealth Is a Magnifier of Character

Money does not change who you are; it simply makes you "more" of who you already are.

If a person is greedy and selfish with $100, they will be a monster with $1,000,000. But if a person is generous, kind, and community-minded with a small budget, wealth will allow them to amplify that impact a thousand-fold. This is why we build our PsyCap in Part 1. We must become the kind of people who can handle the weight of wealth without it changing our hearts.

## The Voice of Doubt: "If I'm Not the Owner, Who Is in Control?"

The shift to a stewardship mindset is perhaps the most difficult mindset shift in this entire book because it requires you to dismantle the very thing that likely made you successful in the first place: your need for control.

When you've spent years building your life from the ground up—especially if you started on a linoleum floor with the world counting you out—the idea of "releasing ownership" feels like a threat to your safety. Let's look at the three most common doubts that arise when we talk about becoming a steward.

**Obstacle:** "My ambition is fueled by the fact that this is MY business, MY brand, and MY legacy. If I start thinking of myself as just a 'manager,' won't I lose the 'hustle' that got me here? I'm afraid I'll become passive or complacent."

**The Mindset Shift:** Stewardship is not the same as passivity; it is high-stakes management.

Think about a professional fund manager who handles billions of dollars for their clients. They don't "own" that money, but they are often more disciplined, more focused, and more aggressive in their pursuit of growth than a casual retail investor. Why? Because they are accountable to a higher standard.

When you realize you are a steward of God's resources, your work ethic shouldn't decrease—it should transform. You aren't working to build a monument to your own ego; you are working to fulfill a mission

(*Continued*)

(*Continued*)

you've been entrusted with. This shift actually *removes* the paralyzing fear of failure. If the business is yours, a setback is a personal indictment. If the business is a resource you are managing, a setback is just a data point that requires a new strategy. Stewardship gives you the "drive" of a CEO with the "peace" of a consultant.

**Obstacle:** "This sounds like a path to poverty. If I'm just a manager, does that mean I'm not allowed to enjoy the fruits of my labor? Am I supposed to live a life of sacrifice while everyone else enjoys their wealth?"

**The Mindset Shift:** Money is a tool, and a good manager knows that a tool must be maintained to be effective.

In the biblical model of stewardship, the manager is always taken care of. You cannot manage a global brand or a community initiative if you are burnt out, stressed over your own bills, or living in a state of lack. Enjoying your wealth—the architecture of flow we built in Part 2—is actually part of your job description as a steward.

The difference is in the attachment. An owner clings to their wealth because they believe it is the source of their security. A steward enjoys their wealth because they know it is a resource provided for their joy and their purpose. You are allowed to live well, but you are no longer a slave to the lifestyle. You are the manager of the blessing, and that includes the blessing of your own well-being.

**Obstacle:** "It's easy for you to talk about stewardship from a veranda in Jamaica. But I'm still in the money moves phase. I'm still trying to get my credit score up and pay off my student loans. I'll worry about 'legacy' and 'stewardship' once I hit my first $100k."

**The Mindset Shift:** This is the most dangerous trap of all. As we discussed, capacity precedes blessing.

If you do not practice stewardship with $100, you will not be able to handle the weight of $100,000. Stewardship is a muscle, not a destination. If you wait until you are "rich" to start managing your resources with integrity, you will likely find that the "revenue trap" is waiting for you at the finish line.

I had to practice stewardship while I was resolving my AT&T roaming fees and negotiating with the utility companies in Jamaica. I had to be a steward of my low iron levels and my physical rest before I could be a steward of a Wiley book contract. Stewardship starts exactly where you are—on the linoleum floor, in the middle of the debt, or at the height of the crisis. By managing the "little" with a steward's heart today, you are literally building the infrastructure for the "much" tomorrow.

# THE 2026 STEWARDSHIP MANIFESTO: A CASE STUDY IN PEACE

To show you what this looks like in practice, I want to share my own Stewardship Manifesto. This isn't a list of "hustle goals"; it is a strategic plan for how I intend to manage my life, my business, and my peace during a season of massive transition.

As I write this, I am preparing for the birth of my child and the launch of this very book. In the past, the Bulletproof Persona version of me would have tried to do it all. I would have worked until the moment of labor and checked emails from the recovery room. But the steward version of me has a different plan.

## The ROI of Pruning

Part of stewardship is knowing when to "cut the cord" on things that are no longer serving the mission.

As a steward of my own mental health and my children's future, I realized that "more business" wasn't the goal—more peace was. By closing necessary doors, I opened up the bandwidth to be a present mother and a focused author. Sometimes, the best money move you can make is to stop doing something that is making you miserable.

## The "Slow" Fourth Trimester

I have set a nonnegotiable goal to limit my work to five hours per week during my first three months postpartum. To the owner mindset, this sounds like a risk. To the steward mindset, this is a requirement. I am managing the most precious resource I have—my health and my bond with my child.

By batch-recording podcast episodes and automating my "digital real estate" (Chapter 18), I have built a system that works while I rest. This is the architecture of flow in its highest form.

## The Peace Fund and the Community

Stewardship isn't just about what you keep; it's about what you put in motion. My manifesto includes maintaining a monthly "Peace Fund" at a high-yield bank and leading two independent community initiatives in my home of Negril.

When you realize you are a manager, you stop asking, "How much can I get?" and start asking, "How much can I move?" Whether it's resolving old charge-offs to fix my credit score or providing groceries for my neighbors after a storm, every move is a reflection of my role as a royal representative.

# TIFF'S TAKEAWAY: DRAFTING YOUR MANIFESTO

I want you to end this book by drafting your own Stewardship Manifesto. This is not a "To-do" list; it is a "To-be" list.

Ask yourself the following questions:

1. What am I currently "owning" that I need to start "managing"? (Is it your debt? Your business stress? Your fear of the future?)
2. What is one "revenue trap" I need to prune to protect my peace?
3. How will I use my wealth to magnify the good in the world?

You are a Cycle-breaker. You have the tools, the math, and the mindset. Now, it's time to take your place as a chief steward of your legacy.

# THE STRATEGIC SABBATICAL: PLANNING FOR YOUR "FOURTH TRIMESTER"

In the world of the Bulletproof Persona, taking a break is seen as a weakness. We are told that if we stop grinding, our momentum will stall, our audience will forget us, and our revenue will evaporate. But as a steward, you realize that a strategic pause is not a retreat—it is a requirement for long-term sustainability.

As I prepare for the birth of my fourth child in February 2026, I am not just planning for a baby; I am planning a Strategic Sabbatical. I am implementing a "Slow Fourth Trimester" where my work is limited to just five hours per week. To the owner mindset, this sounds like a recipe for business suicide. To the steward mindset, it is the ultimate test of the systems we have built.

If you are a founder, a freelancer, or a Cycle-breaker, you will eventually face a season where you need to step back—whether for a birth, a health crisis, or a much-needed mental reset. Here is the framework for planning a sabbatical that protects your peace and your profit.

## The Sabbatical Fund: The Math of Rest

You cannot rest if you are worried about the light bill. Stewardship requires that you fund your peace in advance.

- The Move: Calculate your "survival floor" (your basic Four Walls plus essential business overhead) for three months.
- The Goal: Save this amount into a high-yield "Peace Fund" separate from your business operations.
- The Mindset Shift: This isn't "lost revenue"; it is an investment in your human capital. By funding your rest, you are ensuring that you don't return to work in a state of depletion, which leads to expensive mistakes.

## The Automation and Delegation Audit

A sabbatical is the ultimate "stress test" for your autopilot life. You must identify what must run, what can run without you, and what can simply stop.

- The Strategic Associate Factor: In early 2026, I onboarded a strategic associate to handle the backend tasks that used to keep me tethered to my desk—podcast guest vetting, content optimization, and client audits.
- The Move: Identify your strategic associate. Who can manage the gates while you are away? If you aren't ready for a full-time hire, use tools like Flodesk for automated email sequences and a podcast hosting service to batch-schedule your content months in advance.
- The Mindset Shift: If your business cannot survive a 30-day absence, you don't own a business; you own a high-stress job. Use your sabbatical planning to force the creation of SOPs (standard operating procedures) that make you scalable.

## The Communication Protocol

The biggest source of stress during a break is the "unseen" expectation of others. You must set the guardrails for your peace.

- The Move: Create a "sabbatical auto-responder" that doesn't just say you're away, but directs people to your digital real estate (your FAQs, your blog, or your automated products).
- The Move: Inform your high-level clients three months in advance. As a fractional CFO, I don't just "disappear"; I transition my clients into a maintenance phase where the systems we've built do the heavy lifting while I am in my Slow Fourth Trimester.

## The Cortisol Reset

The final goal of a strategic sabbatical is to lower your biological tax. When I was diagnosed with low iron in late 2025, it was a physical signal that my body was demanding a shift.

- The Move: Use your time away to focus on the "Fifth Wall"—your health. Whether it's daily iron supplements on the veranda or simply sleeping through the night without a 3:00 a.m. dispatch call, your sabbatical is a time to rebuild your PsyCap.

# TIFF'S TAKEAWAY: THE POWER OF THE PAUSE

I want you to remember that the world will not stop spinning because you took a nap. Your business will not fail because you chose your family for a season. In fact, you will often find that your best strategic ideas—the ones that lead to your next $100k or your next book—come during the silence of a sabbatical, not the noise of the grind.

Plan your pause with the same discipline you used to plan your growth. Be a good steward of your rest, and you will find that you return with a level of clarity and efficacy that no "hustle" could ever provide.

# PART 5 ACTION GUIDE

You have reached the summit. You have done the internal work, built the systems, fueled the growth, and automated your life. But as we discussed in Chapter 21, the true measure of a Cycle-breaker isn't just how they live; it's what they leave behind. This Action Guide is designed to help you transition from success to significance. It is time to document your wisdom and prepare the next generation to carry the torch.

## EXERCISE 1: THE FAMILY MONEY MEETING TEMPLATE

One of the most powerful ways to become a financial socializer is to make money a normal, transparent topic of conversation in your home. Use this template to host your first Family Money Meeting.

The Ground Rules:

1. No Shame Zone: This is not a time for lectures or guilt. It is a time for strategy and vision.
2. Age-appropriate Transparency: You don't have to show a seven-year-old your tax returns, but you can show them how you use the "Three Jars" (Give, Save, Spend).
3. Consistency Is Key: Aim for once a month, ideally after a fun family activity.

Meeting Agenda:

- The Celebration: What is one financial win we had as a family this month? (e.g., "We saved enough for our summer camping trip!")
- The Goal Check-in: How are we doing on our big family goal? (e.g., "The new car fund is at 75%.")
- The Lesson: Introduce one concept from this book. (e.g., "This month, let's talk about what an 'Authorized User' is.")
- The Q&A: Ask the kids: "Is there anything about money you're curious or worried about?"
- The Closing: Reiterate your family's core money value. (e.g., "In this house, we use money as a tool for freedom and kindness.")

# EXERCISE 2: THE AUTHORIZED USER LAUNCH PLAN

In Chapter 21, we integrated the "Drawer Method" with a long-term timeline. Use this space to map out the launch for your children (or the young people in your life).

- Child's Name: ________________________________
- Current Age: ________
- Target Phase: (Circle one: Phase 1: Foundation | Phase 2: Training Wheels | Phase 3: Launch)
- The Anchor Account: Which of your credit cards has the longest history and perfect payment record? ______________________
- The Action Date: When will you call the bank or log in to add them? ________________

# EXERCISE 3: YOUR LEGACY LETTER WORKSHEET

In the conclusion, we introduced the Legacy Letter. Use these prompts to draft your first version. Don't worry about making it perfect; worry about making it honest.

1. The Struggle I Overcame: What is the one money ghost or crossroads moment you want your children to understand?
   - *Drafting Thought:* "I want you to know about the time I had to choose between [X] and [Y], and how that taught me about [Value]."
2. The Philosophy of the Umbrella: Why did you build your multiple income streams? What freedom did it give you that you want them to have?
3. The Three Nonnegotiable Values: If your children forget every math lesson in this book, what three values (e.g., Resilience, Stewardship, Generosity) do you want them to live by?
4. The Promise: What is your commitment to them as their financial wellness curator?

# EXERCISE 4: THE LEGACY BINDER CHECKLIST

A legacy is a gift, not a burden. Ensure your family has the technical map they need to manage the wealth you are building.

- The Will/Trust: Is it updated and accessible?
- The Beneficiary Audit: Have you checked the beneficiaries on your 401(k), IRAs, and life insurance policies this year?

- The Password Vault: Does your spouse or a trusted executor have access to your digital password manager?
- The Asset Map: Do you have a single document listing all bank accounts, investment portals, and business entities?
- The Letter: Is your signed Legacy Letter placed on top of these documents?

# THE FINAL COMMITMENT

I, [Your Name], have completed the journey from fear to power. I accept my role as a Cycle-breaker and a Legacy Builder. I commit to teaching the next generation not just how to earn, but how to lead. My story is no longer one of statistics; it is a story of strategy, and my wealth is no longer a secret; it is a heritage.

Signature: ______________________________

Date: ____________

**Client Spotlight:**
**The Thompson Family's Generational Shift**

When David and Sarah first joined one of my workshops, they were already "successful" by most standards. They had stable careers, a healthy emergency fund, and had successfully navigated the architecture of flow (Part 2). But they were haunted by a specific fear: "We've built all of this, but what if our kids blow it all because they don't understand the struggle it took to get here?"

David and Sarah were the first in their families to achieve six-figure incomes. They were Cycle-breakers who had moved from scarcity to abundance, but they realized they were accidentally raising "Financial Tourists"—children who enjoyed the destination without understanding the map.

### *The Shift to Financial Socialization*

We realized that David and Sarah were protecting their children from money rather than preparing them for it. To make the legacy shift, they had to move from being providers to being financial socializers.

**The Authorized User Launch:** David had a credit card account he had opened in college and managed perfectly for 15 years. We used the "Drawer Method" (Chapter 21) to add their 16-year-old daughter, Jasmine, as an authorized user. Jasmine never saw the card, but by the time she applied for her first student loan for college, she already had a credit score of 745. David and Sarah didn't just give her a car; they gave her a "reputation" in the financial world.

**The Family Money Meeting:** They started hosting a monthly "Pizza and Progress" night. It wasn't a lecture; it was a transparent look at the family's Umbrella. They showed the kids how their side business (a small rental property) paid for their summer vacation. They were teaching their children to see the link between human capital and lifestyle design.

**The Legacy Letter:** This was the hardest part for David. He had to sit down and write about the money ghosts of his own childhood—the nights the lights were turned off and the shame he felt wearing hand-me-downs. He realized that by hiding his past struggle, he was robbing his children of the context for their current success.

### *The Result: A Heritage of Power*

The breakthrough happened when Jasmine turned eighteen. Instead of asking for a high-limit credit card to go shopping, she asked her parents if they would help her research how to open a Roth IRA with the money she earned from her summer internship.

She wasn't just thinking about what she could buy; she was thinking about what she could build.

(*Continued*)

(*Continued*)

David and Sarah realized that their legacy wasn't the balance in their bank account; it was the mindset in their daughter's head. They had successfully passed down an Internal Locus of Control. Jasmine didn't view money as a mystery or a lucky break; she viewed it as a tool that she was fully equipped to manage.

**Tiff's Takeaway:** The Thompson family reminds us that the greatest gift you can give the next generation is not a finished building, but the blueprints and the tools. When you make the legacy shift, you aren't just changing your family's net worth; you are changing their trajectory for a century.

# LEGACY BEYOND DNA: FOR THE CHILD-FREE CYCLE-BREAKER

If you don't have children, you might be tempted to skim this chapter or feel that the concept of "legacy" doesn't apply to you. Let's shift that mindset right now.

Legacy is not a biological mandate; it is a spiritual and social one. A legacy is simply the transfer of psychological, human, and financial capital from your life into the lives of others. Whether you are an aunt, an uncle, a mentor, a godparent, or a community leader, you have the power to be the financial socializer for the next generation of your community.

Here is how the legacy shift looks when it isn't defined by parenthood:

- **The "Chosen" Next Generation:** You likely have nieces, nephews, or mentees who are watching how you move. You can still use the Authorized User Strategy for a younger relative, or better yet, you can be the one who gifts them their first "Money Meeting." You can be the safe space where they learn the internal locus of control that their own parents might not yet possess.

- **Institutional Legacy:** Your legacy can be built into the foundations of the organizations you care about. This is where your Umbrella of Income (Part 3) turns into an engine for social change. Whether it's establishing a scholarship fund, supporting a local incubator in a place like Negril, or leaving a portion of your estate to a cause that breaks cycles of poverty, you are ensuring your "why" outlives your "how."
- **The "Legacy Letter" to the World:** Your story of resilience—the crossroads you faced and the ghosts you silenced—is a public asset. By sharing your journey through your brand, your mentorship, or even this book, you are providing a blueprint for thousands of people you may never meet.

**Remember:** A tree doesn't have to produce a sapling from its own seed to be part of a forest. It provides shade, it stabilizes the soil, and it contributes to the ecosystem. Your financial wellness is a gift to the collective. You are breaking cycles for an entire community, and that heritage is just as powerful as any family tree.

Ready to put these shifts into motion? Scan the code below to access the **Cycle-breaker's Resource Vault**, where I've provided downloadable worksheets, budget templates, and video deep-dives for every move in this section.

**Link:** moneytalkwitht.com/moves

# CONCLUSION: YOUR LEGACY IS MORE THAN JUST MONEY

We've come a long way on this journey together. We started with a single step: the courage to face your financial reality. We transformed that courage into a plan, building a budget that put you in the driver's seat. We fortified that plan with faith—in yourself and in a future of abundance. We aimed that faith at a specific destination by setting powerful goals. And finally, we unlocked the entrepreneurial mindset required to build a life of freedom and resilience.

But if you walk away from this book with only a balanced budget and a bigger bank account, I will have failed you.

Because this was never just about money.

Money is a tool. It is a resource. It is an energy exchange. But it is not the end goal. The goal is the life that money allows you to build, the impact it allows you to have, and the legacy it allows you to leave.

# WHAT IS YOUR LEGACY?

Your legacy is not the number in your retirement account. It is the sum of the lives you touch and the values you pass down.

It's being able to support your children's dreams without hesitation.

It's having the freedom to leave a job that is draining your soul to pursue work that sets it on fire.

It's creating opportunities in your community and generously supporting the causes you believe in.

It's breaking generational cycles of financial stress and replacing them with cycles of wealth, knowledge, and confidence.

It's showing your children not what you bought them, but what you taught them about building a life on their own terms.

My personal legacy is rooted in my own story. It's in my work helping Black-owned businesses thrive. It's in my advocacy for the formerly incarcerated, driven by a deep personal connection to the issue. It's in the life I've built for my children in Jamaica, showing them that a life of peace, health, and purpose is possible.

Every financial decision you make is a brushstroke on the canvas of your legacy. Every dollar you save is a vote for your future self. Every debt you pay off is a chain you break. Every side hustle you start is a declaration of your own power.

This deep-seated desire to leave the world better than we found it is what psychologists call *generativity*. First coined by developmental psychologist Erik Erikson, generativity is the hallmark of a healthy, maturing adult. It is the stage of life where our focus shifts from our own survival and success to the "establishment and guidance of the next generation" (Erikson, 1950).

Erikson's research suggests that we face a fundamental choice in our later years: generativity vs. stagnation. Those who fail to find ways to contribute to the future often experience stagnation—a sense of being stuck, disconnected, and lacking purpose. But those who embrace generativity—who mentor, who build, and who pass down wisdom—experience a profound sense of well-being and narrative fulfillment.

By following the steps in this book, you haven't just been "fixing your finances." You have been actively moving toward a generative life. You are ensuring that your story, your struggles, and your successes serve as a bridge for those coming after you. As research in positive psychology shows, the act of intentional legacy-building provides a sense of meaning that transcends our individual lives (McAdams, 2013). You are participating in a timeless human tradition: taking the raw materials of your life and refining them into a gift for the future.

# YOUR FINAL MONEY MOVE: THE LEGACY LETTER

A legacy isn't just about what you leave *for* someone; it's about what you leave *in* them. This letter is your opportunity to put your values, your story, and your "why" into words. Whether you address this to your children, your grandchildren, or your future self, this letter will serve as a North Star for the generations to come.

## The Legacy Letter Template

To my [Children/Family/Future Self],

1. The Story of My Shift:
   *I want you to know where our journey really began. For a long time, I believed that money was [describe your old mindset, e.g., a source of fear/something for other people]. But then, I realized that I had the power to change our story. The moment I decided to [describe your "Crossroads" moment] was the moment everything changed.*

2. The Values I Want You to Carry:

   *If you remember nothing else from my life, remember these three values:*

   - *Value 1: [e.g., Resilience—the ability to start over at any crossroads.]*
   - *Value 2: [e.g., Agency—knowing that you are the driver of your own life.]*
   - *Value 3: [e.g., Generosity—using our tools to build a better community.]*

3. The "Why" Behind Our Wealth:

   *We didn't build our [Emergency Fund/Investments/Business] just to have a high balance in a bank account. We built it so that we could have the freedom to [describe your deep "Why," e.g., spend time together/advocate for others/live a life of peace].*

4. My Greatest Hope for You:

   *My hope is not that you never face a crisis, but that when you do, you remember that you have the PsyCap to overcome it. I hope you use the tools I've shared with you to build a life that feels like permission, not restriction.*

5. My Promise to You:

   *I promise to continue being an honest example of what it looks like to grow, to learn, and to lead with intention. Our legacy is not a destination; it is a path we are walking together.*

With love,
*[Your Name]*

# HOW TO USE THIS LETTER

1. Don't overthink it. Your family doesn't need a literary masterpiece; they need your voice.

2. Be vulnerable. Share a mistake you made and what it taught you. This is how you break the cycle of financial shame.
3. Keep it accessible. Store a physical copy in your "Legacy Binder" (along with your will and insurance papers) and consider reading it aloud at your next Family Money Meeting.

# THE JOURNEY NEVER ENDS

You now have the tools, the strategies, and the mindset shifts to build a life of financial freedom. But the work is never truly done. Your goals will evolve. Your "why" will deepen. Your capacity to give and to build will expand in ways you can't even imagine right now.

Continue to be the CEO of your money. Continue to pay yourself first. Continue to ask, "How can I?" instead of saying, "I can't." Continue to operate from a place of abundance, knowing that you cannot receive with a closed fist.

You are no longer just a passenger in your financial life. You are the architect, the designer, and the builder.

Go build a beautiful life. Go build a lasting legacy.

## The Voice of Doubt: "Is My Legacy Enough?"

As we reach the end of this book, a new kind of doubt might creep in. You might look at the "big" legacies of billionaires or famous philanthropists and feel like your contribution is small. Let's shift that mindset one last time.

**Obstacle:** "I'm just one person. I don't have millions of dollars to leave behind. Can I really have a 'legacy'?"

(*Continued*)

(*Continued*)

**Your Mindset Shift:** Legacy is not measured by the size of the check, but by the depth of the change. If you teach one child to value themselves and their choices, you have changed the trajectory of a family tree for a 100 years. If you support one local business, you are strengthening the fabric of your community. A legacy is a mosaic made of small, intentional acts. Your "small" moves are the foundation of someone else's "big" future.

**Obstacle:** "I started so late. I spent so many years in the scarcity trap. Have I already wasted my chance to leave a legacy?"

**Your Mindset Shift:** Your years in the scarcity trap are not wasted—they are your credentials. The most powerful legacies are built by those who have overcome the most. Your story of resilience is more valuable to the next generation than a pile of easy money ever could be. The fact that you are here, reading this, means your generative work has already begun. You aren't starting late; you are starting with the wisdom that only experience can provide.

**Obstacle:** "What if my kids or my community don't follow the path I've laid out? What if the legacy doesn't 'stick'?"

**Your Mindset Shift:** Your job is to be the architect, not the controller. You provide the blueprint, the tools, and the foundation. What they choose to build on that foundation is their journey. A true legacy is an act of faith—you plant the seeds, knowing you may never sit in the shade of the trees. Your success is in the planting, not the harvest.

# THE FINANCIAL WELLNESS CHECK-UP: YOUR PATH FORWARD

Congratulations. You have traveled from the terrifying crossroads of a crisis to the intentional design of a legacy. You have the mindset, the architecture, the engine, and the autopilot systems in place.

But financial wellness is not a destination; it is a practice. Just as a doctor performs a physical check-up to monitor your health, you must regularly perform a financial check-up to monitor your progress. This quiz is designed to help you see your strengths and identify the areas where your "Money Flow System" needs a tune-up.

## HOW TO TAKE THIS QUIZ

Rate yourself on a scale of 1 (Never/Strongly Disagree) to 5 (Always/Strongly Agree) for each of the following statements. Be brutally honest with yourself—the data is the light.

# PART 1: THE MINDSET (CHAPTERS 1–5)

1. I believe that I am the primary driver of my financial destiny (internal locus of control). [ ]
2. I can identify the money ghosts or inherited beliefs that have influenced my past decisions. [ ]
3. I view education and skill-building as my most powerful investment (human capital). [ ]
4. I have forgiven myself for my past financial mistakes and no longer operate from a place of shame. [ ]
5. I feel a sense of Hope, Efficacy, Resilience, and Optimism regarding my money (PsyCap). [ ]
6. I view a budget as "permission to spend" rather than a restriction. [ ]
7. I am no longer afraid to look at my bank accounts or credit score. [ ]
8. I understand that my current financial situation is a season, not a life sentence. [ ]
9. I have silenced the "external noise" and stopped comparing my journey to others. [ ]
10. I have made a firm commitment to "pay myself first" every single time I receive income. [ ]

Part 1 Subtotal: ____ / 50

# PART 2: THE ARCHITECTURE (CHAPTERS 6–11)

11. I have a clearly defined "why" that is emotionally anchored and drives my financial goals. [ ]
12. I have completed at least one 30-day "Awareness Tracker" mission. [ ]
13. I know exactly where every dollar went over the last month. [ ]
14. I have applied the "Do More, Do Less, Stop" framework to my monthly expenses. [ ]
15. I have a written "Money Flow System" that tells my money where to go. [ ]
16. I have a separate account for my "Four Walls" (Food, Shelter, Utilities, Transportation). [ ]
17. I have established a $1,000 "Baby Emergency Fund" to act as a psychological buffer. [ ]
18. I know my "Survival Total"—the bare minimum I need to cover my Four Walls for one month. [ ]
19. I use the "Drawer Method" or a similar strategy to manage my credit safely. [ ]
20. I have a plan in place for how to handle a sudden loss of income. [ ]

Part 2 Subtotal: _____ / 50

# PART 3: THE ENGINE OF GROWTH (CHAPTERS 12–19)

21. I am actively looking for ways to increase my "Market Value" through new skills or credentials. [ ]
22. I have identified at least one potential "Scalable" or "Passive" income stream. [ ]
23. I am using the "Umbrella Method" to organize my multiple income streams. [ ]
24. I have used the "Side Hustle Selection Matrix" to vet my new business ideas. [ ]
25. I feel confident in my ability to "ask" for what I am worth in a negotiation. [ ]
26. I have a "Tax Buffer" account where I automatically save 30% of my 1099 income. [ ]
27. I have defined my personal or business "Umbrella Brand." [ ]
28. I am building a network of "strategic advisors" (AFC®, CPA, etc.) to support my growth. [ ]
29. I am consistently investing in my own human capital every month. [ ]
30. I view my income as a tool for building wealth, not just a way to pay for a lifestyle. [ ]

Part 3 Subtotal: ____ / 50

# PART 4: THE AUTOPILOT LIFE (CHAPTERS 20–21)

**31.** My "pay yourself first" transfer happens automatically on payday. [ ]
**32.** All of my Four Walls bills are set to autopay. [ ]
**33.** I spend less than 60 minutes a month on bank teller tasks (paying bills, moving money). [ ]
**34.** I have enrolled in "equal payment plans" for my seasonal utilities to create predictable flow. [ ]
**35.** I have a clear vision of what my "Jamaica" moment or "Perfect Tuesday" looks like. [ ]
**36.** I have calculated the actual cost of my "life design" goals. [ ]
**37.** My income is portable—I could earn it from anywhere in the world. [ ]
**38.** I have audited my subscriptions and eliminated all money leaks. [ ]
**39.** I use technology (apps/software) to keep my financial system running with zero friction. [ ]
**40.** I have more time for my "why" today than I did before I started this book. [ ]

Part 4 Subtotal: ____ / 50

# PART 5: THE LEGACY SHIFT (CHAPTERS 22–23)

**41.** I am actively teaching the young people in my life about the Three Jars of money. [ ]
**42.** I have started (or have a plan for) the Authorized User strategy for my children. [ ]

**43.** My family has regular Money Meetings that are positive and transparent. [ ]

**44.** I have a written Legacy Letter that documents my values and my journey. [ ]

**45.** My Legacy Binder (will, passwords, asset map) is organized and accessible. [ ]

**46.** I am a "Cycle-breaker"—the negative financial patterns of my past stop with me. [ ]

**47.** I view my wealth as a heritage to be managed, not just a pile of money to be spent. [ ]

**48.** I am using my resources to advocate for and support my community. [ ]

**49.** I am confident that the next generation of my family will be more financially literate than I was. [ ]

**50.** I am living a life of permission, power, and peace. [ ]

Part 5 Subtotal: ____ / 50

# SCORING YOUR WELLNESS

Add up your subtotals from all five parts to get your Total Wellness Score.

- 225–250: The Financial Wellness Curator. You aren't just managing money; you are curating a life of extraordinary impact. You are a master of the Umbrella Method and your legacy is secure. Your Move: Start mentoring others or deepening your community advocacy work.
- 175–224: The Legacy Builder. You have a solid architecture and your engine is humming. You have broken the major cycles and are now in the autopilot phase. Your Move: Focus on Part 4 (Automation) to reclaim more of your time for your "why."

- 125–174: The Architecture Student. You have made the mindset shift and are starting to build your systems. You might still feel some friction, but you are moving in the right direction. Your Move: Re-read Part 2 and ensure your "Four Walls" and "pay yourself first" habits are nonnegotiable.
- 50–124: The Cycle-breaker in Training. You are at the crossroads. The fact that you are here, holding this book, is your first money move. Your Move: Go back to Part 1. Focus entirely on your locus of control and your PsyCap before you worry about the technical systems.

# THE FINANCIAL WELLNESS CURATOR'S MANIFESTO

You have reached the end of this book, but you are at the beginning of a new era. You have dismantled the ghosts of your past, built the architecture of your present, and designed the legacy of your future. You are no longer a passenger in your financial life; you are the architect. You are no longer a victim of statistics; you are a creator of strategy.

To be a financial wellness curator is to live with intention. It is to recognize that money is not the goal, but the fuel for a life of purpose, peace, and permission. As you step out from these pages and back into the world, carry these 10 commandments as your North Star.

# THE 10 COMMANDMENTS OF THE CYCLE-BREAKER

1. I am the Driver. I reject the external locus of control. My financial destiny is not determined by the economy, my employer, or my upbringing. I take full responsibility for my choices and my growth.
2. I Pay Myself First. I recognize that I am my most valuable asset. Before I fund anyone else's dream, I invest in my own security, my own health, and my own future.
3. I Budget for Permission, Not Restriction. I refuse the "starvation" mindset. My money flow system is a tool that gives me the freedom to spend on what I love by being ruthless about what I don't.
4. I Honor My "Why." I do not chase numbers for the sake of numbers. Every dollar I earn and every move I make is anchored in my deep emotional purpose—my family, my freedom, and my peace.
5. I am a Lifelong Student. I recognize that my human capital has an infinite ceiling. I will never stop learning, evolving, and increasing my value in the marketplace.
6. I Build Umbrellas, Not Just Paychecks. I reject the risk of the single-income stream. I am an architect of multiple flows, ensuring that no single storm can ever sink my boat.
7. I Automate the Boring to Focus on the Beautiful. I use technology to handle the bank teller tasks of my life so I can use my CEO Time for creativity, connection, and contribution.
8. I Am a Financial Socializer. I do not keep my wisdom a secret. I speak the language of money at my dinner table, ensuring that the next generation starts their journey from a position of power.

9. I Choose My Environment. I recognize that my physical surroundings affect my financial and mental health. I have the audacity to design a life that allows me to thrive, whether that's on a veranda in Jamaica or a quiet corner of my hometown.
10. I Am a Cycle-breaker. The negative patterns of my past stop with me. I am the strongest link in my family chain, and the legacy I am building will provide shade for generations I will never meet.

# YOUR VERANDA IS WAITING

My journey began on a linoleum floor in North Carolina, staring at a positive pregnancy test and a future that looked like a dead end. It led me through years of "hustle," through the "ghosts" of credit fear, and eventually, to a veranda in Negril where I now sit as I write these words.

The distance between that floor and this veranda wasn't covered by luck. It was covered by mindset shifts and money moves. It was covered by the decision to believe that I was worth the work.

You are worth the work. Your family is worth the work. Your legacy is worth the work.

The crossroads is behind you. The architecture is built. The engine is humming. Now, go live a life by design.

The work of a steward is never finished, but it is always organized. In the pages that follow, I have provided the tools, the terminology, and the personal blueprints to help you move from theory to legacy. I suggest you start with the mechanics in the Glossary and the Stewardship Stack but allow yourself to end with the heart. Your final move isn't a financial one; it's the letter you leave behind.

One Love.

The journey of a steward is ongoing. To support you as you move from these pages into your new life, I have created a living library of resources that grows as the market shifts. Consider the **Resource Vault** your home base for every move you make from here on out.

**Link:** moneytalkwitht.com/moves

# APPENDIX A

# THE CYCLE-BREAKER'S GLOSSARY

This section is designed to be your North Star as you navigate the money moves and mindset shifts outlined in this book. Whether you are looking to decode the "alphabet soup" of financial credentials or find the best tool to automate your flow, you will find it here.

# PART 1: THE GLOSSARY OF FINANCIAL WELLNESS

The following terms represent the foundational vocabulary of the stewardship mindset. These definitions bridge the gap between traditional financial mechanics and the psychological shifts required for a lasting legacy. As you review these concepts, remember that language has power; by naming the ghosts and traumas of your past, you begin to strip them of their influence over your future.

We begin with the internal landscape. Before you can master the math of your architecture of flow, you must understand the biological and mental frameworks that govern how you perceive value, risk, and responsibility. These terms are the keys to unlocking your Internal Revolution.

## The Psychology of Wealth

- Allostatic load: A term used in environmental psychology and biology to describe the "wear and tear" on the body that accumulates as an individual is exposed to repeated or chronic stress. In this book, we use it to explain why your physical environment (your "Health Wall") is a critical component of your financial plan. High allostatic load impairs decision-making; a healthy environment restores it.
- Decision fatigue: The psychological phenomenon where the quality of decisions made by an individual deteriorates after a long session of decision-making. By automating your finances, you preserve your "cognitive bandwidth" for high-value life and business choices.

- External vs. internal locus of control: A concept developed by psychologist Julian B. Rotter. An external locus is the belief that life happens to you (the victim mindset). An internal locus is the unshakeable conviction that you are the primary driver of your own destiny.
- Financial socialization: The lifelong process by which individuals acquire the values, knowledge, and behaviors that shape their financial future. This happens primarily at the dinner table and through the observation of parental behavior.
- Money ghosts: The inherited financial traumas, fears, and scarcity mindsets passed down through generations. Identifying your money ghosts is the first step in the Internal Revolution.
- Net worth vs. self-worth: The critical distinction between your financial balance sheet and your inherent value as a human being. Net worth is a mathematical snapshot of your resources; self-worth is the foundation of your identity. Confusing the two leads to shame when numbers are low and arrogance when they are high.
- Opportunity cost: The value of the "next best thing" you give up when you make a choice. In stewardship, we don't just ask what a move costs in dollars, but what it prevents us from doing or being. Every "yes" to a low-value expense is a "no" to a future legacy move.
- PsyCap (psychological capital): A scientifically validated framework consisting of four pillars: Hope (willpower and waypower), Efficacy (confidence in your ability), Resilience (bouncing back), and Optimism (positive attribution). PsyCap is the internal currency required to build external wealth.
- Sunk cost fallacy: The tendency to continue investing in a losing proposition simply because you have already spent time or money on it. Breaking this fallacy is essential for escaping the Revenue Trap—it is the courage to prune a dead branch so the rest of the tree can live.

# The Mechanics of Money

- Amortization: The process of spreading out a loan into fixed payments over time. While the payment stays the same, the ratio of interest to principal shifts. Understanding this allows you to see how extra payments "buy back" your future time by attacking the principal early.
- Asset allocation: The strategic distribution of your investments across different categories like stocks, bonds, and real estate. This is the "Umbrella" of your portfolio, ensuring you aren't over-exposed to a single market shift.
- Authorized user strategy: A credit-building move where a primary cardholder adds another person to their account. This allows the authorized user to benefit from the primary holder's positive payment history—a key tool for Cycle-breakers helping their children.
- Choice architecture: The practice of designing environments to "nudge" people toward better decisions. Setting up automatic transfers is an act of choice architecture where you make the "right" choice the "automatic" choice.
- Compound interest: Interest earned on both the original principal and the accumulated interest from previous periods. It is the mathematical engine of wealth when you are saving, but a compound monster in reverse when you are carrying high-interest debt.
- Do More, Do Less, Stop: *The Money Talk with Tiff* framework for expense analysis. Instead of just "cutting," you evaluate spending based on whether it nourishes your "why" (Do More) or drains your resources without adding value (Stop).
- EBITDA: An acronym for Earnings Before Interest, Taxes, Depreciation, and Amortization. It is a "truth meter" for business owners, stripping away accounting noise to show how much cash the core business is actually generating.

- Escrow: A legal arrangement where a third party holds funds until specific conditions are met, often used by lenders to pay property taxes and insurance. Auditing your escrow ensures your capital isn't sitting idle when it could be working in your Peace Fund.
- Geo-arbitrage: The practice of taking advantage of the difference in the cost of living between two locations while maintaining a high income (often through remote work or digital entrepreneurship).
- The Umbrella Method: A strategy for building multiple income streams where various revenue sources (service-based, product-based, and passive) sit under one brand identity, providing financial stability and protection against market shifts.
- Zero-based budgeting: A method of budgeting where your income minus your expenses equals zero. Every dollar is "given a job" before the month begins, ensuring that no money is lost to "leakage."

# PART 2: PROFESSIONAL STANDARDS (THE ALPHABET SOUP)

When you are ready to hire a professional to join your strategic advisory team, it is essential to understand the credentials behind the name. Not all financial professionals are created equal.

- AFC® (accredited financial counselor): This is the gold standard for financial counseling and coaching. An AFC is trained to help clients with the "human" side of money—behavioral change, debt management, and building a solid foundation. This is the credential I hold, and it focuses on empowering you to manage your own flow.

- CFP® (certified financial planner): A professional who has met rigorous requirements for education and experience in comprehensive financial planning, including investments, taxes, and estate planning. They are fiduciaries, meaning they are legally required to act in your best interest.
- CPA (certified public accountant): A tax and accounting expert. While many people only see their CPA at tax time, a great CPA is a year-round strategic partner for your business.
- ChFC® (chartered financial consultant): Similar to a CFP, this professional has deep knowledge in financial planning but often with a specific focus on insurance and employee benefits.
- EA (enrolled agent): A federally licensed tax practitioner who has technical expertise in the field of taxation and is empowered by the US Department of the Treasury to represent taxpayers before the IRS.
- Fiduciary: A legal and ethical obligation for a professional to act in your best interest. This is the nonnegotiable standard for any member of your Council of Stewards. If an advisor is not a fiduciary, they may be a salesperson rather than a partner.
- Fractional CFO: A strategic partner who provides high-level financial oversight and forward-looking strategy on a part-time or project basis. They bridge the gap between looking at the past (bookkeeping) and designing the future (legacy).

# APPENDIX B

# THE STEWARDSHIP STACK (TOOLS AND APPS)

While the list below will show you the individual tools I recommend, I have curated a **Master Stewardship Stack** inside my digital Resource Vault. This includes exclusive discounts for my readers, video tutorials on how I set up my own YNAB buckets, and a "Start Here" guide for your first 30 days.

**Scan to Enter the Vault:**

**Link:** moneytalkwitht.com/moves

# BUDGETING AND TRACKING

- YNAB (You Need A Budget): The ultimate tool for zero-based budgeting. It teaches you to "give every dollar a job."
- Monarch Money: A modern, comprehensive platform for tracking your net worth, spending, and goals across all accounts.
- Quicken Simplifi: A high-performance app for those who want a streamlined, automated view of their finances.
- EveryDollar: A simple, effective zero-based budgeting app based on the Dave Ramsey "Baby Steps" framework.

# BANKING AND SAVING

- Ally Bank: My personal choice for high-yield savings. Their "Buckets" feature is perfect for organizing your "Four Walls" and your "pay yourself first" goals.

# INVESTING AND WEALTH BUILDING

- Robinhood: A user-friendly platform for individual stock and ETF investing.
- Acorns: The best tool for beginners to start "paying themselves first" through spare-change roundups.
- Stash: A great educational platform for those who want to learn while they invest.
- Betterment: A leading "robo-advisor" that automates your investment strategy based on your goals and risk tolerance.
- Capitalize: A specialized service to help you find and roll over your old 401(k)s into a consolidated IRA.

# BUSINESS AND ENTREPRENEURSHIP

- Quickbooks: The gold standard for business bookkeeping. I use this to manage the *Money Talk with Tiff* engine.
- Kajabi: The platform I used for years to host my courses and the "Budget Nirvana" community.
- Shopify: The premier platform for building your own digital or physical product store.
- Coursera: My go-to resource for investing in human capital through professional certifications.

# APPENDIX C

# THE CYCLE-BREAKER'S FAQS

Throughout this book, we have laid out the architecture of a life by design. But as any financial wellness curator will tell you, life rarely follows a straight line. You will encounter "gray areas" where the right move isn't immediately obvious. This section is designed to answer the most common questions I receive from clients who are in the trenches of their own financial revolutions.

## SECTION 1: THE TRIAGE PHASE (MINDSET AND BASICS)

Q: I'm staring at my numbers and my "Four Walls" actually cost more than my total income. What do I do when the math just doesn't work?

Tiff's Move: First, breathe. You are experiencing what I call a "structural deficit," and it is often the most shameful moment for a Cycle-breaker. But remember: this is just data. If your essential survival costs (food, shelter, utilities, transportation) exceed your income, you cannot "budget" your way out of this. You have an income problem, not a spending problem.

- Immediate Action: You must enter crisis triage. Contact your utility providers and ask about hardship programs or "equal payment plans" to lower the monthly hit.
- The Strategic Shift: Every ounce of your creative energy must now shift to Part 3 of this book: Increasing your human capital and building an Umbrella of income. You don't need a better spreadsheet; you need a bigger shovel.

Q: Should I save my $1,000 Baby Emergency Fund even if I have high-interest credit card debt?

Tiff's Move: Yes. Every single time. This is the most debated topic in personal finance, but for a Cycle-breaker, the $1,000 buffer is nonnegotiable. Why? Because without it, you are one flat tire away from backsliding into the very debt you are trying to escape. The $1,000 isn't just money; it's the "break" in the cycle. It allows you to handle a crisis with cash instead of plastic, which protects your new mindset of power.

Q: My money ghosts are loud. I feel guilty every time I spend money on myself, even if it's in the budget. How do I get over the frugality trauma?

Tiff's Move: This is a classic symptom of a scarcity trap upbringing. You've spent so long in survival mode that "thriving" feels like a betrayal. I want you to reread Chapter 5: *Budgeting Is Permission*.

- The Practice: Start small. Create a "Joy Category" in your budget for just $10 or $20 a month. This money *must* be spent on something that has zero "utility" but brings you 10/10 joy. By intentionally spending that money, you are retraining your nervous system to understand that you are safe and that you are allowed to enjoy the fruits of your labor.

# SECTION 2: THE RELATIONSHIP DYNAMIC

Q: I'm all-in on this journey, but my partner is a "spender" and refuses to track their data. How do I break the cycle if we aren't on the same page?

Tiff's Move: You cannot force a mindset shift on someone else; you can only model the peace that comes with it.

- The Approach: Stop talking about "the budget" (which sounds like a restriction to them) and start talking about the "why" (which sounds like a dream). Instead of saying, "We need to stop eating out," try, "I really want us to have that veranda moment in three years. What can we do today to move toward that?"
- The "Yours, Mine, Ours" System: If a joint budget is causing too much friction, move to a three-account system. You both contribute to the "Four Walls" and joint goals, but you each maintain a separate "Permission to Spend" account where no questions are asked and no tracking is required.

Q: How do I talk to my kids about our financial past without scaring them?

Tiff's Move: Transparency is the antidote to trauma. You don't need to share the "binder of credit cards" (Chapter 3) with a five-year-old, but you can share the *lessons*.

- The Script: "Mommy/Daddy used to be afraid of money because I didn't have a plan. But now, we have a system that tells our money where to go so we can be safe and help others."
- The Goal: You want them to see money as a tool that you control, not a monster that controls you. By being a financial socializer (Chapter 22), you ensure they inherit your wisdom, not your ghosts.

# SECTION 3: THE GROWTH AND UMBRELLA PHASE (CHAPTERS 12–19)

Q: I want to start a side hustle, but I'm exhausted from my 9-to-5. How do I find the energy to build an Umbrella when my main job takes everything I have?

Tiff's Move: This is where we return to the PsyCap we built in Part 1. If you are exhausted, it's often because you are using your energy to *survive* rather than to *build*.

- The Strategy: Do not start with a "hustle" that requires more manual labor (like rideshare driving) unless you are in a survival triage. Instead, look for a "rib" that leverages a skill you already use at your 9-to-5.
- The Micro-move: Commit to just 30 minutes a day of "CEO time." Use this time to build your scalable product or your brand identity. When you are building something that you *own*, the energy often

comes from the excitement of the "why" rather than the physical capacity of your body.

Q: At what point should I move from a sole proprietorship to an LLC for my side business?

Tiff's Move: As a Lean Six Sigma Yellow Belt, I'm a fan of efficiency. You don't need the complexity of an LLC for a business that has made zero dollars.

- The Threshold: I generally recommend looking into an LLC once your side hustle is consistently generating enough income to cover its own operating costs and you are beginning to sign contracts or work with clients where liability becomes a factor.
- The Benefit: An LLC doesn't just provide legal protection; it's a psychological "level up." It tells the world—and more importantly, yourself—that this isn't just a hobby; it's a business under your Umbrella.

Q: I'm afraid that if I negotiate for a higher salary (The Art of the Ask), my boss will think I'm ungrateful or fire me. How do I handle the fear of retaliation?

Tiff's Move: This is a money ghost telling you that you are lucky to be there. In reality, your employer is lucky to have your skills.

- The Mindset Shift: Negotiation is not a confrontation; it is a collaboration. You are simply presenting data (your achievements and market value) to help the company make an informed decision about their most valuable asset: you.
- The Safety Net: If a company retaliates against you for professionally presenting market data and requesting a fair wage, that is a clear

signal that your human capital is being wasted. It's time to start looking for a new Umbrella that values your contribution.

# SECTION 4: THE LEGACY AND EXPAT PHASE (CHAPTERS 20–23)

Q: I love the idea of the autopilot life, but I'm worried that if I automate everything, I'll stop paying attention and start overspending again. How do I stay mindful while on autopilot?

Tiff's Move: Automation is not "set it and forget it"; it's "set it and monitor it."

- The CEO Date: You should still have a monthly "CEO date" with your numbers. Because the bank teller tasks (paying bills) are automated, your meeting is focused entirely on strategy. You aren't checking if the light bill was paid; you're checking if your pay yourself first amount should be increased because your income grew.

Q: Moving to Jamaica or becoming a digital nomad sounds amazing, but what about the taxes? Won't the IRS find me?

Tiff's Move: The IRS has a very long reach, and they will definitely find you! Location independence does not mean tax independence.

- The Reality: If you are a US citizen, you are taxed on your worldwide income regardless of where you live. However, there are powerful tools like the Foreign Earned Income Exclusion (FEIE) that can significantly reduce your tax burden if you meet certain residency requirements.

- The Move: Before you buy the plane ticket, consult with an expat tax specialist. This is part of building your strategic advisor network (Part 3). Don't let the fear of taxes stop you from designing your life; just make sure your Tax Buffer is ready.

Q: I don't have children. How does the legacy shift apply to me?

Tiff's Move: Legacy is not restricted to DNA. A legacy is the impact you leave on the world and the people you choose to pour into.

- The Expanded View: Your legacy could be the scholarship fund you start for black-owned businesses, the community relief efforts you organize (like we did in Negril after the hurricane), or the nieces, nephews, and mentees you teach. The Legacy Letter (Chapter 23) is for anyone who will benefit from your wisdom after you are gone. You are a Cycle-breaker for your entire community, not just your household.

# APPENDIX D

# THE SYLLABUS FOR SUCCESS

Building your human capital requires a commitment to lifelong learning. Following is my curated list of the books that have most profoundly shaped my journey from a teen mom in survival mode to a financial counselor on a veranda in Jamaica. I have categorized them so you can choose the "syllabus" that fits your current season.

# CATEGORY 1: THE INTERNAL REVOLUTION (MINDSET AND PSYCHOLOGY)

1. *Mindset: The New Psychology of Success* by Carol S. Dweck
   - The Core Theme: The difference between a fixed mindset (believing your abilities are set in stone) and a growth mindset (believing you can develop through effort).
   - Tiff's Key Takeaway: This is the foundation of the internal locus of control. If you believe you are "just bad with money," you will stay stuck. Dweck's work taught me that financial literacy is a skill to be learned, not a talent you're born with. When you shift to a growth mindset, your debt stops being a life sentence and starts being a problem you are capable of solving.
2. *The Soul of Money* by Lynne Twist
   - The Core Theme: An exploration of our relationship with money as a reflection of our values and the "myth of scarcity."
   - Tiff's Key Takeaway: This book was instrumental in my move toward stewardship. Twist explains that we live in a culture that tells us we are "never enough." Learning to move from a mindset of scarcity to one of sufficiency allowed me to stop the frantic "grind" and start making moves from a place of peace. It's the ultimate guide for anyone feeling the money ghost of never-ending lack.
3. *Atomic Habits* by James Clear
   - The Core Theme: How small, 1% changes in your daily systems lead to massive results over time.

- Tiff's Key Takeaway: Wealth is the lagging measure of your habits. You don't "hustle" your way to a legacy; you automate your way there. Clear's framework for "Identity-Based Habits" is exactly how we build a Bulletproof Persona. You don't just "save money"; you become a person who prioritizes their future self.

4. *The Psychology of Money* by Morgan Housel
   - The Core Theme: Doing well with money isn't necessarily about what you know; it's about how you behave.
   - Tiff's Key Takeaway: Housel reminds us that "logical" and "reasonable" are not the same thing. You might have a "logical" reason for keeping a high-interest credit card, but is it "reasonable" for your peace of mind? This book validates the emotional side of finance that I teach—reminding us that our personal history with money (our financial socialization) dictates our current moves more than any spreadsheet.

# CATEGORY 2: THE ARCHITECTURE OF FLOW (TACTICAL FINANCE)

5. *I Will Teach You to Be Rich* by Ramit Sethi
   - The Core Theme: A no-guilt, no-excuses approach to automating your finances and focusing on "Big Wins."
   - Tiff's Key Takeaway: Ramit is the king of Choice Architecture. His focus on "conscious spending"—spending extravagantly on the things you love while cutting costs mercilessly on the things you don't—is the exact philosophy behind my Do More, Do Less, Stop framework. This is the book for the person who wants to enjoy their life *while* they build their wealth.

6. *Your Money or Your Life* by Vicki Robin and Joe Dominguez
   - The Core Theme: Transforming your relationship with money by viewing it as "life energy."
   - Tiff's Key Takeaway: This is the book that introduces the concept of geo-arbitrage without calling it that. It forces you to calculate your "Real Hourly Wage" (including commuting, stress, and work clothes). When I realized how much of my "life energy" I was trading for a high-cost lifestyle in the United States, the move to Jamaica became a mathematical necessity.
7. *Profit First* by Mike Michalowicz
   - The Core Theme: A behavioral approach to business accounting that ensures you take your profit before paying expenses.
   - Tiff's Key Takeaway: This is the pay yourself first philosophy applied to entrepreneurship. Most business owners wait until the end of the month to see if there is money left over; Michalowicz teaches you to flip the formula. As a fractional CFO and financial counselor, I use a modified version of this to help my clients escape the revenue trap. If your business doesn't pay you, it's not a business—it's an expensive hobby.
8. *The Total Money Makeover* by Dave Ramsey
   - The Core Theme: A "Baby Step" plan for getting out of debt and building a foundation using the debt snowball method.
   - Tiff's Takeaway: While I don't agree with every one of Dave's "rules" (especially his stance on credit cards for those who have mastered their behavior), his focus on the Psychology of the Win is undeniable. The debt snowball works because it builds Efficacy. Seeing a small balance disappear gives you the "Hope" you need to tackle the big ones. Use his steps for the foundation, but use my Umbrella Method for the legacy.

# CATEGORY 3: THE ENGINE OF GROWTH (BUSINESS AND LEGACY)

9. *Think and Grow Rich* by Napoleon Hill
    - The Core Theme: The power of thought and persistence in the pursuit of wealth.
    - Tiff's Key Takeaway: This is a classic for a reason. Hill's concept of the "Mastermind" is what led me to create the council of stewards. You cannot reach the highest levels of success in isolation. You need a team of people who see the vision you're building and can help you navigate the blind spots.
10. *The Color of Money* by Mehrsa Baradaran
    - The Core Theme: A history of the racial wealth gap and the systemic barriers to black wealth in America.
    - Tiff's Key Takeaway: To be a Cycle-breaker, you must understand the cycle you are breaking. Baradaran's work provides the historical context for why many of our money ghosts exist. It's not just "bad choices"; it's a systemic "external locus" that we must fight against with intentionality and education.
11. *Financial Feminist* by Tori Dunlap
    - The Core Theme: How to use money as a tool for protest and power in a system that wasn't built for you.
    - Tiff's Key Takeaway: Tori's message aligns perfectly with my mission to empower women and marginalized founders. Money is a tool for autonomy. When you have a "Peace Fund," you have the power to say "no" to toxic situations, whether they are in the boardroom or the bedroom.

# CATEGORY 4: THE STEWARDSHIP SHIFT (SPIRITUALITY AND PEACE)

12. *Boundaries* by Dr. Henry Cloud and Dr. John Townsend
    - The Core Theme: How to set healthy boundaries in your relationships and your work to protect your soul.
    - Tiff's Key Takeaway: You cannot be a good steward if you have no boundaries. Many Cycle-breakers struggle with "financial enabling"—trying to save everyone else while their own ship is sinking. This book gave me the permission to say "no" to unpaid workshops and "no" to family members who were draining my resources, allowing me to protect my capacity for my children and my purpose.
13. *It's Not About the Money* by Brent Kessel
    - The Core Theme: Integrating your spiritual life with your financial life by identifying your "Money Archetype."
    - Tiff's Key Takeaway: Kessel helps you identify if you are a "Saver," a "Spender," or an "Avoider" (the Ostrich). Understanding your archetype is the key to resolving your financial socialization. It moves the conversation from "What am I doing?" to "Why am I doing it?" which is the heart of the Internal Revolution.
14. *The 7 Habits of Highly Effective People* by Stephen Covey
    - The Core Theme: A principle-centered approach for solving personal and professional problems.

- Tiff's Key Takeaway: Habit 2—"Begin with the End in Mind"—is the core of legacy planning. If you don't know what you want your Legacy Letter to say at the end of your life, you can't make the right money moves today. Covey's "Circle of Influence" is one of the most accessible practical applications of the internal locus of control concept.

15. *The Four-Hour Workweek* by Timothy Ferriss
    - The Core Theme: Escaping the 9–5 grind, living anywhere, and joining the "New Rich."
    - Tiff's Key Takeaway: While some of the tactics are dated, the philosophy of lifestyle design is timeless. Ferriss's concept of "Mini-Retirements" is what inspired my strategic sabbatical and my move to Jamaica. Why wait until you're 65 to find peace? Use the Expat Math and the Umbrella Method to build a life you don't need a vacation from right now.

# APPENDIX E

# THE LEGACY BINDER

Being a steward means ensuring that if you were called home tomorrow, the people you love wouldn't have to hunt for passwords, bank accounts, or legal documents while they are grieving. A Legacy Binder (some call it a "Peace of Mind Folder") is the ultimate gift of order.

Following is the checklist of what should live in your binder. I recommend keeping a physical copy in a fireproof safe and a digital version in a secure, encrypted cloud drive.

# SECTION 1: THE LEGAL FOUNDATION

These documents prove who is in charge and what your wishes are. Without these, the state decides your legacy—and the state doesn't know your heart.

- ☐ Last Will and Testament: The primary document outlining how your assets should be distributed.
- ☐ Revocable Living Trust: (If applicable) To help your estate avoid the cost and delay of probate.
- ☐ Durable Power of Attorney: Naming the person authorized to handle your financial affairs if you become incapacitated.
- ☐ Healthcare Proxy/Medical Power of Attorney: Naming the person to make medical decisions on your behalf.
- ☐ Living Will/Advanced Directive: Outlining your specific wishes for end-of-life care and life support.

Tiff's Take: Don't just sign these and forget them. Review them every time you have a "Life Shift"—a birth, a move (like my move to Jamaica), or a significant change in assets.

# SECTION 2: THE FINANCIAL MAP

Your family needs to know where the "flow" is. Many people have "hidden" accounts that are lost to the state because no one knew they existed.

- ☐ List of All Bank Accounts: Include the institution name, account type (Checking/Savings), and the last four digits of the account number.

- ☐ Investment and Retirement Accounts: Details for your 401(k), IRAs, brokerage accounts, and any crypto-wallets (including "seed phrases" kept in a separate, secure location).
- ☐ Insurance Policies: Life, health, disability, homeowners, and auto insurance. Include policy numbers and agent contact information.
- ☐ Debt Inventory: A list of all mortgages, car loans, student loans, and credit cards.
- ☐ Real Estate Deeds and Titles: Proof of ownership for your home, land, or vehicles.

Tiff's Take: As an AFC, I see people lose thousands in "unclaimed property" simply because they didn't keep a map. This list is the GPS for your Council of Stewards.

# SECTION 3: THE DIGITAL KEYS

In the twenty-first century, our lives are digital. If your family can't get into your phone or your email, they can't manage your legacy.

- ☐ Master Password List: I recommend using a password manager, but your binder should contain the "Master Key" to that manager.
- ☐ Social Media Directives: Instructions on whether you want your accounts memorialized or deleted.
- ☐ Subscription Inventory: A list of recurring payments (Netflix, software, gym memberships) so they can be canceled to prevent "leakage" from your estate.
- ☐ Phone and Laptop Passcodes: Essential for accessing two-factor authentication (2FA) codes.

Tiff's Take: Digital legacy is often overlooked. Make sure your "digital steward" knows how to access your primary email, as that is the "skeleton key" for almost every other account.

# SECTION 4: THE BUSINESS CONTINUITY PLAN

If you are an entrepreneur, your business is a major part of your legacy. It needs its own set of instructions.

- ☐ Standard Operating Procedures (SOPs): Where do the files live? Who are the key contractors? How do clients get billed?
- ☐ Business Licenses and Tax IDs: Essential for the formal dissolution or transfer of the business.
- ☐ Buy-Sell Agreements: If you have partners, how is your share of the business handled?

Tiff's Take: My decision to dissolve a business in early 2026 is part of my continuity plan. I am "cleaning the house" so my heirs don't have to manage a business they don't understand.

# SECTION 5: THE PERSONAL INSTRUCTIONS

This is where the "soul" of the binder lives.

- ☐ Funeral and Memorial Wishes: Do you want a celebration of life? Where do you want to be laid to rest?

- ☐ The "Legacy Letter": (See Appendix F). Your final words of wisdom and love to your children and community.
- ☐ Ethical Will: A document where you share your values, life lessons, and hopes for the future, rather than just your money.

Tiff's Take: This section provides the most peace. When your family knows exactly what you wanted, they don't have to argue or guess during a time of grief. You are stewarding their emotional health even after you're gone.

# APPENDIX F

# THE LEGACY LETTER

To my children—Deric, Christian, Angel, and the little soul I am preparing to welcome into this world:

As I sit here on our veranda in Negril, watching the sun dip below the horizon, I am struck by the silence. For most of my life, silence was a luxury I couldn't afford. My life was defined by noise: the noise of survival, the noise of sirens in the city, the noise of a business that never slept, and the internal noise of a young woman trying to prove a doubting world wrong.

I am writing this letter because while this book is for the world, the legacy is for you. I want you to understand the "why" behind the moves I made, the shifts I endured, and the peace I finally chose.

## TO DERIC: MY FIRST PARTNER IN THE GRIND

Deric, we practically grew up together. You were there when I was seventeen, sitting on that linoleum floor, trying to figure out how to be a mother while I was still a child myself. You watched the "High-functioning Survival Mode" up close. You saw me go to school, work multiple jobs, and grind until I was bone-tired, all because I was determined to break a generational cycle.

In our family, for too many generations, mothers didn't get to raise their own children. My mother didn't raise me; my grandfather's mother didn't raise him. I made a vow that I would be the one to break that chain. I fought for years to ensure you stayed with me, even when the world made it difficult.

Moving to Jamaica and leaving you in the United States to finish your path there was the hardest decision of my life. It hurt me deeply, but I did it because I knew that to be the best version of myself for you, I had to find a place where I could breathe. I hope that as you enter young adulthood, you see those sacrifices not as an abandonment, but as a strategic move for our family's longevity. Be strong, Deric. Never be afraid to make the hard decisions that improve your life. You are the first proof that the cycle is broken.

## TO CHRISTIAN: THE WITNESS TO THE RISE

Christian, you saw the birth and the rise of *Money Talk with Tiff*. You saw the "CEO version" of your mom. I know there were many days when I wasn't as present as I wanted to be because I was chasing degrees and building an empire to ensure we were okay.

You have a natural gift for making money, and I love that about you. But the mindset shift I want you to carry into your teenage years is the art of Balance. You don't have to spend every dollar that enters your pocket. In this book, I talk about the architecture of flow—I want you to build that flow early. Save for the future you haven't met yet, so that money remains your tool and never becomes your master.

## TO ANGEL: THE COURAGE OF THE MOVE

Angel, you were only a year old when we boarded that plane for Jamaica. You are my "Veranda Baby." I want you to grow up remembering the courage it took for us to choose peace over the Revenue Trap.

I want you to know that just because a person makes a lot of money doesn't mean they are happy. I chose to get out of my comfort zone—and yours—to find a culture and an environment that valued our souls more than our output. Always strive for happiness over a high balance. It is okay to be different. It is okay to leave the "grind" to find your grace.

## TO MY NEWEST BLESSING: THE STEWARDSHIP ERA

You are coming into a world where your mother is finally the best version of herself. You won't know the "Survival Tiff" or the "Bulletproof Tiff." You are being born into the Stewardship Era.

My goal for you is stability and presence. My businesses no longer need me to work 24 hours a day because I built them to serve our life, not consume it. I am choosing to be a present mom, spending every moment I can with you all, because I finally understand that time is the only resource we can't earn back.

# THE INHERITANCE: YOUR THREE NONNEGOTIABLES

Regardless of how much money is in the bank when I leave this earth, I want these three values to be your true inheritance.

## 1. Integrity: The Audience of One

Always be honest, regardless of the consequences. Honesty is not just a policy; it is a shield. There have been so many times in my life where a lie could have made things "easier" in the short term, but the truth always worked out in my favor in the long run. Remember that God is always watching, even when no one else is. If you have integrity, you have a foundation that no market crash can take away.

## 2. Stewardship: You Are a Manager, Not an Owner

Always be a good steward of what God blesses you with. I have learned that when I manage my resources well, the blessings multiply. But the moment I start acting like an "owner"—clutching things too tightly or becoming arrogant—everything goes down the drain. You don't own anything in this life. You can't take it with you. You are simply a manager for a season. Manage it well and use it to help others.

## 3. Resilience: The Strongest Soldiers

Life will not always go your way. You will face battles that feel too heavy to bear. But remember: everything happens exactly as it is supposed to. You will never be given more than you can handle. The toughest battles are reserved for the strongest soldiers. Never let fear of failure—or fear of success—deter you from the greatness I know is inside of you.

# A FINAL WORD ON ENVIRONMENT

I moved us to Jamaica because I wanted to live longer. I was facing health issues in the United States that I now know were caused by my environment. Your environment—the weather, the food, the people, the culture—affects your PsyCap.

Don't ever feel trapped by where you are. If your environment is killing your peace or your health, make the move. It will be hard, and it will require a "Bulletproof" level of courage, but it could be the best decision of your life.

I love you all more than words can put on these pages. Use this book as your map but use your heart as your compass.

With all my love,
Mommy

# APPENDIX G

# HOW TO WRITE YOUR OWN LEGACY LETTER

The final legacy shift in your financial journey isn't about a will or a trust—though those are important. It's about the transfer of Wisdom Capital.

A Legacy Letter is a document that outlines your values, your history, and your hopes for the next generation. It ensures that your heirs don't just inherit your money, but the *mindset* that allowed you to build it.

# THE LEGACY LETTER FRAMEWORK

If you are ready to write your own, use this four-step framework to guide your thoughts.

## Step 1: The Context Audit

Start by reflecting on your own "linoleum floor" moments. What were the struggles that defined you?

- *Prompt:* "I want you to know about the time I almost gave up, and why I didn't ..."
- *Prompt:* "The hardest money move I ever made was ..."

## Step 2: The Individual Address

If you have children or mentees, write to them individually. Acknowledge their unique strengths and the specific lessons you hope they learn from your journey.

- *Prompt:* "I saw [Strength] in you when you were young, and I hope you use it to ..."
- *Prompt:* "My biggest regret in our early years was [X], and here is what I learned from it ..."

## Step 3: The Value Declaration

Identify your nonnegotiables. If your bank account was emptied tomorrow, what are the principles you would still want your family to live by?

- *Prompt:* "If you remember nothing else about money, remember this …"
- *Prompt:* "Our family stands for [Value 1], [Value 2], and [Value 3] because …"

## Step 4: The Vision for the Future

Describe the world you are trying to build through your stewardship. Why does your wealth matter beyond your own comfort?

- *Prompt:* "I am building this legacy so that you have the freedom to …"
- *Prompt:* "I hope our family's wealth is used to solve the problem of …"

# WHEN TO WRITE IT

Don't wait until you are "successful" or "old" to write this. Your legacy is being built every day. Write your first draft today, even if you are still in the middle of your Internal Revolution. As your mindset shifts and your wealth grows, you can update the letter to reflect your new level of stewardship.

# BIBLIOGRAPHY

**Allegretto, Sylvia A.** "Basic Family Budgets: Working Families' Incomes Often Fail to Meet Living Expenses Around the U.S." Economic Policy Institute Briefing Paper 165 (2005). https://www.epi.org/publication/bp165.

**Brand, Jennie E.** "The far-reaching impact of job loss and unemployment." *Annual Review of Sociology* 41 (2015): 359–375. https://doi.org/10.1146/annurev-soc-071913-043237.

**Carr, Nicholas.** "Digital Sharecropping" *Rough Type* (blog). December 2006. http://www.roughtype.com/?p=634.

**Cascio, Christopher N., Matthew B. O'Donnell, Francis J. Tinney, et al.** "Self-affirmation activates brain systems associated with self-related processing and reward and is reinforced by future orientation." *Social Cognitive and Affective Neuroscience* 11, no. 4 (2016): 621–629. https://doi.org/10.1093/scan/nsv136.

**Chen, J. A., E. Fearey, and R. E. Smith**. "'That which is measured improves': A theoretical and empirical review of self-monitoring in self-management and adaptive behavior change." *Journal of Behavior Therapy and Mental Health* 1, no. 4 (2017): 19–38. https://doi.org/10.14302/issn.2474-9273.jbtm-16-1180.

**Donahue, Amy K., and Philip G. Joyce.** "A framework for analyzing emergency management with an application to federal budgeting." *Public Administration Review* 61, no. 6 (2001): 728–740. https://doi.org/10.1111/0033-3352.00143.

**Erikson, Erik H.** *Childhood and Society*. New York: Norton, 1950.

**Gifford, Robert.** "Environmental psychology matters." *Annual Review of Psychology* 65 (2014): 541–579. https://doi.org/10.1146/annurev-psych-010213-115048.

**Goldsmith, Kelly, Vladas Griskevicius, and Alison Ahlstrom**. "Economic scarcity and the mind of the consumer." In *The Cambridge Handbook of Consumer Psychology*, edited by M. I. Norton, D. D. Rucker, and C. Lamberton, 332–358. Cambridge: Cambridge University Press, 2020.

**Gudmunson, Clinton G., and Sharon M. Danes.** "Family financial socialization: Theory and critical review." *Journal of Family and Economic Issues* 32, no. 4 (2011): 644–667. https://doi.org/10.1007/s10834-011-9275-y.

**Hall, C. C.** "Promoting savings for financial resilience: Expanding the psychological perspective." *Current Directions in Psychological Science* 30, no. 1 (2021): 49–54. https://doi.org/10.1177/0963721420979603.

**Haushofer, Johannes, and Ernst Fehr**. "On the psychology of poverty." *Science* 344, no. 6186 (2014): 862–867. https://doi.org/10.1126/science.1232491.

**Huang, S. C., L. Jin, and Y. Zhang**. "Step by step: Sub-goals as a source of motivation." *Organizational Behavior and Human Decision Processes* 141 (2017): 1–15. https://doi.org/10.1016/j.obhdp.2017.05.001.

**Hunter, MaryCarol R., Brenda W. Gillespie, and Syue-Yuan Chen.** "Urban nature experiences reduce stress in the context of daily life based on salivary biomarkers." *Frontiers in Psychology* 10 (2019): 722. https://doi.org/10.3389/fpsyg.2019.00722.

**Lee, Jinkook, and Sherman D. Hanna**. "Savings goals and saving behavior from a perspective of Maslow's hierarchy of needs." *Journal of Financial Counseling and Planning* 26, no. 2 (2015): 129–147. https://doi.org/10.1891/1052-3073.26.2.129.

**Locke, Edwin A., and Gary P. Latham**. "Building a practically useful theory of goal setting and task motivation: A 35-year odyssey." *American Psychologist* 57, no. 9 (2002): 705–717. https://doi.org/10.1037/0003-066x.57.9.705.

**Mani, Anandi, Sendhil Mullainathan, Eldar Shafir, and Jiaying Zhao**. "Poverty impedes cognitive function." *Science* 341, no. 6149 (2013): 976–980. https://doi.org/10.1126/science.1238041.

**McAdams, Dan P.** "The positive psychology of adult generativity: Caring for the next generation and constructing a redemptive life." In *Positive Psychology: Advances in Understanding Adult Motivation*, edited by Judith M. G. A. M. van Hoof, 191–205. New York: Springer, 2013.

**McDonald, J. T., and S. Kennedy**. "Insights into the 'healthy immigrant effect': Health status and health service use of immigrants to Canada." *Social Science & Medicine* 59, no. 8 (2004): 1613–1627. https://doi.org/10.1016/j.socscimed.2004.02.004.

**McEwen, Bruce S.** "Allostasis and Allostatic Load: Implications for Neuropsychopharmacology." Neuropsychopharmacology 22, no. 2 (2000): 108–124. https://doi.org/10.1016/S0893-133X(99)00129-3.

**Mullainathan, Sendhil, and Eldar Shafir.** *Scarcity: Why Having Too Little Means So Much*. New York: Times Books, Henry Holt and Company, 2013.

**Ong, Q., W. Theseira, and I. Y. H. Ng.** "Reducing debt improves psychological functioning and changes decision-making in the poor." *Proceedings of the National Academy of Sciences* 116, no. 15 (2019): 7244–7249.

**Portal, S., R. Abratt, and M. Bendixen.** "The role of brand authenticity in developing brand trust." *Journal of Strategic Marketing* 27, no. 6 (2019): 514–529.

**Ryan, Richard M., and Edward L. Deci.** "Self-determination theory and the facilitation of intrinsic motivation, social development, and well-being." *American Psychologist* 55, no. 1 (2000): 68–78. https://doi.org/10.1037/0003-066X.55.1.68.

**Shany, O., G. Gurevitch, G. Gilam, et al.** "A corticostriatal pathway mediating self-efficacy enhancement." *Npj Mental Health Research* 1, no. 6 (2022). https://doi.org/10.1038/s44184-022-00006-7.

**Shaw, Colin N., and Daniel P Longman.** "Homo sapiens, industrialization and the environmental mismatch hypothesis." *Biological Reviews*, (2025). https://doi.org/10.1111/brv.70094.

**Starcke, K., and M. Brand.** "Decision making under stress: A selective review." *Neuroscience & Biobehavioral Reviews* 36, no. 4 (2012): 1228–1248. https://doi.org/10.1016/j.neubiorev.2012.02.003.

**Stilley, K. M., J. J. Inman, and K. L. Wakefield.** "Spending on the fly: Mental budgets, promotions, and spending behavior." *Journal of Marketing* 74, no. 3 (2010): 34–47. https://doi.org/10.1509/jmkg.74.3.034.

**Thaler, Richard H.** "Mental accounting matters." *Journal of Behavioral Decision Making* 12, no. 3 (1999): 183–206. https://doi.org/10.1002/(SICI)1099-0771(199909)12:3<183::AID-BDM318>3.0.CO;2-F.

**Thaler, Richard H., and Shlomo Benartzi.** "Save more tomorrow: Using behavioral economics to increase employee saving." *Journal of Political Economy* 112, no. S1 (2004): S164–S87. https://doi.org/10.1086/380085.

**Thaler, Richard H., and Cass R. Sunstein.** *Nudge: Improving Decisions About Health, Wealth, and Happiness*. Revised and Expanded Edition. New York: Penguin Books, 2018.

**Tversky, A., and D. Kahneman.** "Judgment under uncertainty: Heuristics and biases." *Science*, New Series, 185, no. 4157 (1974): 1124–1131. https://doi.org/10.1126/science.185.4157.1124.

**Whitebread, David, and Sue Bingham.** *Habit Formation and Learning in Young Children*. London: Money Advice Service, 2013. https://www.thekidzmoney-project.com/wp-content/uploads/2021/02/University-of-Cambridge-Study-Habit-Formation-and-Learning-in-Young-Children.pdf.

**Xiao, Jing Jian, and Nilton Porto.** "Present bias and financial behavior." *Financial Planning Review* 2, no. 2 (2019): e1048. https://doi.org/10.1002/cfp2.1048.

# INDEX

Note: Page numbers in *italics* indicate figures.


**A**

abundance mindset, 30, 98, 116, 127–8

Accredited Financial Counselor® (AFC), 21, 158, 167, 307

active income, 146, 201

affirmations
  cringe factor, overcoming, 121–2
  examples, 120
  personal, 120
  scriptural
    discipline to stick to plan, 91
    future anxiety, 89
    next generation, building for, 90
    scarcity trap, 90
    tracking and planning, 90

anchoring, 182–3

architecture of flow, 57, 230, 257

attraction marketing, 189

authorized user strategy, 251–3, 259, 282

automation, 188, 205–7
  cognitive bandwidth preservation, 211
  equal payment plans, 213–14
  fear, overcoming, 215–16
  personal finances
    bills, 212
    debt repayment, 213
    emergency fund, 212
    investing, 213
    paycheck, 212

autonomy, 219, 325

autopilot spending, 75–6

awareness, self-monitoring and, 65

**B**

Baby Emergency Fund
  as buffer, 97
  pay yourself first and, 101–2
  savings challenges for, 101
  $1,000 in savings, 96, 99

bandwidth tax, 98, 156
behavioral self-monitoring, 65
branding, 188
  attraction marketing, 189–90
  authenticity in, 189, 195–6
  community building, 193–5
  content platform
    comparison, 191–2
    digital sharecropping, 190
    domain name selection, 191
  free content strategy, 192–3
  *see also* lead magnets
budget billing *see* equal payment plans
budgeting
  decision fatigue and, 53
  obstacles, 54–5
  peace of mind from, 53
  permission to spend, 51–4
  reframing of, 50
  as restriction, 52
  as stewardship, 89–91
  strategic plan for, 54
Budget Nirvana, 54, 211
Bulletproof Persona, 6, 7, 162, 273
  high-functioning survival mode, 7–8
  hyper-independence, 7
  post-traumatic growth (PTG), 13

C

Certified Financial Planner (CFP), 168
CFO mindset, 231, 234
Chartered Financial Analyst (CFA), 168
choice architecture, 39–40, 82, 211
cognitive impairment, 107
cognitive slack, 39, 99
cognitive tests, 98–9
commission system, 257
compound interest, 255
cortisol ROI, 233–4
COVID-19 pandemic, business
    disruption, 155–6
credit action plan
  automatic payments, setting up, 35
  recurring charges, automating, 35
  reports, obtaining, 34
  training wheels card, selecting, 34–5
  utilization ratio, maintaining low,
    35–6
credit cards
  family financial habits, 29
  retail promotions, 30
  as tools for credit building, 32
crisis buffer, 41, 102
crisis-management protocol, 108
Custodial Roth IRA
  compound interest calculation, 255
  earned income requirement, 254
  parent contribution match, 254–5
  tax-free growth, 254
cycle-breakers
  commandments of, 300–1
  common questions answered,
    313–19
  negotiation as daily tool, 177–8
  relocation as strategic decision, 230
  tax planning for, 169

D
data, 63
data leaks, 67–8
decision fatigue, 53, 210
deferred life plan, 219
digital sharecropping, 190
domain name selection, 191
domestic geo-arbitrage, 220–1
Do More, Do Less, Stop framework, 50, 68
  audit framework, 73–6, 79
  *see also* architecture of flow

E
education
  audit, 24–5
  economic returns, 21–2
  financial aid, 20
  human capital, 18, 22
  as investment, 18–19
  lifetime value (LTV), 24
  online study, 18–19
  payback period, 23–4
  persistence, 19
  ROI, 21–3
  self-efficacy, 20
Emergency Buffer, 50
emergency funds
  financial resilience, 100
  initial funding goal, 96
  peace of mind from, 100
  *see also* Baby Emergency Fund
employee assistance program (EAP), 185
entrepreneurs, mental energy of, 210–11
environmental psychology, 223–4
equal payment plans, 213–14
expat finances
  fixed costs, 232
  food and local economy, 232–3
  geo-arbitrage, 235
expat life
  Foreign Earned Income Exclusion (FEIE), 239–40
  geo-arbitrage, 237–8
  global banking infrastructure, 238–9
external locus of control, 9, 45, 250

F
family money meeting
  money date, 262–3
  parental leadership in, 264
Fear Of Missing Out (FOMO), 72
fiduciary, 168
financial buffer
  Baby Emergency Fund as, 97
  psychology of, 97–8
financial crisis
  four walls framework, 106
  panic response, 105–6
  psychological impact, 107
financial insecurity, 39
financial nourishment, 72–3
financial pulse check, 64
financial resilience, 100

financial safety net
bandwidth tax, 98
buffer, 96–8
cognitive control, 98–9
cortisol connection, 99–100
$1,000 reset, 99
*see also* Baby Emergency Fund
financial socialization, 249
age-by-age guide
allowance introduction, 251
family economy, 257–8
foundation, 256–7
generational partner, 260
give, save and spend concept, 250
launchpad, 251, 259
training wheels, 258
financial starvation, 72–3
financial trauma, 30, 52
Five Whys, 59–60, 111
Foreign Earned Income Exclusion (FEIE), 239–40, 318
four walls framework
as cognitive shortcut, 107
community, 224–6
cost, 226
financial stability and, 109
food, 108–9
health, 222–4
housing, 108–9
safety, 224
in survival mode, 222
transportation, 108, 110
utilities and basic clothing, 108, 110

**G**

generativity *vs.* stagnation, 286
generosity, 128
geo-arbitrage
lower-cost living environments, 231
remote work and relocation, 221
worksheet, 228–30
goals, 132
accountability and, 138
adjusting as needed, 138
affirmations and, 138
budget, integrating with, 137
commitment, 59
emotional connection to, 58, 59
long term, 137
short term, 137
small wins, 136
SMART goal framework, 132–5
starting with why, 134
subgoals, 133
surface-level *vs.* deep, 59
visual reminders, 138

**H**

Health Savings Account (HSA), 184–5
health wall, 222–4, 234, 240
healthy immigrant effect, 223
HERO framework, *13*
high-functioning survival mode, 7, 155, 157
high-velocity asset, 23–4
human capital theory, 21–2
hyper-independence, 7, 8, 170

**I**

income
- active/service, 142, 146
- issue, 78, 86, 140
- multiple income, building, 141, 144, 145
- passive/residual, 142, 146–7
- scalable/product, 142
- streams
  - alignment with values, 151
  - digital asset, building, 148–9
  - existing skills and knowledge, leveraging, 147–8
  - gig economy and task-based work, 148
  - neighborhood services, 149
  - skills inventory, listing, 150

inner game of wealth, 117–18
- affirmation, 119–20
- faith as strength, 118–19
- gratitude, practicing, 119
- visualization, 119, 121–4

internal locus of control, 9, 46, 144, 248–50
- *see also* external locus of control; locus of control

intrinsic motivation, 59

**L**

launchpad, 128, 251, 259

lead magnets
- problem-solving focus of, 193
- types of, 193–5

legacy
- binder
  - business continuity plan, 332
  - digital keys, 331–2
  - financial map, 330–1
  - legal foundation, 330
  - personal instructions, 332–3
- generational wealth, 248
- internal locus of control, 246
- letter
  - to children, 335–9
  - framework, 342–3
  - template, 287–8
  - usage, 288–9
  - values, inheritance of, 338–9
  - writing, timing of, 343
- parent's financial fear, overcoming, 261
- passing down values and systems, 246, 286–7
- practical toolkit for, 255–6

levelized billing *see* equal payment plans

lifetime value (LTV), 24

locus of control, 9, 159
- *see also* external locus of control; internal locus of control

**M**

market signals, 25

Maslow's Hierarchy of Needs, 108

mental accounting, 211

mental bandwidth, 31, 32, 39

mental energy, 210–11
mental imagery *see* visualization
micro-flow strategy, 87
micro-investing, 25
money flow, 50
  architecture of, *80*
  bi-weekly paycheck, 87
  data leaks, 67–8
  financial pulse check, 64
  irregular income, 88–9
  monthly paycheck, 88
  90-day grace period, 92–3
  semi-monthly paycheck, 87–8
  syncing, with pay cycle, 86
  30-day no-judgment rule, 64–7
    for awareness, 64–5
    mindfulness of spending, 65
    self-efficacy, building, 65
    for tracking, 66
  tracking method, 66–7
  weekly paycheck, managing, 87
  zero-based budgeting, 81
    assigning every dollar, 85–6
    Do More, Do Less, Stop framework, 84–5
    expenses, listing, 84
    four walls, 83–4
    fun money in, 85
    monthly income, listing, 82
    paying yourself first, 82–3
money ghosts, 45, 167, 170
multiple income streams, 141, 144
    scaling, *188*

**N**

negotiation
  fear of rejection in, 180–1
  phases
    confidence, 180
    conversation, 182–3
    preparation, 179–80
  power of asking, 178
  resource optimization and, 177–8
noise, silencing, 6
notebook/journal, recording, 67

**O**

online study, 18–19
Ostrich Approach, 10

**P**

passive income, 146–7
pause, power of, 276
payback period, 23–4
pay yourself first, 44
  automation, 82–3, 212
  Baby Emergency Fund and, 101–2
  non-negotiable priority, 82
  peace of mind from, 39, 40
  present bias and, 40
  savings, automating, 40
  wealth building through, 38
  *see also* three-legged stool of wealth
Peace Audit, 160
Pell Grant, 20

permission to spend *see* budgeting
personal branding
  authenticity, 195–6
  fear of visibility, 196–7
personal finances
  automation
    bills, 212
    debt repayment, 213
    emergency fund, 212
    investing, 213
    paycheck, 212
  as team effort, 166–7
portable skills, 25
post-traumatic growth (PTG), 13
present bias, 40
psychological capital (PsyCap), 2, 11, 13–14, 20, 248
  efficacy, 13, 14, 45
  hope, 13, 14, 46
  optimism, 13, 14
  resilience, 13, 14, 46

**R**

ranking strategy, 76–7
resourcefulness, 20
rest deficit, 110
return on investment (ROI)
  education, 21–3
  lifetime value, 24
  peace matrix, *161*
  personal peace, 160–1, 172
  ROI of Peace, 154, 160–2, 233
  *see also* cortisol ROI
revenue trap
  audit, 163–4
  hidden tax, 157
  high performance in wrong environment, 158
  illusion of success, 154–5
  pandemic-driven pivot, 155–6
  shame and debt, 171
  spending to maintain success image, 162
  steward *vs.*, *161*
  stewardship mindset, transition to, 171
  work-life imbalance, 156–7
  *see also* return on investment (ROI)

**S**

safety net *see* financial safety net
scalable skills, 25
scarcity mindset, 30, 97–8, 126
  beliefs, identifying, 128–30
  shift to abundance mindset, 127–8
self-actualization, 108
self-affirmation, 123
  *see also* affirmations
self-determination theory (SDT), 76, 218–19
self-efficacy, 65, 123
SMART goal framework, 132–3, 136–7
  achievable goals, 134–5
  Ask Why Five Times exercise, 134
  measurable goals, 134
  relevant goals, 135

SMART goal framework (*Cont.*)
for relocation, 219–20
specific goals, 134
time-bound goals, 135
Society for Human Resource Management Certified Professional (SHRM-CP), 21
someday syndrome, 227–8
spending tracker
aligning with values, 75
Do Less category, 74
Do More category, 74–5
Stop category, 73–4
stagnation *vs.* generativity, 286
starvation budget, 50, 72
Stewardship Manifesto
drafting, 273
peace fund and community, 272
postpartum prioritization, 272
ROI of pruning, 271–2
stewardship mindset
automation and delegation audit, 274–5
capacity building, 268
character magnified by wealth, 268–70
communication protocol, 275
money as tool, 267–8, 270
ownership, shifting to, 266, 269
sabbatical fund, 274
safety through surrender, 267
stewardship stack
banking and saving, 310
budgeting and tracking, 310
business and entrepreneurship, 311
investing and wealth building, 311
strategic education audit, 24
strategic sabbatical, 273–5
subgoals, 133

**T**

tax preparers, red flags in, 169
tax steward mindset, 144
30-day no-judgment rule, 64–7
three-legged stool of wealth, 248, *249*
Tiffany-isms, 5, 17, 29, 37, 51, 57, 63, 71, 79, 95, 105, 117, 125, 131, 139, 153, 163, 165, 177, 187, 209, 217, 247, 265
*see also* stewardship mindset
Toxic Partnership Tax, 157
tracking method
digital tracker (apps), 66
notebook/journal, recording, 67
spreadsheet, 66–7
tunneling, 31, 98
tunnel vision, 126
2008 financial crisis, 30–1

**U**

Umbrella Method
case study, 143
core brand as handle and canopy, 141
one brand, many ribs, 141–2
side hustle selection matrix, 142–3

tax steward mindset, 144
*see also* multiple income streams

V
value-congruent living, 75
value incongruence, 75–6
values-based budgeting, 73
value score, 76–7
vetting checklist, 173–5
Visionary Mindset, 10
visualization, 121–4

W
wealth building, 115–16
why, power of, 59–60
workplace financial wellness
employee assistance program (EAP), 185
Health Savings Account (HSA), 184–5
insurance benefits, 186
retirement matching, 184
tuition reimbursement, 185–6

Z
zero-based budgeting, 81
assigning every dollar, 85–6
Do More, Do Less, Stop framework, 84–5
expenses, listing, 84
four walls, 83–4
fun money in, 85
monthly income, listing, 82
paying yourself first, 82–3